SELECTED PAPERS FROM THE SECOND WORLD CONGRESS FOR SOVIET AND EAST EUROPEAN STUDIES

GARMISCH–PARTENKIRCHEN

SEPTEMBER 30–OCTOBER 4, 1980

Sponsored by

INTERNATIONAL COMMITTEE FOR SOVIET AND EAST EUROPEAN STUDIES

and

DEUTSCHE GESELLSCHAFT FÜR OSTEUROPAKUNDE

General Editor

Roger E. Kanet

University of Illinois at Urbana-Champaign

EDITORIAL COMMITTEE MEMBERS

Patrick L. Alston, Bowling Green State University
Oskar Anweiler, Ruhr-Universität Bochum
Evelyn C. Bristol, University of Illinois at Urbana-Champaign
Georg Brunner, Universität Würzburg
Marianna Tax Choldin, University of Illinois at Urbana-Champaign
R.W. Davies, The University of Birmingham
Dennis J. Dunn, Southwest Texas State University
R.C. Elwood, Carleton University
Zbigniew M. Fallenbuchl, University of Windsor
Frank Y. Gladney, University of Illinois at Urbana-Champaign
Bohdan Harasymiw, The University of Calgary
Roger E. Kanet, University of Illinois at Urbana-Champaign
Thomas F. Magner, The Pennsylvania State University
Sidney Monas, The University of Texas at Austin
Temira Pachmuss, University of Illinois at Urbana-Champaign
Peter J. Potichnyj, McMaster University
T. Harry Rigby, Australian National University
Hans Rogger, University of California, Los Angeles
Gertrude Schroeder Greenslade, University of Virginia
Jane Shapiro Zacek, Governor's Office of Employee Relations (New York)
Günther Stökl, Universität Köln

RUSSIAN LITERATURE AND CRITICISM

SELECTED PAPERS FROM THE SECOND WORLD CONGRESS
FOR SOVIET AND EAST EUROPEAN STUDIES

Edited by

Evelyn Bristol

University of Illinois at Urbana-Champaign

BERKELEY SLAVIC SPECIALTIES

Berkeley, 1982

PRINTED IN U.S.A.

ISBN 0-933884-27-3

CONTENTS

PART I — LITERATURE

FOREWORD BY THE GENERAL EDITOR

The articles published in this volume have been selected from among those presented at the Second World Congress for Soviet and East European Studies, held in Garmisch-Partenkirchen, Federal Republic of Germany, September 30 – October 4, 1980. The Congress was sponsored by the International Committee for Soviet and East European Studies in conjunction with the Deutsche Gesellschaft für Osteuropakunde and was attended by well over 1,400 scholars from around the world.

Among the approximately five hundred formal papers and additional papers presented at the Congress, more than 150 were submitted for consideration to the editorial committee for the official English-language Congress publications. From among these a substantial number have been accepted for publication in the series of thirteen volumes to be published by Berkeley Slavic Specialties, (Berkeley, California, U.S.A.), Pergamon Press (New York, N.Y., U.S.A.), Russica Publishers (New York, N.Y., U.S.A.), Allen and Unwin (London, England), Praeger Publishers (New York, N.Y., U.S.A.), and Martinus Nijhoff Publishers (The Hague, The Netherlands). In addition, several other volumes are scheduled for publication in Germany.

As general editor of the series of English-language Garmisch Congress publications, I wish to express my sincere appreciation to all of the individuals and organizations that made the conference and the resulting publications possible. This includes the numerous organizations that provided financial support for the Congress itself, the Executive Committee of the International Committee for Soviet and East European Studies (including the past president, Adam Bromke) and in particular, the members of the German Planning Committee who organized the Congress (including the chairman and current president of the International Committee, Oskar Anweiler). Finally, I wish to thank the Congress participants who submitted their papers for consideration, the members of the editorial committee that selected the essays to be included in the various volumes, and the editors of those volumes. Their contributions and cooperation have made possible the publication of this volume and the other volumes in the series.

Roger E. Kanet

University of Illinois
  at Urbana-Champaign

INTRODUCTION

These papers read at Garmisch-Partenkirchen reflect not only the variety of scholarly interests among Western Slavists, but a tendency to highlight previously neglected or oppositional literature. The World Congress series was, indeed, founded as a forum for Western scholars; the only stipulation for subjects at the Congress was, however, a concentration on the twentieth century. Modernism, from Decadence through Futurism, attracted several papers, apparently not only because of the relative silence about these movements in the Soviet Union, but also because of their inherent air of defiance. Relatively little attention was given to the literature of the twenties; its individualistic current was still strong, but derivative of Modernism, and its best authors were, in any case, published. Instead, Western scholars have begun, if these articles are indicative, to turn their attention to contemporary subjects, particularly to the wave of village prose. Dissent, if present in this genre, is both subdued and altered: individualism has been replaced by a nostalgia for a primitive communal harmony. Contemporary prose works devoted to urban life tend to feature, by contrast, alienation and intellectualism; they do not constitute a coherent movement, and are the subject of fewer papers. Russian literary criticism is shown in its tendency to rise to the level of social or linguistic theory. Particularly the idealistic current of the twenties, its antecedents and aftermath, is examined here.

Modernism owed its capacity to shock in part to its elitism, in part to new and pointedly uncivic criteria for morality and amorality. Symbolism endowed its mystical element with a moral coloring, but accompanied that uplift with Decadence, an arrogant amorality. Intuition, whatever its message, became the only infallible spiritual guide. The innovative role of women authors in this upheaval has allegedly been neglected, with the exception of Zinaida Gippius. They brought into question, it seems, the conventional roles of women while the men still revered some hypostasis of the Eternal Feminine. Andrei Belyi must be counted among the would-be mystics, but his "symphony," *The Return* is seen here as an ironic treatment of the premises of his own school. Perhaps the work is an esoteric refutation of Viacheslav Ivanov's eternal return and Dionysian redemption by death and resurrection, derived from Nietzsche. The Futurists did not claim an alliance with divinity as had the Symbolists, and vitality, or the intensity of experience, replaced intuition for them as a measure of spiritual rectitude. They viewed society as a constant philistine menace to individualism. Citizenship, the idealization of women, and other tendencies which they resisted, can be shown to ascend through nineteenth-century Realism to Sentimentalism.

Unaligned authors contemporary to these movements displayed equally individualistic tendencies. The conventions which Marina Tsvetaeva is shown to have violated were those of language; her poetry reflects the coherent systems of her own idiosyncracies. Her natural voice was not demure, but astringent, even fierce. The science fiction of Aleksandr Grin sounds a familiar warning that mere human fantasy will be persecuted as an enemy by a coercive society.

After the revolution Russian literature returned to the investigation of an essentially nineteenth-century premise — the necessity of public life for personal fulfillment. Simplistically, realism has been taken to signal an affirmation and avantgardistic traits an equivocation. But one author suggests here that ideology is not really a fit basis for aesthetic judgments. Instead, the wealth or paucity of ideological choices and of constructive methods within the work are offered as more viable criteria. Then Pasternak and Nikolai Ostrovskii turn up, disconcertingly, as bedfellows. Moreover, richness appears to derive less often from ideological alternatives than from a complex fabric.

Village prose is welcomed among these papers as a wholesome departure from the recent past, but a development with obvious connections with Russian traditions. Grigorovich, Turgenev, and Bunin are named among others as predecessors. Moreover, village prose is shown on the basis of a comparison with Zhdanovist narratives to echo broader currents of Russian populism. A realistic method and an avoidance of individualism enables village prose to appear to fit within the frame of Socialist Realism while rejecting its essence. As a pastoral current embodying an impulse to praise the ideals of the peasant, it is also related to neo-Slavophilism, and Solzhenitsyn's "Matrena's Yard" is seen as a kindred phenomenon. A repertory of village themes was established already in the sixties, when Vasilii Belov represented the genre. Naturalness, a communal spirit, and stabile peasant traditions in remote areas are compared favorably with urbanization, collectivization, mechanization, and the bureaucratic trivialization of life, processes inescapably associated with Marxism. Belov also initiated an emphasis on childhood, seen as an era of purity, and on a closeness to animals and nature. Valentin Rasputin, the trend's leading practitioner in the seventies, is concerned about the loss of traditional values, whose vessels he portrays as the old people, particularly the women, for they are centers of families.

The popularity of Chingiz Aitmatov, who writes of his native Kirghiz area, belies the necessity of a Slavic cast to the pastoral form. His somewhat exotic characters and ethnography show that village prose has a Romantic strain. His emphasis on children and on a protective mother point to a renewed Sentimentalism. Authors of village prose have been able also to revitalize personal (if not individualistic) subjects, and have given the pastoral tradition contemporary ironies and psychological subtleties, which bring it closer to Western literature. At the same time village prose continues the moralizing tendency of Russian literature; it shows an anxiety for the conscience, but its subject is family, communal, or tribal, not public, life.

The current literature of disaffection, individualism and criticism is not only miscellaneous in direction, but relatively divested of its former signs of dissent. Iurii Trifonov combined ennui and moral weakness with realism in stories critical of the modern city, but he also tried, like his predecessor, Chekhov, to point to more universal sources of malaise. The former Socialist Realist Valentin Kataev has belatedly turned to avantgardism in his "mauvism," which rests on an intense awareness of individuality; his works are fragmented memoirs; and the ornamentalism of his style is an expression of the uniqueness of his utterances. Recent science fiction is shown to warn of the Faustian temptations of modern scientists to play God and of the dangers of privilege, warnings which sort well with the fears seen in village prose, but which do not call Soviet policies into question.

Russian literary criticism, itself seen as visions of Russian society, is subjected here to approval or disagreement. Bakhtin, a dissenting voice of the early Soviet period, is shown to have used subterfuge to publish his un-Marxist message: the word (langauge and literature) is the spirit made flesh, a dialogue (*parole* not *langue*) between the individual and his culture; thus Bakhtin's concept of language rests on a religious concept of community in which the individual plays an indispensable role. Elsewhere Russian criticism, from Belinskii to Berdiaev, is taken to task for tending to usurp the role of philosophy within culture. Literature, it is alleged, was mistaken for a true representation of reality, and genuine philosophy, deprived of its natural object, was intimidated and failed to provide Russians with a perspective on their own culture. Finally, an argument is raised against Likhachev's thesis that medieval Russian humor is related to the institution of carnival, said to be a Western tradition. Medieval Westerners laughed, it is shown, at the remission of accepted rules, while Russians, being less disciplined, laughed instead at the imposition of rules from above. The function of Christianity within Russian culture figures as an essential element in each of these papers. Although written from a bird's-eye view above the traffic of current events, they are partisan exclamations or subdued polemics with Russian culture. Nowhere is criticism asked to make aesthetic judgments about literature, to say what should endure and what be forgotten. Thus the volume reflects as a whole not only the scholarly interests, but the constant, if mild, oppositional tone of Western Slavic studies.

Evelyn Bristol

University of Illinois
  at Urbana-Champaign

PART I

LITERATURE

FUTURIST REJECTIONS OF SENTIMENTALISM

EVELYN BRISTOL

In their manifestos the Futurists rejected all of the literature
of the past, but in practice they intuitively opposed most strenu-
ously those values which had come into nineteenth-century literature from Sentimentalism.[1] The latter movement had once signalled the *embourgeoisement* of literature, whereas the Futurists
appeared at the high tide of a reactive sensitivity to society's im-
pingements on the individual. When in "Vo ves' golos" (1930)
Maiakovskii parodied earlier poetry as the mandolin playing of
intellectual and prettified men, he was objecting not only to its
being delicate and attenuated, but to its being conventional; he
disliked the approval of society. Aleksei Kruchenykh was ridiculing the utilitarian purpose of nineteenth-century literature
when he portrayed it in his essay "Chort i rechetvortsy" (1913)
as a dog called Norma, after Bellini's operatic heroine, charged
with destroying the scorpion of evil in the world.[2] He also understood that women had been idealized so as to serve as moral mea-
suring sticks. *Pamela* (1740) and *Clarissa* (1747–8) had, indeed,
been lessons in acceptable behavior. Chernyshevskii unwittingly
demonstrated the link between Sentimentalism and Realism when
in "Russkii chelovek na rendez-vous" (1858) he showed that the
incapacity of the new hero for responsible citizenship was often
symbolized by his failure to establish a conventional family.[3]

The Futurists, however, did not see society as a stage for the
individual's productive activity, but as a threat to his personal
integrity and expressiveness. As Benedikt Livshits wrote in *Polutoraglazyi strelets* (1933), they were united more by their ego-
centrism than by any constructive program or aesthetic.[4] In their
various tendencies they fought the traditional identification of

the Good, the True, and the Beautiful. In the works of some, transense language circumvented both utilitarianism and beauty. Although they specifically opposed philistinism rather than Sentimentalism, a comparison with the traits of the earlier school will serve to focus the animosities of the Futurists and show that they had an inner coherence.

The Futurists regarded the social aggregate, the shibboleth of Sentimentalism, with pessimism or indifference. James Thomson in *The Seasons* (1730) extolled English patriotism, orderly government, agriculture, and commerce, while he deplored the uncultivated lands (and disasters) of Africa and the "torrid zones." Cubo-Futurists, however, suspected that any civilization is unavailing, sometimes for the reason that human nature is not in itself civilizable. In Khlebnikov's poetry the prevalence of violence and rapine belies the possibility of stable governance, whether in primitive or historical times. In "Deti vydry," a cosmogony and history of the world, he shows that life began only after the destruction of prohibitive suns, and has continued only through such legendary struggles as those of Prometheus, Achilles, and the Cossacks; in the fifth "parus" the narrator reflects that everywhere life is sad and ends in death. Violence also characterizes Khlebnikov's lyrics; "Bekh" is spoken by the disillusioned bones of the medieval war dead. Defenseless victims such as women and animals seem especially pathetic, but in other poems they also commit violence and wage war. In "Semero" horses battled in ancient Hylaea; in "Chto byl — v nashem tonet" even maidens do. Kruchenykh's poems, when they are not in *zaum,* usually feature a similar violent primitivism. "Pustynnik" (1913) is narrated by a "merciless warrior" who subsists on raids, and "Pustynnitsa" (1913) is related by a helpless old woman facing death. Kruchenykh even wrote of savagery with evident enjoyment. Nor is human nature shown by him to be improved by material well-being; together with Khlebnikov he wrote "Igra v adu," a mirror of civilization's corruptions. The urban population of the early play *Vladimir Maiakovskii* (1913) suffers existential woes even without being prey to violence; their ills are symbolized by physical malformations and deprivations, as well as by various tears. Only one happy man is rumored to exist somewhere in

Brazil. Thus Cubo-Futurist poetry sometimes displays not so much an aversion to a stable community as a collapse of belief in it.

Sentimentalists instituted a line of compassionate social criticism that preceded the nineteenth-century faith in progress. Thomas Gray in "Elegy in a Country Churchyard" (1750) sounded a note of animosity to militarism and vainglory; Oliver Goldsmith in "The Deserted Village" (1770) warned against pollution; humble members of society, such as the farmer, were extolled, and the question whether a gentleman should be prepared to marry a peasant was raised, as in Karamzin's "Bednaia Liza." But Cubo-Futurists tended to anticipate deterioration rather than improvement; several saw in social evils the evidence of malice and insensitivity from above and the justification for rebellions.

Khlebnikov was a foremost denigrator of the civilization of advanced technology. In his "Zhuravl'" machines eat children; in other poems trains destroy figures which symbolize the pastoral world, such as a shepherd, or frogs. His initial response to war was the promise (in "Byli veshchi slishkom sini") of a bloody revenge for the Russian deaths at Tsushima. But he became an outspoken pacifist; in "Voina v myshelovke" the personified figure of war speaks of its insatiable need for the deaths of young men. In "Volga! Volga!" the river is implored to cease the cannibalization of children during the famine and Civil War. Maiakovskii's most pacificistic protest came in *Voina i mir* (1916) where he shows that the sacrifices made by the common people serve only the greed of the sated and the expansionism of nations. Pasternak portrayed war in "Durnoi son" (1914) as an intolerable chaos and carnage.

The struggle against an ensconced bourgeoisie was such an overwhelming motivation in Maiakovskii's verse that it even brought aridity to much of it.[5] Where Khlebnikov was the champion of the innocent victims of violence, Maiakovskii was the spokesman first of syphilitics, prostitutes, and tuberculars, and later of the proletarian. His animosity to philistinism appeared in such early poems as "Moe k ètomu otnoshenie" (1915), reached its height by *Misteriia-buff* (1918) and *150,000,000* (1920), and is manifest in his astounding capacity for propaganda, as in his work for ROSTA. When Maiakovskii admired technology, more-over, his praise was lyrical and occasioned more by monumental-ness, as in "Bruklinskii most" (1925), than by any service to the public weal. Khlebnikov's protests against class oppression had a resemblance to Sentimental literature in that he tended to por-tray women as its victims and as models of moral fortitude. He broke with the Sentimental tradition, however, in that he implied the right of the injured to revenge. In "Noch' pered sovetami" the female narrator had nursed the master's pup; in "Prachka. (Goriachee pole)" a woman describes the misery of her fellow residents in the city dump. In "Nochnoi obysk" the moral supe-riority of the women — the mother, the sister (and the Madonna of the icon) — justify the conflagration at the end.

The Sentimentalists anticipated that societal ameliorations would come through the concerted efforts of responsible citizens. Throughout *The Seasons* Thomson teaches that philosophy and morality together will lift civilization ever higher; in "Summer" he evokes those virtues required by the empire; the first is Pub-lic Zeal; among others are Peace, Social love, Charity, Truth, Dignity, and Courage. Insofar as the Futurists allowed for the possibility of improvement, they turned, as Romantics, to uto-pian solutions. Khlebnikov relied on the achievements of vision-aries. He pictured in "Gorod budushchego" a city of glass whose society is ordered by a hierarchy of priests. Elsewhere he dreamed that mankind would learn to war like flowers with aromas ("È— è! y—ym! ves' v potu"), or live according to a single religious awareness ("Edinaia kniga"). He relied excessively on the con-cept of a body of world presidents, whose insights would be en-hanced by his study of numbers in relation to history. The remedy for social ills in *Vladimir Maiakovskii* was likewise not in construc-tive citizenship, but the redemptive suffering of the poet. When Maiakovskii later exhorted the population to the production of coal and iron, it was heroic efforts he urged, rather than ordinary, fruitful labor.

The core of Sentimentalism was the idealization of the "social" emotions and institution of the family, while the Futurists mani-fested an equally essential aversion to convention and to *byt*. In this sphere the movements were diametrically opposed. Both

Thomson and Young dwell on the necessity of a moderate (not passionate) love and friendship for the spiritual health of the individual. Marital morality as seen from the allegedly feminine point of view became an issue for Richardson; the goal of *Night Thoughts* (1747–8) is the spiritual salvation of the author's friend, "Lorenzo"; in "Elegy in a Country Churchyard" children are shown to vie for a place on their father's knee. But the Futurists depicted compelling passions, irresponsible eroticism, exclusive and idyllic loyalties, and, in general, relationships that cannot be enmeshed in society. They also cast new perspectives on friendship, and dealt, as well, with the lonely person apart, or those in self-sufficient isolation.

Love is portrayed in Khlebnikov's verse as highly erotic or sweetly idyllic. In the lyric drama "Devii bog" the maidens' capacity for promiscuity brings them into conflict with their prehistoric community, and especially with their families; their god is ostracized. The impulsive behavior of *rusalkas, vilas* and forest sprites, seen as Slavicized nymphs and satyrs, is the subject of several of Khlebnikov's long poems, such as "Vila i leshii," and a number of lyrics. "Liudi, kogda oni liubiat" is a tribute to the ubiquitous "passion" which affects humans, animals, and gods. Eroticism may entail violence; "Lesnaia deva" is a girl's reproach to an interloper who has murdered her lover, a singer. Women also perpetrate abuses, as in "Liubovnik Iunony," whose hero perished despite the efforts of his mother to save him. Idyllic and faithful loves, usually set in distant times and places, tend to incur the wrath of the community; in "I i È" the lovers are in danger of being burned, and when they have triumphed instead, they became rulers. In "Sel'skaia druzhba," a revival of the idyl genre, an exclusive friendship also arouses the uneasy interference of the community. Figures who are isolated from social ties tend not to be pathetic, but emblematic, larger than life. Venus sojourns with a shaman until recalled to Europe by a swan. The sisters of "Tri sestry" are like primitive priestesses, privy to religious secrets, at home in nature, and sexually promiscuous. In Khlebnikov's very few love poems he tends himself to be rejected; in "Lasok" her eyes are filled with stepmothers. If Stenka Razin was a favorite subject with Khlebnikov, as well as with several other Futurists, because he was a rebel, it may also be because his feat was the sacrifice of his bride — his own domestic life — to his calling as a rebel. A note of regret appears in the lyric "Ia videl iunoshi proroka" whose hero, Protivo-Razin, creates a maiden out of water.

In Vasilii Kamenskii's long works idyllic unions are contrasted with oppressive, obligating marriages on the background of a pastoral nostalgia. In *Zemlianka* an urban marriage dissolves in favor of a rural retreat which the hero shares with a child, a dog, and a bird, ultimately to wed a peasant. The bird, significantly, was enabled by the gift of song to live in freedom apart from any society; and Kamenskii's lyrics show a yearning for placidity in nature. In several long works on Razin, the rebel becomes an object of pity when he must sacrifice his second wife, a Persian princess, and when he falls a victim to the vindictive rage of his first wife.

The escape from parental authority, a motivation no doubt germane to the entire Futurist movement, was depicted graphically by Kruchenykh in a small poem which begins "kopi bogatstva begi ottsa." The father's pursuit is facetiously depicted, yet the message of the poem seems a valid expression of the movement's attitude to society and to tradition. Kruchenykh has been described as characteristically setting forth the tenets of the school in a bald way that is instructive, because of his daring.[6] His preference for *zaum,* which cannot be given a meaning, was a manifest evasion of authority.

Just as Khlebnikov saw violence in both public and private matters, so Maiakovskii confronted at the helm of the state and in society's stifling conventions the same enemy — philistinism. In "Chelovek" (1917) he is defeated, in the guise of Everyman, first by greed, which reigns through finance, war, Law, and Religion, and then by his desire for a woman who is married. His opposition to domesticity was tragically in conflict with his need for love. His first loss to the institution of marriage was in *Oblako v shtanakh* (1915); his dilemma is presented in *Pro èto* (1923) as the necessity of a moral choice between his lover and the man on the bridge, or love for humanity. Unable to imagine other than Sentimental roles for women, he succeeded best in portraying his own frustrated hunger for love. Sometimes he recalled his "mama," as in *Oblako v shtanakh*. He fought the Sentimental understanding of love by portraying it as a physical need, as of the heart or flesh. In "Lilichka" (1916) he compares himself in his pain to massive animals, an ox or elephant; in *Pro èto* he becomes a bear in order to howl. These animal comparisons probably reveal a deep-seated conviction about human love. At the end of *Pro èto,* when he has suffered martyrdom for the cause of the man on the bridge, he returns to wait for his love in the zoo. At the end of *Klop* (1929) Prisypkin's last menage is a cage with a bedbug, a pathetically reductive, but unmistakable, symbol of natural life; no woman is present. In *Bania* (1930), the Phosphorus Woman is a new figure in that she is disassociated from Sentimental roles, but she has the ominous function of leading out of this world into another.

Elena Guro, being a woman, protested in her work against the assigning of conforming or submissive roles to anyone, and especially to women and children. In an early prose piece, "Tak zhizn' idet," a girl who is beaten emerges through puberty to link love itself with sadism and violence. Philistinism, however, is more often confronted in Guro than physical cruelty, because her deepest fear was for the imagination. In that she depicted herself in her works as a loving wife and mother, she pled for the recognition of the isolated, or bohemian, family. She shows family relationships which are protective, rather than destructive, of the creative faculty; for example, she relied (painfully, in fact) on her husband's high estimate of her artistic gift. Several fantasies show how she would have protected her deceased son from society's demands for conformity. In general she portrayed humdrum social events so as to reveal the pain they cause awkward individuals, especially young ones. She was religiously inclined when alone in nature. Like Khlebnikov she returned to the Sentimental theme of friendship with a corrective; in "Poryv" she portrayed a loyalty between two women; Sentimentalists had idealized friendship only as it occurred between men.

The Centrifugists did not oppose Sentimental values so directly or abrasively as the Cubo-Futurists; nor had they much recourse to primitivism, violence, or the idyllic. Pasternak's *Sestra moia*

zhizn' (1922) and "Temy i variatsii" (1923) each have at their core
a rapt and inward-looking love story that is conducted in near-
obliviousness to society and the momentous political events of
the times. The seasons have more effect on the lovers. In "Step'"
even the mosquitoes' whine is capitalized. Love tends to the exultant and partakes more of the universal than of the societal. The
lovers are conscious of the eternal, but their love is transient in
earthly time. The plot of the later *Doktor Zhivago* resembles
Kamenskii's *Zemlianka,* distant as the two works are in execu-
tion, in that a conventional marriage disintegrates in favor of an
love.

Igor' Severianin opposed to the marital virtue esteemed by Sentimentalists a moral laxness. His message (often addressed to
women) is that self-indulgence is more gratifying than virtue; an
example is "V grekhe — zabven'e" (1911). The Ego-Futurists
claimed in their manifestos a rectitude assured through an identification with the universal ego.[7] But Severianin's verse embodies
the mere idle daydreams of the philistine who chafes at rules and
wishes to enjoy the liberties allowed bohemians. Marriage and
children are set at naught; family tedium leads nearly to suicide
in "V berezovom kotèdzhe" (1911). Love itself may be either
obsessive or frivolous, depending on the caprice of the moment.

The aesthetic pronouncements that appeared in the Futurist
manifestos were meager in content; the Cubo-Futurists merely
rejected the art of the past, the Ego-Futurists elevated the ego,
and both advocated the use of words as an artistic medium. But
every program was sufficient to obviate the didactic tendency of
Sentimentalism, and occasionally "feminization" was also repu-
diated.[8] When the heart displaced the rational capacity as the seat
of moral discernment, women were pronounced more sensitive
than men to its delicate stirrings. Young's *Night Thoughts,* which
exhorts to religious faith, was inspired by the death of a wife.
Karamzin argued in "K zhenshchinam" (1796) that literary taste
is also a moral judgment, and that the artist attunes his work to
the good, the true, and the beautiful by writing for women. Pushkin adopted the convention only facetiously, but in subsequent
Russian prose female characters were indeed held up as a moral
measure in the way that so angered Kruchenykh: men were made

to fail beside women, as Oblomov beside Ol'ga.

The Futurists' poetic depictions of art and the artist are, however, much more revealing than their manifestos, and the works point to a common belief that art captures a unique moment in the flow in the essential universal process. Whether the artist is pictured as a priest, as Khlebnikov did himself in "Truba Gul' Mully," or as the self-effacing spokesman of inanimate things, as Pasternak did when he exhorted his poetry to be a Greek sponge in "Chto pochek, chto kleikikh zaplyvshikh ogarkov," is immaterial. Both views display a faith in the coincidence of the innermost and the elemental. Having rejected the conventional identification of the good, the true and the beautiful, the Futurists yet believed that their art was indicative of the universal or could be of use to society. But their utility was to stem from within, rather than from without. For Khlebnikov the poet was a visionary who foresaw the forms of the future utopia; he was the author of the "Edinaia kniga" which would replace the world religions of the present. In his last poem he reproached society for its failure to recognize him as a guiding star. For Maiakovskii the poet was a savior or a democratic institution, a factory, or a proletarian. The Ego-Futurists' declarations that the artist intuitively identifies with the world Ego probably expresses a wider Futuristic belief in religious terms.

Democratic inclinations dictated the Futurists' tendency to the prosaic and the everyday, their use of colloquial language, and impatience with mellifluous sounds.[9] But the cultivation of vulgarities and harsh sounds with the intent to shock was also a flouting of what was considered to be false, as well as feminine. Maiakovskii instituted his programmatic use of mundane imagery in "A vy mogli by" (1913); in "Vo ves' golos" he pictured conventional poetry as a capricious and aristocratic old lady tending a garden, and himself as a latrine-cleaner. Kruchenykh ascribed moral (and immoral) attributes to the nonlexical aspects of language. In *Slovo kak takovoe* (1913) he protested that language should no longer be required to be pure and honest, as those virtues were more appropriate to women. In *Vzorval'* (1913) he predicted that "Out of base (podlogo) disdain for woman (sic) and children our language will have only the masculine gender."[10]

His peom "Dyr bul shchyl" features grating sounds, and else-where he defended their use theoretically. Pasternak's prosaic imagery results, however, only from a salutary sense of democracy among phenomena.

The Futurists were uniformly without the belief in a personal deity which the Sentimentalists had once defended in the face of Romantic doubts and theories of a world soul. They did not tend as a group to espouse, or even oppose, any metaphysical positions; they deemphasized the entire sphere, and their individual positions are sometimes difficult to discern. But their evident demands or yearnings for a sense of ultimate belonging while in the present were alien to the Sentimental resignation to earthly sufferings in the anticipation of a more gratifying afterlife. Futurists wrote either as pantheists or as atheists; in either guise they sometimes posed as cosmic rebels. In Khlebnikov's poem "Gody, liudi i narody" he sadly evoked a universe whose whole essence is transience and shadow; but in "V tiazhelykh sapogakh" the difficulty of that passage is said to be recorded in words (art), which are a reproach (a knife in the heart) to God. Khlebnikov in some poems appears as a minor Prometheus. Maiakovskii's derisive pictures of God and heaven indicate not only an atheist's revolt against clericalism, but a metaphysical frustration which prompted him to assume, even if ironically, a savior's role, whether as Prometheus or as Christ. Thus, in the place of the divinity, the Futurists variously perceived either essence or emptiness, but the figure of God was posited as a straw man. They were more consistent in discerning either in nature or in natural man the locus of their values. Khlebnikov, Guro, and Kamenskii venerated nature and the pastoral way of life. In "Mne vidny — Rak, Oven" Khlebnikov recorded a moment of cosmic ecstasy when he felt as a younger brother to the constellations. The intensity of the sense of existence was highly valued among the Futurists. In this respect, Pasternak, who was more given to religious emotions and premises than to the societal concerns of the Cubo-Futurists, was an exemplary Futurist.[11] His universe is characterized by an omnipresent vitality which is the opposite of Young's leading idea in *Night Thoughts,* which is that true life begins only after death.

In summary, Sentimentalism had taught the individual to value the rewards of accepting society's framework, but the Futurists did not believe in or did not value that framework. They found that despite rulers and governments life is dangerous and painful, or that states are oppressive. They found their private needs did not match the conventions intended to provide for private gratifications. They (and other avantgardists), having inherited a Romantic individualism, intensified still further its potential for a delight in opposing society or a need to fight society. Thus they viewed art as a self-justified embodiment of their own perceptions of self, society, and the universe.

University of Illinois
at Urbana-Champaign

NOTES

1. The rejection of the past *in toto* was made in the Cubo-Futurists' initial manifesto, "Poshchechina obshestvennomu vkusu" (Moscow, 1912). A general history of Futurism appears in Vladimir Markov, *Russian Futurism: A History* (Berkeley and Los Angeles: University of California Press, 1968). A history of Cubo-Futurism appears in Vahan D. Barooshian, *Russian Cubo-Futurism 1910–1930* (The Hague and Paris: Mouton, 1974). N. Khardzhiev and V. Trenin, *Poèticheskaia kul'tura Maiakovskogo* (Moscow: Iskusstvo, 1970) contains general comments about the Futurists' literary technique.

2. Aleksei Kruchenykh, "Chort i rechetvortsy," *Apokalipsis v russkoi literature* (Moscow, 1923), p. 9. When Futurists attacked any specific literary schools, their objects were Symbolism or Realism; they seem to have remained oblivious to the fact that Russian Realism had been strongly influenced by Sentimentalism.

3. N. G. Chernyshevskii, "Russkii chelovek na rendez-vous," *Polnoe sobranie sochinenii v piatnadtsati tomakh,* Vol. 5, Part I (Moscow: GIKhL, 1950), pp. 156–174.

4. Benedikt Livshits, *Polutoraglazyi strelets* (Leningrad, 1933), p. 144.

5. Maiakovskii's works are analyzed in the following: Edward J. Brown, *Mayakovsky: A Poet in the Revolution* (Princeton: Princeton University Press, 1973); Victor Erlich, "The Dead Hand of the Future: Vladimir Maiakovskii," *The Double Image: Concepts of the Poet in Slavic Literatures* (Baltimore: The Johns Hopkins Press, 1964); Lawrence Leo Stahlberger, *The Symbolic System of Majakovskij* (The Hague: Mouton, 1964).

6. Vladimir Markov, *Russian Futurism: A History,* p. 129.

7. See several examples translated by Vladimir Markov in *Russian Futurism: A History,* pp. 65–75.

8. An analysis of the material contained in the manifestos appears in Anna Lawton, "Russian and Italian Futurist Manifestos," *Slavic and East European Journal,* Vol. 20, No. 4, pp. 405–420

9. I discussed the contrast between the Futurists' use of the elevated and the low in "Romanticism and Naturalism in the Works of the Russian Futurists," *American Contributions to the Eighth International Congress of Slavists,* Vol. 2. Edited by Victor Terras. (Columbus, Ohio: Slavica, 1978), pp. 82–95.

10. A. Kruchenykh, "Iz knigi 'Slovo, kak takovoe'," *Apokalipsis v russkoi literature* (Moscow, 1923), p. 42; "Iz 'Vzorval'"," *Manifesty i programy russkikh futuristov.* Edited by Vladimir Markov (Munich: Fink Verlag, 1967), p. 62.

11. See A.D. Siniavskii, "Poèziia Pasternaka," in Boris Pasternak, *Stikhotvoreniia i poèmy,* 2nd ed. (Moscow and Leningrad: Sovetskii pisatel', 1965. Biblioteka poèta, Bol'shaia seriia), pp. 9–62.

VALENTIN RASPUTIN: A GENERAL VIEW

DEMING BROWN

A great amount of perceptive, analytical and appreciative commentary on the writing of Valentin Rasputin has appeared in Soviet and Western literary criticism.[1] He is widely recognized as one of the most promising of Soviet authors — perhaps, in fact, the most gifted writer of the 1970s. In considering four of his *povesti* (*Den'gi dlia Marii* — 1967, *Poslednii srok* — 1971, *Zhivi i pomni* — 1974, and *Proshchanie s Materoi* — 1976), what I find most striking is the enormous range of his talent.

The various aspects of Rasputin's writing are so closely integrated and so well-balanced that it is difficult to single out separate features, much less to establish a hierarchy among them. I shall therefore list what I consider to be Rasputin's most prominent virtues, in no particular order of importance.

Rasputin displays a profound knowledge of human nature, and of the ways in which individuals, consciously or unconsciously, manifest their emotions, their likes and dislikes, their allegiances and their sense of right and wrong. All of Rasputin's *povesti* are concerned with important moral issues, which he keeps in clear and constant focus, and which he explores in all their complexity and many-sidedness. His characterizations do not spare the uglier sides of behavior, but they also include a great deal of compassion for the fallible human race. Examining his characters both individually and in groups, Rasputin shows a remarkable sense of the social organism — the rhythms and unwritten laws of its existence, its cohesive and divisive forces. This virtue, of course, is most evident in his portrayal of the Siberian village.

All four of the *povesti* feature situations of crisis. Rasputin's favorite strategy, it would seem, is to set up ominous, threat-

ening, or even doomed circumstances and to examine how people
behave in these conditions. Although there are highly dramatic
incidents and confrontations, there is no resolution, as a rule,
nor is one needed. The function of the story is to probe the
psyches of individual Russians, to test their moral fibre, and to
trace in detail the patterns of their lives with one another in a
native Siberia to which the author is extremely devoted.

Particularly noteworthy is Rasputin's sensitive use of the natural environment — vegetation, the river Angara, the seasons and
the weather, birds — together with domestic animals and crops.
The critic Starikova has pointed to the striking quality of *anima-
tion* in his portrayal of nature, which lends a dynamic, poetic
aura to his depiction of the environment and of man's relationship to it.[2] The acuteness of Rasputin's eye for detail in both the
natural and the man-made worlds, and his subtle emphasis on
the close relationship between these two worlds, endow his writing with an extraordinary sense of life.

Another special quality of Rasputin's writing is its unity and
compactness. Each of the four *povesti* focuses on a single problem or situation, and almost everything in the narrative bears
upon it. There are no subplots or digressions, and nearly all
characters, episodes and images contribute to an exploration of
the central issue. Although the *povesti* are rich in physical and
psychological detail, contain many descriptions of settings, and
include abundant dialogue and monologue, they give an overall
impression of narrative economy, discipline and control. Likewise, despite their localized, rural Siberian setting and atmosphere,
all four *povesti* have a manifestly universal human relevance. For
Rasputin explores many of the darker and more poignant aspects
of human existence with remarkable courage and insight.

Rasputin's works gain authenticity from the ingredient of village culture that is embodied in them. Folk beliefs and standards
of conduct, traditional ways of doing and seeing things, in large
measure motivate the behavior of his characters, particularly that
of the older ones among them. Of course, Rasputin is not unique
among Soviet writers in his ability to suggest such motivation.
What lends his works a special authority in this respect is his ingenious use of local language, in the speech of his narrator as well

as that of his characters, to suggest, intimately, his villagers' points of view. It is particularly significant that he does this so successfully, since a major concern of his stories is the present threat to his villagers' way of life and the precious human values it represents.

Rasputin is similar to other contemporary village writers in several respects. Among these is his striving to convey a sense of reality in the depiction of social surroundings and cultural detail. He writes with the precision, meticulousness and inclusiveness of a careful ethnographer. I have already mentioned his close attention to the nuances of localized rural speech. Also, he indirectly describes his characters by listing the objects they use in their daily lives. In *Proshchanie s Materoi,* for example, there is a fascinating catalogue of peasant implements and household things, and a touching account of the villagers' attachment to these objects — most notably the samovar that is destroyed when Katerina's house burns down: "Without it, Katerina was completely orphaned."

Like most Soviet writers about rural life, Rasputin seems to argue that the best qualities of his villagers come from their closeness to the soil. In *Den'gi dlia Marii,* one of the most endearing traits of the hero Kuz'ma is the fact that money has meant nothing to him because he has lived so intimately and exclusively with the land. More specifically, it is *work* — what men do with their hands when they live on the soil — that ennobles them and provides them with spiritual support. The malaise of Anna's son Mikhail in *Poslednii srok* comes to a great extent from the fact that mechanization and the breakup of his kolkhoz prevent him from engaging in hard, communal labor. One of the finest of many splendid scenes in *Proshchanie s Materoi* is the last joyous hay-cutting, a bittersweet festival of labor celebrating the final efflorescence of the doomed island.

A tendency to emphasize the dichotomy between the city and the countryside is another trait that Rasputin shares with most village writers. Like them he views urbanization, technology, and the modern industrial, bureaucratic society, with anxiety. With the growth of cities the preservation of precious folk customs and traditions is threatened, and the cultural and moral values of the countryside are being eroded. These fears are expressed primarily in *Poslednii srok,* in which those children of the dying Anna who have been urbanized (her daughters Liusia and the absent Tan'chora), or who have otherwise been uprooted from their native village (son Il'ia), are seen to have lost a great deal of their humanity. Both this story and *Proshchanie s Materoi* feature groups of people whose demoralization is attributable to encroachments from the city on their way of life.

Closely related to this concern is another which Rasputin shares with many village writers — alarm over disruption of the natural environment. This is a major burden of *Proshchanie s Materoi.* (It is typical of Rasputin's tightly integrated thematics that this issue in the story is virtually inseparable from the issue of the threat to rural culture.) I see *Proshchanie s Materoi* as primarily a work of social protest (albeit the author's best-written *povest'*), directed against those who are altering the environment and disrupting a time-honored mode of existence in the name of material progress. It is also, of course, a loving tribute to a disappearing way of life and set of values and a poetic lament over their passing. But the undertone of moral indignation over the drowning of this beautiful, fertile island and the three centuries of peasant civilization it has nourished, of hatred for the planners who are forcing this ugly transformation, is unmistakable. In this respect, *Proshchanie s Materoi* is closer in spirit to much of the rest of "village prose" than any other work of Rasputin.

Until the appearance of this *povest'*, Rasputin could not have been properly considered a writer of immediate and direct social protest. Social pathos had indeed been present in the three previous *povesti,* but as a rule it had been subordinated to other concerns. Rasputin was clearly partial to the village, but he showed his devotion by describing it in detail, without overtly asserting his partisanship. Unlike other writers, for example, he did not linger on the poverty, deprivation and discontent in the countryside. Rather, he seemed to accept the difficulties, and sometimes the injustices, of village life, as a matter of course, as something to be lived with and not dwelt upon. The village as an entity was important for him, but not as a matter of central interest. What did interest the author were more general questions of a universal nature, and the village was an interesting and familiar setting in which to explore these questions. It is this circumstance, I think, that explains the difference between Rasputin and other village writers, and which helps to explain the broad range of his accomplishments.

However, before embarking on a discussion of these accomplishments, as reflected in the first three *povesti,* I should like to linger for a moment on Rasputin's use of nature, the presence of which is felt constantly, and which is closely integrated with many different features of his narration. The author uses landscapes of varying dimensions, to create atmosphere, to establish mood, and as indirect moral commentary. Thus, the lovingly beautiful descriptions of Matera make its impending passing all the more deplorable. An example is the mysterious nocturnal prowl through the ill-fated village by the goblin "Khoziain" — an account which captures the subtle sounds, smells, sights, and the very feel of the place as it breathes in its sleep. Nature provides much of the imagery in the stories. *Proshchanie s Materoi* includes numerous tree images, of which the most prominent is the huge, indestructible larch which, tradition has it, serves as the island's "anchor." Near the end of *Poslednii srok* a lone, semi-transparent cloud appears in the clear sky — a delicate reminder of the impending death of the venerable and noble peasant Anna. In *Zhivi i pomni* the image of Nastena fighting her way through a snowstorm to visit her misanthropic, fugitive husband suggests her tragic plight in general.

The author carefully chooses the seasons of the year in which his narratives occur. *Den'gi dlia Marii* is set in the time of transition between autumn and winter — dull, grey, ugly days in which everyone is "waiting . . . waiting . . . waiting" — which contributes to the mood of threat and apprehension essential to the story. In *Zhivi i pomni,* the coming of spring, through emphatic contrast, provides an ironic background for the criminal acts of the deserter Andrei and the anguish of his pregnant wife Nastena, who is his victim. Poetic coloration and mood are also provided by the weather. In *Den'gi dlia Marii,* the roaring and wailing of the wind, and its banging of shutters, give a sense of alarm, and the long-expected snow, which finally falls at the end of the story, suggests a resolution. In the closing pages of *Proshchanie s Materoi,* a sudden fog impedes the effort to evacuate the final holdouts among the island's inhabitants; nature has flung up a last, desperate barrier.

Bird and animal imagery is especially prominent in *Zhivi i pomni.* Nastena, trapped in her tragic circumstance, finds temporary relief in the return of the swallows, which also coincides with the end of the war against Germany. She also pities the hawk, a predator which reminds her of her husband Andrei Gus'-kov. Gus'kov himself learns to howl from a wolf; his killing of a wild she-goat (and morbid curiosity over her lingering death), and his subsequent killing of a bull calf in the presence of its mother, foreshadow the destruction of Nastena and her unborn child.

In large measure the strong effectiveness of Rasputin's writing comes from his humanizing of nature, to give an intimate, peasant's-eye view of the world. In *Poslednii srok,* the weather and seasons are described in villagers' dialect, in terms of their effect on the potato harvest and haymaking, and the author further animates the weather, for example, by comparing its errant behavior to that of an old woman who has lost possession of her faculties. For the eighty-year-old Anna on her deathbed, nature remains the strong source of wonder and consolation it has been all her life. In both this story and *Proshchanie s Materoi,* elder Siberian peasants are shown to be inextricably close to nature. To a great extent, the psychology of the characters in these novels, and *Zhivi i pomni* as well, is shown to be inseparable from the rhythm of nature.

I have asserted that ultimately what makes Rasputin stand out among writers who use the village setting is his concern with questions of a universal nature. *Den'gi dlia Marii* is an examination of a community's response to the emergency of one of its families, an emergency that can be met only through comradeship, generosity and self-sacrifice. Mariia, an honest and simple woman, has been exploited by her neighbors, who have persuaded her to take the job of village storekeeper even though she totally lacks the necessary experience and is fearfully reluctant. An inventory discloses a shortage, and although everyone knows she is not guilty of embezzlement, she faces a prison term if she cannot cover the shortage. The heart of the story is the attempt of her husband Kuz'ma to save her (and therefore their family) by borrowing a thousand rubles from his friends and neighbors, and ultimately, with little reason to hope, from his brother in the city. Kuz'ma is only partially successful, and the story ends with his and Mariia's problem unresolved. Within the framework of this test of communality, the story offers a fascinating and sharply individualized gallery of characters as they react in various noble and ignoble ways to Kuz'ma's timid appeals for help. Rasputin has put the human race on trial, with only mixed results. The story is tightly compressed, suspenseful, and rich in psychological insight.

Poslednii srok recounts the last days in the life of Anna, an old Siberian villager. Four of her five living children (she has borne thirteen) come to her deathbed. A temporary improvement in her condition enables three of her children to persuade themselves that Anna is not yet dying, and they leave abruptly. They have come not to comfort their mother but to bury her, and are frustrated, disappointed, even angry at her stubborn refusal to die. That night Anna does die.

We are shown a family that has become fragmented and has lost its soul in the process. Anna's children have not merely been geographically dispersed and out of touch; they are spiritually remote from one another and are clearly unworthy of their mother. (One wonders, in fact, how such an exemplary peasant woman could have produced such an ugly and shallow brood.) At the same time, they are a fascinating group, acutely individualized and vividly memorable.

Each of Anna's children is portrayed in a deft combination of perspectives: direct authorial description; through the eyes of Anna (both in the present and in retrospect); through the eyes of his or her siblings and in interaction with them; through the eyes of five-year-old Ninka; and through his or her own behavior. The two sons Mikhail (the only one who has remained in his native village) and Il'ia (a pathetically stupid failure who lives in the city and whose face, to his mother, seems anonymous "as if he had sold his own or lost it at cards"), consume the bottles of vodka purchased for the wake. The eldest daughter Varvara, dim-

witted and confused, flaps about hysterically in search of rituals
to suit the occasion. Although all of Anna's children are callous
and lacking in spiritual depth, the most repulsive is the quarrelsome daughter Liusia, a hardened, self-righteous city-dweller who
views everything in the village, including her own family, with an
attitude of critical superiority, and who even scolds her mother
for pretending to be sicker than she is.

It should be emphasized that *Poslednii srok* is a multi-dimen-
sional work of art, more mature in several aspects than *Den'gi
dlia Marii.* Anna, who with her old friend Mironikha represents
a disappearing generation and its values, is a profoundly conceived character, particularly in the portrayal of her steadfast,
welcoming approach to death. Also of great interest is her son
Mikhail, who, despite his scandalously sodden behavior, is the
least selfish in his attitude toward his mother. In one of the story's
psychologically most interesting scenes, Mikhail, over a bottle,
speculates at length to his equally broken-spirited brother Il'ia on
"why we drink" and says: "We've gotten very tired, and not,
you know, from work, the devil knows what from." There are
numerous other arresting scenes in this account of a family in
which, as O. Salynskii has observed, "Anna has a soul, her children have psychology."[3] Perhaps the most powerful scene is the
story's swiftly dramatic ending, in which Liusia, Il'ia and Varvara
leave their mother in a rush, forever.

Rasputin's talent for the dramatic is best shown in his skillful
construction of a tragedy in *Zhivi i pomni,* the story of a front-
line deserter, Andrei Gus'kov, who hides out near his native village with the aid of his wife Nastena. A loving, loyal woman
whose purity of heart blinds her to her own welfare, Nastena sacrifices herself by becoming an accessory to her unworthy husband's crime. As an outlaw, Gus'kov becomes vicious; his humanity disintegrates. Increasingly tormented by guilt, fear of apprehension, and mental torture sadistically inflicted on her by
Gus'kov, Nastena kills herself and their unborn child by drowning
in the Angara. Andrei and Nastena are portrayed with impressive
psychological depth and moral acuity, so that the reader understands them and pities their situation without necessarily con-
doning their acts. The movement of the story is masterful in its

relentless accumulation of harrowing circumstances that lead to Nastena's suicide.

Rasputin shows a remarkably imaginative and tough-minded ability to understand and portray situations of psychological and moral complexity, and to create casts of characters that embody these situations vividly and convincingly. Although his situations and characters are indigenous to Soviet society, they are by no means exclusive to it, and though written with ethnographic precision, the stories have a manifestly human relevance. I think it can be predicted with confidence that this writer, who is still in his early forties, will have made a major contribution to world literature by the end of this century.

University of Michigan

NOTES

1. Two Soviet commentaries are listed below. An excellent commentary in English is in Geoffrey Hosking, *Beyond Socialist Realism: Soviet Fiction Since Ivan Denisovich* (New York, 1980), pp. 70–81.

2. E. Starikova, "Zhit' i pomnit'," *Novyi mir,* 1977, no. 11, p. 247.

3. O. Salynskii, "Dom i dorogi," *Voprosy literatury,* 1977, no. 2, p. 15.

ZHDANOVIST FICTION AND VILLAGE PROSE

KATERINA CLARK

Consider a recently published Soviet novel (1978–79) with the suggestive title *Privol'e* (the wide open spaces or the vast expanses). The novel is set in a village — Privole — in the steppe of Southern Russia. Not surprisingly, the plot of the novel follows a pattern often met in that most popular vogue in contemporary Soviet literature, "village prose."

"Village prose" is more than mere ficiton on the rural theme, it is a literary movement whose authors treat the decline of the Russian village as a metaphor for the passing of what they see as the traditional Russian way of life and explore the possibility that it might be revived. The mood of "village prose" varies, but is usually nostalgic, elegiac, bitter, or skeptical.

The common pattern of "village prose" seen in *Privol'e* is the return of a hero from the city, where he now lives, to the countryside of his roots, a move which brings into focus those issues about the old and the new which "village prose" explores. In *Privol'e* the hero is Mikhail Chazov, a young journalist. He now has a good job in Moscow, but "some strange force" draws him back to Privole. As we encounter him, he longs for "the smell of wormwood" (a traditional Russian symbol for the home of one's roots). Against the advice of his colleagues, and even of his girlfriend, all of whom think he is crazy, he gives up his job and returns to the village. He is not disappointed, for there he finds that true village where the people feel real bonds with their surroundings. The villagers dress as they have "since time immemorial."[1] They are said to have a unique, special nature deriving from those vast expanses of the steppe which have surrounded them and their forebears for centuries.[2]

36

As "village prose," *Privol'e* is closest to that of Valentin Rasputin. In particular, it follows the custom of venerating the simple old woman — uneducated, but selfless and hardworking — as an incarnation of the old moral virtues, a tradition which began with Solzhenitsyn's Matrena of "Matrenin dvor" (1963), but reached an apogee in Rasputin's *Poslednii srok* (1970) and *Proshchanie s Materoi* (1976). In *Provol'e* the simple old woman is Chazov's own grandmother who raised him in part and with whom he now lodges. The grandmother, like the heroine of *Proshchanie s Materoi,* regales her grandson with freshly baked bread and milk straight from the cow.[3] The story of Chazov's grandmother seems closer, however, to that of the old woman in *Poslednii srok.* Chazov's grandmother presides over a dynasty, but her six children are scattered over the country — one has even been sent to the Congo — and as her death approaches she longs to see them again. Shortly before her death, she realizes that she is going to die without seeing her youngest again, and she breaks down and cries.[4]

In view of the fact that the story of Chazov and his grandmother seems close to patterns of quintessential "village prose," it might come as a surprise to learn that *Privol'e* was written by Semen Babaevskii, an infamous author of Zhdanovist kolkhoz novels, novels typical of the Stalinist forties and therefore representative of the sort of hackneyed occasional writing which the authors of "village prose" decry. One might have thought that after all the gibes made at Babaevskii's expense by critics of the early Khrushchev years for his *lakirovka,* or varnishing of reality, he would not have dared to show himself in print again. Indeed, inasmuch as Babaevskii has adopted some of the trappings of "village prose," he seems to be trying to rehabilitate himself in the eyes of the public. As if to confirm this, throughout the novel he insists (speaking through his hero) that a writer must show life as it is without embellishment. Also, in a 1979 review of one of Brezhnev's memoirs, *Tselina,* Babaevskii cites as one of the book's three major virtues its "sincerity" (*iskrennost'*), the very quality whose absence caused Babaevskii's works to be attacked under Khrushchev.[5]

The difference between Zhdanovist fiction and "village prose" entails more than how "sincere" or how embellished the repre-

sentation of Soviet rural life is. The two movements stand for
fundamentally different values. Zhdanovist fiction presents the
official Stalinist version of a Soviet countryside transformed by
collectivization. The idea behind collectivization was not merely
to nationalize farms, but also to organize agriculture along the
lines of industry or, as it was expressed in Stalinist catchphrases,
to "take the city into the countryside": everything was to be large-
scale, centrally planned, and mechanized. This modernization
would lead to greater efficiency, and therefore material progress.
"Village prose" implicitly questions the basic assumptions behind
that scenario as it points to the ills that have flowed from trying
to impose "the city" on the countryside: the rape of nature, ugli-
ness, graft, breaking the bonds that tied man to man and man to
soil, and so on.

Given this clash of fundamental values, it seems highly unlikely
that a Zhdanovist writer could make a transition to "village prose"
with any ease. And, indeed, although the "smell of wormwood"
haunts Chazov over the pages of the entire novel, *Privol'e* is not
really "village prose." On closer examination, even the close-to-
the-earth grandmother does not fit the part of the typical "village
prose" heroine. This is most glaringly apparent when she has died
and Chazov is moved by the sight of all her Soviet medals glint-
ing in the sun as she is placed in her grave.[6] And when the local
officials decide to mark her passing with a monumental statue to
the Soviet shepherdess, placed by the road to impress passing mo-
torists, one understands that this cannot be "village prose."[7]

"Village prose" usually chooses for its subjects figures who
are outside the system, people who have a small or marginal role
in the running of the country — such as the retired women who
figure so prominently in Rasputin's works. If characters do hold
an office, this fact is often not especially relevant. In *Privol'e,*
however, the narrator may sing the praises of his old grandmother,
but whenever he leaves her house and goes out into the countryside he enters a world of kolkhoz chairmen, district Party secre-
taries, etc. and his thoughts are not drawn to village life, but
rather to the question, "What are the qualities of a good *rukovoditel'*?" This time-honored question of Soviet literature dominated Zhdanovist fiction and certain varieties of fiction under

Khrushchev (notably the Ovechkin school) but has more or less died out in recent prose. Moreover, in *Privol'e* the question is presented in a way reminiscent of Zhdanovist literature: in a schematic contrast of three local officials, each of whom represents an excess, one is too liberal and bookish, one too independent, and a third too high-handed and materialistic, too neglectful of ideology.

In addition to such fossilized Zhdanovist thematics, *Privol'e* makes certain points which suggest that, in a covert way, the book is a polemic against "village prose." Its polemical stance can be sensed not only in a number of details (such as the comment that certain characters would do well to shave off their beards)[8] but also in major themes, such as the contempt shown for those who resist modernization and the advance of technology. Such people are given the familiar Stalinist tag, "those whom time has passed by,"[9] while positive characters are described as "young, energetic, and educated."[10] The heroes of "village prose" are typically old and uneducated. In short, *Privol'e,* while making gestures in the direction of "village prose," also attacks its basic values. The novel seems confused and never manages to establish what it is *for.* The hero's tragic death in a fire conveniently breaks off his search for the true *rukovoditel',* and there the novel ends. Perhaps Babaevskii could not make it into "village prose," after all. Perhaps, to use the old adage, "time had passed him by . . . ."

One should not conclude from Babaevskii's failure that "village prose" and Zhdanovist fiction have nothing in common. Their incompatibilities are obvious; nevertheless, they have more similarities than one might expect. Particularly we in the West do not expect to find similarities because we consider Zhdanovist prose discredited, whereas "village prose" is taken seriously.

One reason why "village prose" might have some features in common with Zhdanovist fiction is that there are aspects of the social and cultural climate of the Soviet Union today which are similar to those which obtained in the Zhdanov period. These include: firstly, World War II's central role in official culture as a major symbol; secondly, an increasing chauvinism and xenophobia; thirdly, an aging administration which resists major innovation; fourthly, problems in feeding the populace which have made the question of what to do in the rural sector more urgent; and, finally, a low birthrate. In both Zhdanovist fiction and "village prose" some themes reflect these political realities. For instance, in both there is a stress on the value of the family and dynastic roots, on woman's role as a bearer of children, on the sufferings and human loss brought by World War II, and (though in the Zhdanov era only in kolkhoz fiction) on how much more rewarding it is to stay in the village, close to nature (and to the country's efforts to increase the food supply), rather than to work in a city. There have in both instances also been examples of an insidious *Blut and Boden* kind of writing.

Although "village prose" seems in these themes to be responding to its times, one cannot write it off as merely a well-disguised "social command" writing, that is, writing whose direction is officially prescribed. Zhdanovist fiction, by contrast, was subject to pressures which ensured that it obeyed most "social commands." Moreover, the two themes which the Zhdanov era most insistently "commanded" to its writers make Zhdanovist fiction *dissimilar* to "village prose" — i.e., the cults of technology and of the Stalinist leadership. There are indications that had writers then enjoyed as much freedom as they now have in the Soviet Union, they might have produced a fiction that was closer to the ethos of "village prose" than was the case even of literature in the Khrushchev years, when the writer was freer in many respects than he is today.

While fiction of the Khrushchev period was obsessed with destalinization and related issues in Soviet public life, Zhdanovist fiction and "village prose" both betray a greater interest in private life and personal sorrows and joys. Much of the fiction of the seventies, and especially "village prose," is dominated by the monologues of ordinary people who relate universal events such as loves and hardships, deaths in the family, disappointments in children, and so on. Children are born out of wedlock, family members are estranged, and many couples divorce. In Zhdanovist fiction one can detect, beneath the veneer of the saga about how the plan was fulfilled and the cadres trained, beneath the stock themes of public life, this same concern with the ordinary lives of individuals.

In almost all novels of the forties (other than those about the war), the hero's love plays a central role. Moreover, in most cases the threat of divorce or adultery hangs over the lives of the protagonists. Writers could not allow their heroes to indulge in adultery, or even to experience sexual passion. One's love and one's work had to be inextricably intertwined. Characteristically for the Zhdanovist novel, in G. Nikolaeva's "Zhatva" (1950), the heroine falls in love with her future husband as she sees him driving a tractor.[11] Heaven forfend that her passion or love-making should be described to the reader, though its occurence is always intimated.[12] In Babaevskii's Stalin prize kolkhoz novel *Kavaler zolotoi zvezdy* (1947–48), we infer what is happening when the hero is obliged to spend the night at his fiancee's house on one visit "because of the rain." He wakes in the night to find her standing in his room "in a white dress." They go out for a walk in the steppe (the rain having conveniently stopped). Break. The action resumes next morning when the hero feels so renewed that he is able to work better than before — "as if the night had poured new strength into him."[13] In *Privol'e* Babaevskii responded to the more liberal conventions of Soviet literature today and even allowed his hero to impregnate one woman in an access of passion while another already awaited his illegitimate child. The contrast between Babaevskii's two books says more about changing literary conventions regarding the depiction of sexual passion than it does about the relative concern for matters of the heart in the fiction of the seventies as compared with that of the forties.

Of course human interest themes — love, passion, and melodrama — can be utilized in the service of virtually any ideology. To point to the common themes in Zhdanovist fiction and "village prose" might be to obscure their fundamentally different stances. The nostalgia of "village prose" for traditional peasant life seems completely at odds with the Zhdanovist celebration of progress, electrification, and machines.[14] But a closer look at Zhdanovist novels reveals a surprising degree of ambivalence about modernization. In V. Panova's industrial novel *Kruzhilikha* (1947), for instance, children find much more spiritual sustenance in the woods and the steppe than they do in the dreary city.[15]

In Zhdanovist novels one even finds sections describing the "pull of the soil." In E. Mal'tsev's *Ot vsego serdtsa* (1948), for instance, a ne'er-do-well husband feels quite exultant while mowing in the fields with his fellow villagers: "He was filled with a proud feeling he hadn't felt for some time, a feeling of being at one with everyone."[16] As his wife drives across the steppe she is filled with joy at its boundlessness and exclaims to herself involuntarily "O Rus! What do you want of me? What is that mysterious bond between us that can never be broken?"[17] In P. Pavlenko's *Shchast'e* (1947), the hero, Voropaev, a wounded army officer retired to work in the rural Crimea, finds there a richer world than the one of epaulettes and promotions he left behind. We hear echoes of Tolstoi when Voropaev confounds an ambitious young officer of his acquaintance by rejecting his offer of a prestigious military post saying he prefers to be where he is, among the tillers, for "I have always felt drawn to the soil."[18]

In Zhdanovist fiction such bucolic transports are prudently juxtaposed with other events. In *Ot vsego serdtsa* the husband feels ecstatic about mowing just after he is flattered to be invited to work in a new electric station, and the wife is moved by the vastness of the steppe as she returns to her village after being inducted into the Party. In *Shchast'e,* Voropaev expresses his attachment to the soil as he rejects a path of careerist opportunism in favor of remaining where he has been posted. Such events do not cancel out the pastoral sentiments, nevertheless.

The thematic similarities between Zhdanovist fiction and "village prose" should not be exaggerated. Although the two have many more themes and attitudes in common than one might have expected, there remain obvious differences between them. A purely mechanical, thematic approach — such as comparing the amount of sentiment favoring nature in Zhdanovist fiction with the amount favoring the machine — would not be very fruitful. We have to examine this question at a less superficial level.

The first question which must be asked is what is the "village" of "village prose," anyway? Especially Babaevskii's mock- "village prose" novel throws this question into focus. It is clearly not enough to "folks-up" one's fiction in order to produce "village prose." Yet do we want to go as far as some critics who accept as "village prose" writers only those whose work is clearly informed by a religious faith? Then we must ask whether "village prose" writers represent any sort of consensus on the meaning of the village. Are they, for instance, really advocating a return to the village as they lament its decline? Here there seems to be great ambivalence. At times, some writers such as V. Belov seem to want to resurrect the entire peasant culture (to judge from works like "Lad" of 1979 and "Beskul'tur'e" of 1968). Some even imply that all those who leave the village are lost people, as do P. Oroshin in "Tiaga zemli" and E. Nosov in "Ob"ezdchik." Others, however, are haunted by the idea that their vision of the traditional Russian village is a chimera that never existed or a dream that could never be recaptured. It is an Eden lost in the past and those who try to return to the village of their youth or their forefathers discover the age-old truth that you can never go home again, as V. Belov implies in "Sluchainye etiudy."

In the past decade not only "village prose" has told of alienation, discontinuity, fractured families, and vain strivings to rediscover bonds among people. This tendency has been apparent in most recent Soviet fiction. Indeed, Belov's excursion into urban fiction with works like "Vospitanie po doktoru Spoku" and "Moia zhizn' (Avtobiografiia)" (both 1974) demonstrates how close "village" and urban fiction are in this regard. Recent fiction has obsessively shown estrangement from and disillusionment in the family as a metaphor for the failure of the ideal of true community which the Communist experiment promised.

A second, and more important, reason why "village prose" has more features in common with its seeming antagonist, Zhdanovist fiction, than one might expect is that the Russian intelligentsia has been concerned, at least since the latter half of the nineteenth century, with the problem of alienation and especially with what happened to Russia as it became westernized and entered the industrial and urban age. Many intellectuals believed that a solution to Russia's many social ills could be found in a return to the traditional way of life. Some even advocated that Russian society be organized along the lines of the old peasant commune. Those who looked to Marxism believed that its doctrines offered a surer route to their ideal of true community.

"Village prose," then, is but another expression of the intelligentsia's perpetual dream of *Gemeinschaft*. Its practitioners yearn not so much for the village as such, as for the sense of wholeness and organic unity they associate with the village and which they believe has been lost. Some seek that ideal in a *place,* the Russian village, others in a time, pre-Muscovite Russia when city-states were small communities not yet subjected to the evils of Muscovite centralism. Most authors choose the village, however, and their fiction is haunted by the ideal of a rhythmic life in a close community which is still in touch with its age-old traditions and where man is not cut off from the soil. Belov conveys this vision in a recent account of peasant culture with the suggestive title "Lad" (harmony):

> Everything was interconnected and nothing could live separately, without the other parts. Everything was assigned its place and time. Nothing could exist outside the whole or appear out of turn.[19]

"Village prose" is a pastoralization of Soviet reality. Here I mean pastoralization not just in the literal sense that writers cover the landscape with quaint villages. "Village prose" represents a pastoralization in the more modern usage of the term whereby literature is called "pastoral" if, to use the definition provided by Peter Marinelli,

> [it] deals with the complexities of life against a background of simplicity. All that is necessary is that memory and imagination should conspire to render a not too distant past of comparative innocence as more pleasureable than a harsh present . . . .[20]

A striking feature of almost all "village prose" is that it is set in some remote part of Russia, usually in Siberia, the Altai, or the north of European Russia. In these remoter areas the traditional Russian village has been better preserved than it has been near dense population areas. The setting is thus cut off in both space and time — not absolutely, but relatively — from the rest of the country. Rasputin even set his award-winning novella *Zhivi i pomni* (1974) in a village on the Angara where no boats called and, as he said pointedly, "no news penetrated."[21]

Somewhat analogous in Zhdanovist fiction was the practice of setting novels "far away from Moscow" (to use the words of the title of V. Azhaev's novel of 1949), that is, distant from major urban centers such as Moscow or Leningrad (this tendency began to erode in the last years of the Zhdanov era with novels like Y. Trifonov's *Studenty* of 1951). Even when a novel was set in a major city, action focused so exclusively on the place of work of the protagonists as to make its actual location virtually irrelevant.

The action of a Zhdanovist novel was set not only "far away from Moscow," but usually in a finite microcosm such as a factory, kolkhoz or army unit which was represented as isolated from the surrounding areas. One reason for this, I would suggest, was that writers felt ideologically bound to portray Soviet society as an incipient *Gemeinschaft* and in these small settings it was easier to tone down the "harshness" and "complexity" of modern Soviet life; they made a "village" of life in an advanced industrial nation. Moreover, the "pastoral" element in Zhdanovist fiction was often intensified by individual writers. Many of them had inherited anti-urban prejudices from their intelligentsia forebears, and these sentiments colored even their telling of the standard Zhdanovist tale of how technology brought progress and plenty to the countryside.

Writers of today are more fortunate in that when they write of the countryside they are no longer obliged to turn their fiction into production novels. They are able to set their novels in the village itself, rather than in the office of the kolkhoz president or district secretary. They are not obliged, as were their Zhdanovist predecessors, to seat their heroes on tractors or in positions of authority. Hence, they can take their heroes even farther "from Moscow" than could Azhaev in his novel about a pipeline project in the Far East of Siberia. In both Zhdanovist fiction and "village prose," the setting in a small, closed world relatively cut off from the rest of the country is a way of creating an ecosystem, an environment pared of much of the complexity of present reality where *Gemeinschaft* can flourish.

There is often an element of idealization in "village prose," a *lakirovka* (albeit a less insidious one than in Zhdanovist fiction). Much of "village prose" is starkly realistic, but lurking beneath the surface of the grim narrative you find an opposite impulse, and it surfaces periodically. The most idealized figure is, of course, the old peasant: uneducated and humble, he (or most often, she) becomes the last remaining source of morality and spirituality and, in Belov's "Lad," of aesthetics. It is even suggested that those truly close to the soil are more industrious and don't drink to excess.

"Village prose" writers have the same lust for the transcendental and extraordinary as was carried to such ludicrous extremes in Stalinist culture. They make the poor, overburdened Russian peasant its vessel. It should not be forgotten that Stalinist culture also developed in the Stakhanovite movement a cult of the extra-systemic and uneducated. Kolkhoz fiction of those years also had truly wondrous people. In G. Nikolaeva's "Zhatva," for instance, the heroine falls in love with her tractor driver because there is something "extraordinary" in his speech.[22]

"Village prose" writers are not always less extravagant than Zhdanovist authors in depicting positive heroes. You can even find a distinctive kind of hagiography about "village prose" writers themselves which is uncannily reminiscent of the sort of hagiography written about culture heroes in the Stalin era. Particularly striking in this regard is the description published in *Moskva* in 1980 of an interview with Dmitry Balashov at a conference of Northern writers. Balashov was dressed in folk costume and sported a beard, but the reporter was especially struck by Balashov's "unusual face":

> It was pale and — I do not spurn the use of lofty words — spiritual, and concentrated on some great and important thought. It was such a great and such an important thought that it occupied his whole being without any reserve. It was as if he stood here in this vast vestibule yet at the same time was somewhere else, far, far away. No doubt it was the deep, penetrating eyes which gave such an impression. He gazed at you and saw what was behind you and beyond, beyond the walls of this hall.[23]

In Stalinist rhetoric the mighty *"vozhd'"* (and, by analogy with him, lesser *"vozhdi"*) was often said to be so "concentrated on some great and important thought" that he would see "far, far away . . . beyond the walls . . . ."[24] And the cliches for the positive hero in fiction of those years included an "intense gaze" and "penetrating eyes."

The hackneyed idealization we find in this description of Balashov is not normally found in "village prose" itself. "Village prose" is more sophisticated: a complex structure, a complex point of view, a narration approaching stream of consciousness, irony, humor, self-irony, character exploration, and ambivalence are all common features. They undermine the epic wholeness which characterized Socialist Realist fiction under Stalin and often turn "village prose" into the mere country cousin of the so-called *byt* prose which tells of the everyday lives of the Soviet Union's urban dwellers.

Yet there is also a wild, utopian strain in "village prose," an expression of the impulse which caused Solzhenitsyn to say in his *Letter to the Soviet Leaders* that much of the Soviet population should be resettled in the Northeast in small towns where all petrol-powered machines would be banned and the people would be saved from the pollution of the cities.[25]

Since the Russian intelligentsia has traditionally felt ambivalent about modernization and has yearned for a sense of community and a reality that transcends the mundane and earthly, something like "village prose" has existed for some time. For instance, Tolstoi, a figure much venerated by the Soviet establishment, provides convenient precedents to which "village prose" writers can point.

There are also precedents which are less acceptable politically. One that comes to mind is Georgii Grebenshchikov who commenced his multivolume dynastic saga of the Altai region, *Churaevy,* in 1913 and finished it in emigration in 1936. In *Churaevy* the informing ideology is cruder and more directly presented than in "village prose," yet we can recognize sentiments much like those informing much "village prose," and Rasputin's in particular; examples are a concern for the graves of the forefathers, a love of the soil, a belief that agricultural labor leads to spiritual fulfillment, and that village folks are "closer to God" than are their cousins in the "so-called cultured world."[26]

This is not to suggest that Rasputin himself is a sort of émigré writer manqué. The list of possible precursors for a writer like Rasputin is long, indeed, for "village prose" belongs to a tradition that is very strong in Russian literature. It predates Socialist

Realism, was carried into emigration, and very likely will postdate Socialist Realism as well. It is so strong that it crept into that unlikely vessel, Zhdanovist fiction, even though in those days the official ideology would have had the city take over the countryside.

Indiana University

NOTES

1. S. Babaevskii, "Privol'e," *Moskva,* 1978, no. 9, p. 110.

2. Ibid., p. 114.

3. Ibid., p. 110.

4. "Privol'e," *Moskva,* 1979, no. 10, p. 38.

5. S. Babaevskii, "Skazanie o tseline," *Moskva,* 1979, no. 1, p. 5.

6. S. Babaevskii, "Privol'e," *Moskva,* 1979, no. 9, p. 61.

7. *Moskva,* 1979, no. 10, p. 125.

8. *Moskva,* 1978, no. 9, p. 179; no. 11, p. 136.

9. *Moskva,* 1979, no. 10, p. 86.

10. *Moskva,* 1978, no. 9, p. 125.

11. G. Nikolaeva, "Zhatva," *Znamia,* 1950, no. 5, p. 20.

12. Ibid., p. 38.

13. S. Babaevskii, "Kavaler zolotoi zvezdy," *Oktiabr',* 1947, no. 4, pp. 37-38.

14. Eg., G. Nikolaeva, "Zhatva," *Znamia,* 1950, no. 5, p. 75.

15. V. Panova, "Kruzhilikha," *Znamia,* 1947, no. 11, pp. 67-9, 81, 104.

16. E. Mal'tsev, "Ot vsego serdtsa," *Oktiabr',* 1948, no. 10, pp. 118, 139.

17. Ibid., p. 164.

18. P. Pavlenko, "Shchast'e," *Znamia,* 1947, no. 2, pp. 4-6.

19. V. Belov, "Lad. Ocherki o narodnoi estetike," *Nash sovremennik,* 1979, no. 10, p. 117.

20. Peter V. Marinelli, *Pastoral* (*The Critical Idiom,* vol. 15; London: Menthuen, 1971), p. 2.

21. Valentin Rasputin, *Povesti* (Moscow: Molodaia gvardiia, 1976), p. 203.

22. *Znamia,* 1950, no. 5, p. 38.

23. Semen Shurtakov, "Vossozdanie istorii," *Moskva,* 1980, no. 3, p. 203.

24. Eg., Akademik I. Vardin, "Ispolin-mudrets," *Vstrechi s tovarishchem Stalinym,* ed. A. Fadaev (Moscow: Gos. izd. polit. lit., 1939), p. 53.

25. A. Solzhenitsyn, *Pis'mo vozhdiam Sovetskogo soiuza* (Paris: Y.M.C.A. Press, 1974, pp. 29-33.

26. Georgii Grebenshchikov, *Churaevy* (7 vols.; New York: Alatas, 1925-52), vol. 3, pp. 134, 141; vol. 7, p. 28.

THE THEME OF "BYT" — EVERYDAY LIFE —
IN THE STORIES OF IURII TRIFONOV

CAROLINE DE MAEGD-SOËP

In contemporary Russian prose Iurii Trifonov is a pioneer in depicting the everyday life — *byt* — of the Russian intelligentsia. This interest is expressed in the themes, structure, and vocabulary of his Moscow stories. However, the word *byt* is seldom used, and Trifonov came to dislike the word. As he told us in Moscow, "I do not write about *byt* but about people's lives."[1] The writer became annoyed by the fact that many Soviet critics and literary scholars define his short stories as *"proizvedeniia bytovogo zhanra"* (works in the *byt* genre).[2] Many Western critics also stress the social aspects of his Moscow stories. Such an approach naturally means that the writer's purely artistic creativity is insufficiently appreciated! Trifonov himself defined the term *"bytopisatel'stvo"* as "literature related to the *ocherk* (sketch), *publitsistika,"* "ethnography and geography." The author also noted the extent to which Soviet writers were concerned with the problem of *byt* and in this context he cited the names of A. Bitov, I. Evdokimov, M. Ganina, D. Granin, V. Iskander, S. Krutilin, G. Semenov, I. Velembovskaia, S. Zalygin, etc. We could certainly add the name of the talented writer I. Grekova to this list.[3]

Trifonov thus categorically denied that the theme of his short stories can be defined as *byt*. Nevertheless it is fascinating to examine the evolution of his attitude towards the term. After all, in 1972 he still not only took the word most seriously but even defended its use. He said: "At that time I could still stand the word, it did not annoy me so much." Indeed, in the early period of his popularity the critics did not yet bandy the term about as a general label for his work. In those days Trifonov himself provided an excellent definition of *byt* when he wrote: "*Byt* is a

great trial. It should not be talked about contemptuously as if it
were a lower side of human life unworthy of literature, for *byt*
is ordinary life, the trials and tribulations of life which reveal
and test the new morality of today . . . . *Byt* is war which knows
no truce."[4]

If the author became so strongly opposed to the use of the term
byt, it was because many critics did not understand his work or
its deeper significance. What is in fact fascinating in Trifonov's
work is the deeper *podtekst,* the undercurrent which is concealed
beneath the seemingly guileless descriptions of everyday routine
with all its prosaic details. In Trifonov's work the moral, philosophical, sociological, historical, political and even economic
podtekst has an essential role. It is not by chance that the word
"nezametno" (unnoticed) occurs so frequently in the Moscow
stories. Sometimes Trifonov is reproached with "not saying everything." His reaction to this accusation was: "As an artist I do
say everything but you have to be able to read properly!" In
other words Trifonov could well have repeated Chekhov's famous remark: "When I write, I rely entirely upon the reader in
the assumption that he will himself add the subjective elements
lacking in the story."[5]

Although Trifonov became annoyed by the term *byt,* he was
correct when in 1976 he pointed out its complexity. At the Sixth
Writers' Congress in Moscow he declared: "There is perhaps no
more enigmatic, polysemantic and incomprehensible word in the
Russian language . . . . It is not for nothing that this concept
does not exist in any other language and that it is impossible to
translate the word *byt* . . . . Foreigners evidently conclude that
the mysterious *byt* is some special form of Russian life." Trifonov also referred to the emotive nature of the "elastic" term,
which is used "now in the form of the simple communication
of information, now in the form, as it were, of a term of reproach,
of condemnation and even of scorn."[6]

Literary polemics about the concept of *byt* have a long tradition. Arguments about it had already begun in Pushkin's day.
Every time a great Russian writer depicts new aspects of prosaic
reality he has to endure the reproach that he was artistically wrong
to use material which lies outside the sphere of "true literature"!

Thus Pushkin's contemporaries reproached him for giving too concrete a picture of reality in *Evgenii Onegin*. But Pushkin taught his readers that everyday reality can serve as the object of highly artistic depictions. When Gogol' in his turn delved deeply into the life of the ordinary man and his apparently banal environment, he too had to endure the reproach that this was no fit subject for an artist! Tolstoi and Dostoevskii also recreated *byt* with their great artistic abilities, but they systematically linked it to questions about life and death. When Chekhov's work appeared, this acute observer of Russian *byt* in a *fin de siècle* atmosphere was severely reproached with being nothing more than a *"byto-pisatel'."* The artistic significance of his work was denied especially by the Symbolists. The poet Z. Gippius even commissioned V. Briusov to write a sharply critical review of the premiere of Chekhov's "naturalistic" *Cherry Orchard,* which was staged in the Moscow Art Theatre on 17 January 1904.[7]

Many Symbolists dreamed of a more exalted existence where there was no place for Chekhov's overly realistic depictions of banal reality. However, the more cautious A. Blok considered that even a Symbolist writer could safely use "some earthy sap" in his work and thus stated that *byt* should be depicted, as Chekhov was doing.[8] Chekhov's honor was "redeemed" by this pronouncement and because of certain symbolistic elements in his work he was even able to influence the Symbolist movement.

In the early twentieth century the problem of *byt* was one of the central themes featured in controversies raging in the Russian artistic world. *"Byt"* was bound up with polemics about man's existence. The possibility of a "new *byt*" forced itself strongly upon the Futurists. Maiakovskii dreamt of an entirely new *byt*. His defeat in the struggle against down-to-earth *byt,* which ended in his suicide, is signalled by a line of his poem "Neokonchen-noe" (Unfinished): "The barque of love has been wrecked on *byt*."[9] In the revolutionary decade of the twenties, the principal question which many Russian artists were asking was: To what extent can man change as a result of the influence of the new social structure? Influential writers such as the humorist M. Zo-shchenko, the philosopher M. Bulgakov, the romanticist Iu. Ole-sha and others showed that in spite of everything man had remained himself! Trifonov too pointed to this phenomenon with his statement: "Man's character does not change as quickly as do cities and river beds."[10]

When considering the traditions of Soviet fiction behind Trifonov's work it should be noted that the principal writers who dealt with the theme of *byt* were Zoshchenko, Bulgakov, and Olesha, each of whom treats the subject in his own particular way. Each also differs in his narrative style and his characters from Trifonov. Zoshchenko was the first writer after the revolution to depict day-to-day life. With his fine sense of humor and occasional irony he describes the adventures of the little man. His heroes are ordinary people without much culture who are removed from the great problems of the general human condition. The author very seldom voices his own point of view but allows his characters to tell and comment upon their own stories. Trifonov told us that Zoshchenko had in fact had an influence upon him from the stylistic point of view. He called him "a perfect master of intonation in Russian literature." In contrast to Zoshchenko Trifonov directs his attention to the intellectual who leads an intense inner life. Nor is it possible to call the "magical" Bulgakov a direct forerunner of Trifonov. Bulgakov reveals to us, especially in his novel *Master i Margarita* (*The Master and Margarita*), the diabolical forces which permeate Moscow *byt*. His depiction is far removed from that of Trifonov who does not recognize the devil at all.[11] In his novel *Zavist'* (*Envy*) Olesha expresses an interest in *byt* but he is a romantic who can only depict the new *byt* in an ironic way.

Beginning in the thirties we notice a striking hiatus in the treatment of the theme of *byt* in Soviet literature. During the Stalinist period a literature emerges which could be considered *byt*-less. The writer's attention is concentrated upon heroic characters who are engaged in the task of constructing the new socialist society. The lengthy novels lack conflict and have no room for *byt,* which highlights man's personal life and psychological state. The theme emerges once more beginning in the 1950s in the works of V. Panova, V. Aksenov, A. Bitov, D. Granin, I. Grekova, S. Krutilin, G. Semenov, I. Velembovskaia, and S. Zalygin.

In his treatment of *byt* Trifonov follows above all the Chekhovian tradition.[12] This is especially noticeable in the way he treats the power of daily routine, people's mutual estrangement, indifference, and the real and the pseudo- intelligentsia. Trifonov, just as Chekhov did, is describing a period of stabilization in Russia. Trifonov's characters find it difficult to remember the war, but in apparently peaceful, contemporary Russian life the writer reveals forces which incite people to wage their own little wars anew every day!

Moscow is the central setting of the action and also determines the atmosphere of Trifonov's stories. In Moscow he unmasks the standardization characteristic of every modern large city and points to its "rapacious" character; a large city constantly expands its boundaries at the expense of nature. Trifonov also poses the problem of the village life sometimes led by the city intelligentsia. Indeed, the theme of the *dacha* plays an essential role in all of the Moscow stories. The *dacha* appears often as the symbol of true beauty, freshness, youth, and peace. For certain of Trifonov's heroes *dacha* life is in fact the sole refuge where they can escape from the difficult conditions of the city. Frequently the most beautiful moments in the lives of Trifonov's characters are experienced in the poetic atmosphere of the *dacha*. The latter symbolizes the "other life" for which Trifonov's heroes strongly yearn!

The transformation of man and human relationships under the pressure of the nervous bustle of city life is an important theme of the Moscow stories. Trifonov wrote of this phenomenon in 1972: "Interrelations between people are also *byt*. We find ourselves in a confused and complicated structure of *byt*, at the crossroads of a multitude of relations, opinions, friendships, acquaintances, enmities, psychologies, ideologies. Every person living in a large city feels at every moment of the day the persistent magnetic currents of this structure acting upon him and sometimes pulling him apart. Choices have constantly to be made, something to be decided, something to be overcome, something to be sacrificed.[13]

The tearing pace of Moscow life affects the Muscovites most during their daily pursuit of elementary comfort. Trifonov depicts the many material problems of contemporary Soviet society down to the last concrete detail. In so doing he makes skillful use of *bytovaia leksika*. However, this depiction is intended to reveal the psychological state of the characters and this is at the heart of the stories' general human significance. In Trifonov's work it is in *bytovye* conflicts that people's varying characters and their outlooks on life are expressed. *Byt* in Trifonov's work is not merely bound up with the concrete problems of a flat, food, clothes, career, and travel abroad. The principal problem posed by the author is: "How must man live?" And above all: "How must man behave towards his fellowmen?" In a discussion with us Trifonov remarked that he considered the most important aspect of life to be the way in which people live together. For him the love of one's fellowmen is the most precious thing in our existence. The author has shown this conviction in a work where the remark is made that the love of one's fellowmen is "the oxygen" without which man cannot live (p. 73).

In particular Trifonov points out the danger inherent in the loss of human contacts as a result of the new consumer ethic. However, he reacted just as strongly to the use of the term *meshchanstvo* (philistinism) with regard to his work as he did to *byt*. He remarked scornfully: "They say that my short stories are not only *'bytovye'*, but even *'meshchanskie'*."[14] Nevertheless Trifonov unmasks philistinism, especially in intelligentsia circles. The author even coined a new term to denote the phenomenon: *olukianit'sia,* from the name of the petit bourgeois Lukianov family in the story "Obmen" ("The Exchange," 1969, p. 37). Here Trifonov depicts the unremitting hunt for greater material comfort. The hero, Viktor Dmitriev, reproaches his wife, Lena Lukianova, for wanting to obtain at any price his dying mother's room so as to exchange that room together with their own room for a large flat. Horrified by his wife's callous behavior, Viktor says bitterly: "You have some sort of spiritual defect. Some sort of underdeveloped feelings. Something . . . subhuman" (p. 10). The author depicts Lena's possessive impulse as something animal-like: "For she clamped onto her desires like a bulldog . . . she did not let go until the desires — held right between her teeth — had turned into flesh" (p. 51). Under pressure from his energetic wife, the weak-willed Viktor is driven to commit an act of which he disapproves and finally he compromises with his conscience and seeks salvation in resignation. His evolution is depicted by Trifonov thus: "He agonized, was amazed and racked his brains but then got used to it. Got used to it because he saw it was the same for everybody and everybody had got used to it" (p. 8).

In all of his Moscow stories Trifonov depicts the process of the sensitive, good-natured, but weak-willed intellectual who abandons his ideals under the pressure of everyday life and is reduced to frustration. He shows that many will not shrink from any quid pro quo, deceit, or treachery in the name of material and intellectual comfort. For this reason the term *"meshchanstvo"* must be viewed in the deeper meaning which the author gives to it. It is not merely an unbridled lust for possessions, but also a weltanschauung steeped in egoism and soullessness.

Trifonov makes frequent use of his *bytovaia leksika* to ironize about people "who have the ability to get their own way" (p. 9), but who in fact reveal a "lack of intelligence and a truly piratical lust for acquisition." He calls them the "gentlemen of success" (p. 111). For such people *byt* is no trial to bear but rather a kind of sport. They build up an indispensable circle of influential connections who can help them in their ascent of the social ladder. In Trifonov's world these artful people assert: "Whoever has the necessary connections can really live!" This is the simple logic of all those characters of whom it is said in his work that they are "ideally adjusted to this life" (p. 51).

Most conflicts in Trifonov's short stories are caused by the collision of these sober "energetic people" with the idealistic heroes, who are not at all adjusted to *byt*. They are distinguished by their rich spiritual interests and their striving for inspired creativity. However, their "sober" environment regards these people as "dreamers," "eccentrics," and "fantasts." They are said to have no "talent for living"! For Trifonov's idealistic heroes *byt* is a real trial. Chekhov too depicts the constant conflict between the idealist and his sterile environment. Trifonov's characters are so firmly rooted in prosaic *byt* that they form part of it and can no longer escape. In this then lies the tragic significance of Trifonov's work. However, the author also uses *bytovye* conflicts to reflect the indecisiveness and irresolute behavior of the idealistic hero. In his work the protagonists are repeatedly revealed as lacking the force required to oppose their own way of living (p. 90). But Trifonov, humane and understanding, also reveals the inexorability of *byt,* which is why the despondent, agonizing intellectual so frequently asks himself: "What is to be done?" or "Who is guilty?" He thus attempts to understand why he has behaved in his daily life in precisely such and such a way and not differently.

In the Moscow stories the question of "Who is guilty?" is given the most varied of answers. In "Drugaia zhizn'" ("Another Life," 1975) Ol'ga, tormented by the premature death of her husband Sergei, searches for the causes: "Try to understand, there must be a meaning, somebody must be guilty, those near to you are always guilty" (p. 225). In the case of Sergei, a gifted historian, his struggle with his colleagues of the research institute has apparently accelerated the fatal outcome. Ol'ga speaks of intrigues which Sergei's former friend, Klimuk, started in connection with her husband's dissertation: "If only he had reached an agreement with Klimuk then! . . . Everything would have turned out differently. He would still be alive . . . . Sergei did not know how to intrigue, it disgusted and infuriated him . . ." (p. 336). In fact Sergei was the victim of the unrelenting struggle between innovatory, honest, scholarly work and the unoriginal activity of scholars resembling Professor Serebriakov in Chekhov's play *Diadia Vania (Uncle Vania).* This age-old conflict is also portrayed in "Dom na naberezhnoi" ("The House on the Embankment," 1976). Here there are no "guilty people" but the times are the guilty force: "Neither Glebov nor people are guilty, the times are" (p. 375). However, in this story Professor Ganchuk ascribes the guilt above all to the *"melkoburzhuaznaia stikhiia."* His wife, Iuliia, says of an article by one of her husband's assistants, "He wrote about the main thing: the danger represented by the petit-bourgeois element" (pp. 471–72, 426).

In all of the Moscow stories Trifonov also depicts the protagonist's conflict with his conscience. In contrast to the revolutionary hero who acts in a social conflict, the conflict of Trifonov's contemporary hero is with himself. Professor Ganchuk points this out: "Today man does not entirely understand what he is doing . . . . For this reason he is in conflict with himself . . . . He

is trying to convince himself . . . . The conflict is situated deep
within man" (p. 501).

Trifonov's stories illustrate the revival of psychological prose
in present-day Soviet literature.[15] The writer is also following in
the Chekhovian tradition in that he gives a penetrating analysis
of the emotional and spiritual state of his characters. He too
structures his stories mainly in the form of an interior monologue. The narrator or protagonist analyses both his personal
and his social life in order to understand his own personality.
In so doing he sometimes ascribes the guilt for his failure to his
own character, disposition, and upbringing. Moreover, the hero
judges both his own behavior and that of other people from a
well-determined moral standpoint.

Taking concrete *bytovye* events as a starting point, Trifonov
shows far-reaching changes which take place in the spiritual world
above all in his idealistic characters. The melancholy leitmotiv of
"I have become a different person" runs like a thread through
all the Moscow stories. Under the pressure of *byt* the good-natured,
but also selfish and reticent hero usually turns into a prematurely
aged man who suffers from all sorts of ailments. This is very aptly
confirmed by the poetry translator Gennadii Sergeevich in "Predvaritel'nye itogi" ("Preliminary Reckoning," 1970) when he says:
"We have some justification: we are ill" (p. 107). Trifonov frequently penetrates the inner world of his characters like a psychiatrist establishing the correct connection between the psychic and
the physical state of man. This is illustrated by Gennadii's con-
fession when he says: "My earnings were low, orders were difficult to come by and I fell ill" (p. 100). By using an apposite medi-
cal terminology the author shows how every time his characters
find themselves in a difficult situation they are stricken by some
illness. Heart disease, high blood pressure, vegetative neuroses,
fainting fits and such like all figure systematically in Trifonov's
world. His ailing characters frequently look to nature for their
salvation, or to a long journey, a dream, an illusion, or even to
parapsychology.

But there is no remedy which can alleviate the ailments caused
by dislocated relations between people. In "Drugaia zhizn'" this
phenomenon is defined as "the disease of incompatibility" (*bo-*

lezn' nesovmestimosti, pp. 344–45). The drama of many of Trifonov's characters lies precisely in the fact that to the extent that
byt drains their living forces they are no longer able to have real
relations with other people. The consequence is loneliness, mis-
understanding, and an inability to help and to love. This failure
is naturally felt most acutely in the relationship between husband
and wife. "He lived a separate life" Olga recalls of Sergei (p. 353).
In the same way Gennadii Sergeevich dreams of a divorce from
his second wife in order to begin his life anew. The latter also sees
the causes of his difficulties in *byt* when he remarks: "There's no
need to look for complicated reasons! Everything became tense
and snapped because *byt* suddenly became strained" (p. 102).

But Trifonov also uses the term *byt* to render our general human
condition. He depicts a series of characters who prove that not
only *byt* acts as a brake, but also the temperament of certain characters who are not able to tackle effectively the daily struggle for
existence. In "Dolgoe proshchanie" ("A Long Goodbye," 1971)
it is said of the protagonist, Grisha Rebrov: "It is not a question
of acting or of the environment, it is a question of character"
(p. 160). In "egoism" Trifonov sees the greatest obstacle to human
relations. He calls it "the oldest of all human illnesses"[16] and
depicts its nefarious consequences in many different forms. In
"Drugaia zhizn'" the conflict between the spouses is caused not
only by the differences in their characters and outlooks but also
by what the author calls "the clash of two egoisms" (p. 281). In
"Predvaritel'nye itogi" a similar explanation of the family conflict is given and it is also noted that: "Every egoist has a way
out . . . . To find a good person who will forgive him everything"
(p. 116).

In Trifonov's world forgiveness is an essential element of love.
His ideal heroines are imbued with a spirit of all-forgiving love.
They strive to save the man whom they love and to be for him:
"both shield and mother and wife . . ." (p. 210), but they are
frequently helpless because they love an "unhappy, maladjusted,
hungry and poor but pure man . . ." (p. 298). The women are
also much more realistic and practical than the men and cope
more effectively with daily routine. In the context of the theme
of "love and *byt,*" which is treated by many contemporary Soviet

writers, Soviet critics note that a man's value is determined by his attitude towards love: "soullessness" is regarded as the archenemy of true love.[17] Trifonov also exposes the heartless insensitiveness of his heroes towards the woman they love. In "Predvaritel'nye itogi" we hear: "Egoism? It is a lack of love. All unhappiness comes from this uniform cause" (p. 121).

Trifonov sees in true love an exalting force which can oppose the draining power of routine. This vision coincides with Chekhov's conception of love, which is exemplified in "Dama s sobachkoi" ("The Lady with the Dog"). An echo of this story can be heard in "Obmen" where the protagonist, Viktor Dmitriev, says of his extramarital liaison with Tania: "It seemed to him that he had only become associated with that normal, truly human condition in which people should — and with time will — always live" (p. 29). Grisha Rebrov also considers love to be the essence of existence and expresses this original thought: "It is not *cogito ergo sum* but *amo ergo sum*" (p. 205).

Trifonov also sees in love a force which should permeate all humanity. The leitmotiv of love for one's fellowmen runs through all his stories and resounds clearly in the words: "It is possible to be ill, it is possible to do an unfulfilling job all one's life, but one must feel a man. For this one thing is necessary — an atmosphere of simple humanity . . . . Nobody can achieve this feeling by himself, autonomously, it arises from others, from those near to us" (p. 73).

Trifonov often uses the verb "to pity" (*zhalet'*) and we consider this word to be the key to an understanding of his weltanschauung. His vision is expressed in "Drugaia zhizn'": "All at once a love of one's fellowmen will appear, the ability to feel pity and compassion will emerge" (p. 327). Trifonov told us in Moscow: "I pity those heroes and heroines." We indeed feel pity especially for those characters who at the moment of a decisive choice either become ill or seek refuge in flight. Sometimes the "restricted consciousness" of Trifonov's confused heroes reminds us of Dostoevskii, who is named more than once in Trifonov's stories.

His philosophical reflections about man's common lot gives Trifonov's work a general human significance. He does not judge people harshly because he understands the complexity of the human condition. He says in "Obmen": "It just dawned on him — the inexorability of life. Lena had nothing to do with it, she was but a part of that life, a part of that inexorability" (p. 9). Trifonov makes us realize that man is not merely an enigma to his fellowmen, but also to himself. Ol'ga in "Drugaia zhizn'" expresses this melancholy thought: "To understand oneself for a start. Good heavens! We do not have the strength, nor the time or perhaps we lack the ability, the courage . . ." (p. 365). Because of this human failing Trifonov opposes any form of contempt. In "Predvaritel'nye itogi" he says of one of Chekhov's characters: "Professor Serebriakov is a man too. Why despise him so much? . . . People cannot be blamed for not being Leo Tolstois or Spensers" (p. 118). Trifonov also reflects the relativity of all *bytovye* problems and conflicts when he says in "Obmen": "There is nothing in the world except life and death. And everything that is subordinate to the former is happiness but everything that belongs to the latter . . . is the destruction of happiness . . ." (p.31).

A leitmotif of contemporary *byt* as depicted by Trifonov is the period of the revolution; it is most strongly exemplified in his late story "Starik" ("The Old Man," 1978). In Trifonov's work a melancholy longing for Russia's revolutionary past can be felt in the appearance of many historical figures and motifs. Thus in his novel *Neterpenie* (*Impatience,* 1974) Trifonov turns his attention to the young idealists of the terrorist movement *Narodnaia Volia,* which was responsible for the assassination of Tsar Alexander II in 1881. However, for Trifonov's idealistic, powerless heroes Russia's revolutionary history is a spiritual refuge as it offers the possibility of escaping, albeit in thought only, from the grip of prosaic *byt*. For them the revolutionary is "the true hero" as he knows "how man must live." Through the person of the revolutionary Trifonov also stresses the immense power of one's conscience. The answer to the question: "How should one live?" is found in "Dolgoe proshchanie," where it is said of a revolutionary: "He executed the will of his own conscience . . . . This is a tremendous strength" (pp. 198–99). In "Obmen" it is said of the old revolutionary, Fedor Nikolaevich, that he had little understanding of "contemporary life" and that any "*Lukianopo-*

dobie" (similarity to the Lukianovs) was foreign to him (pp. 44–45). The thematic richness of Trifonov's work in which *byt* and historic past are interwoven is determined by the complex structure of the Moscow stories. Present and past, daily occurrences and historic events are constantly alternating. By means of reminiscences the narrator or the protagonist continually compares past and present. The problem of the evolving times so fascinates the author that he even chose "time" as the principal figure in a next novel, *Vremia i mesto* (*The Time and the Place*), which has yet to appear.[18] In the Moscow stories memory itself plays a capital role. The narrator constantly ponders on the significance of *byt*, history, life, and death, with the aim of reaching a definite conclusion. But the "open finale" in Trifonov's stories indicates that any conclusion is premature. Thus the hero, sadly reflecting on his past, so often says: "If only . . . " (Esli by . . .) but does not finish his thought.

The many suggestive thoughts and unfinished statements in Trifonov's work confirm that the author, like Chekhov, is relying on the reader as coauthor. Like Chekhov, Trifonov is a master of the art of objective depiction without a priori judgments, didactic declarations, and easy solutions. But Trifonov's work makes us understand that it is sometimes easier for a man to perform a historic deed than to live out every day in his prosaic existence of "inexplicable and incomprehensible *byt*"!

State University of Ghent
Belgian National Fund for Scientific Research

NOTES

1. In April and December 1979 and in January 1980 we had many conversations with Iurii Trifonov in Moscow. All references to his views are taken from these discussions.

2. V. Pertsovskii, "Ispytanie bytom," in *Novyi mir,* 1974, no. 11, p. 236. The critic also reckons the works of D. Granin, S. Krutilin, I. Velembovskaia and S. Zalygin's "Iuzhno-amerikanskii variant" as belonging to this genre.

3. "Rech' Iu. Trifonova," *Shestoi s"ezd pisatelei SSSR, 21 iiunia–*

25 iiunia 1976 g.: stenograficheskii otchet (Moscow: Sovetskii pisatel',
1978), pp. 138–39.

4. Iu. Trifonov, *Prodolzhitel'nye uroki* (Moscow: Sovetskaia Rossiia,
1975), p. 71.

5. Letter to A.S. Suvorin, 1 April 1890, in A.P. Chekhov, *Polnoe sobranie sochinenii* (30 vols; Moscow: Nauka, 1976), vol. 4, p. 54.

6. "Rech' Iu. Trifonova," p. 138.

7. G. Brodskaia, "Briusov i Chekhov," *Teatr,* 1972, no. 2, pp. 97–100,
cited by E.A. Polotskaia, "Teatr Chekhova v vospriiatii Briusova," *Briu-
sovskie chteniia 1973 goda* (Erevan: Sovetakan Grokh, 1976), p. 237.

8. A. Blok, "O realistakh," *Sobranie sochinenii* (8 vols.; Moscow and
Leningrad: Khudozhestvennaia literatura, 1962), vol. 5, pp. 99–129.

9. V. Maiakovskii, *Polnoe sobranie sochinenii* (13 vols.; Moscow: Khudozhestvennaia literatura, 1958), vol. 10, p. 287.

10. Iu. Trifonov, *Prodolzhitel'nye uroki,* p. 70.

11. In his Moscow stories Trifonov only once names Bulgakov's Woland
and this in connection with the careerist Klimuk in the story "Drugaia
zhizn'." Iu. Trifonov, *Povesti* (Moscow: Sovetskaia Rossiia, 1978), p. 284.
Page references to this volume will subsequently appear in the text.

12. We have dealt with this aspect of Trifonov's work in "Traditsii Chekhova v sovremennoi russkoi proze," *Slavica Gandensia,* 1978, no. 5,
pp. 39–58 (Belgian Contributions to the 8th International Congress of
Slavists, Zagreb-Liubliana, September 1978).

13. Iu. Trifonov, *Prodolzhitel'nye uroki,* p. 71.

14. "Rech' Iu. Trifonova," p. 139.

15. The revival of psychological prose is illustrated by the works of
F. Abramov, V. Aksenov, V. Astaf'ev, V. Belov, A. Bitov, D. Granin,
I. Grekova, V. Iskander, V. Rasputin, V. Shukshin et al.

16. Iu. Trifonov, *Prodolzhitel'nye uroki,* p. 70.

17. F. Kuznetsov, "Chelovek 'estestvennyi' i 'obshchestvennyi'," *Literaturnoe obozrenie,* 1973, no. 6, p. 28.

18. Iu. Trifonov, "Kazhdyi chelovek — sud'ba," *Sovetskaia kul'tura,*
10 November 1980.

VALENTIN RASPUTIN'S *PROSHCHANIE S MATEROI*

JOHN B. DUNLOP

> You think people don't understand
> that Matera shouldn't be flooded?
> They understand all right. But
> they're going to flood her none-
> theless.[1]
>
> — Dar'ia Pinigin to her
> grandson, Andrei

Valentin Rasputin's *Farewell to Matera* is one of a handful of important novels published in the Soviet Union during the 1970s.[2] An ambitious, resonant work, it recounts the fate of the inhabitants of an island, Matera, located in the midst of the Siberian river Angara, in the last few summer months preceding their evacuation to the mainland. The island's evacuation is required by the construction downstream of a huge hydroelectric plant, which will cause the level of the river to rise, inundating Matera and other nearby islands. The majority of the island dwellers whom we come to know are elderly peasants who have spent their entire lives on Matera. Their imminent removal to an ur-banlike *sovkhoz* settlement or to similar semi-industrial settings fills them with apprehension. Their plight offers Rasputin an opportunity to examine the rapidly disappearing life of the traditional Russian village and to compare it with the urban settlements sprouting up on the banks of the Angara.

Rasputin accomplishes this task in part by focusing upon three generations of the Pinigin family — the grandmother, Dar'ia, who is in her eighties, her son, Pavel, who is about fifty, and Pavel's youngest son, Andrei, who appears to be in his early twenties. The "debate" which breaks out several times between grandmother and grandson illuminates much of the ideational and emotional thrust of the novel. The author also lingers over the fates of a number of Dar'ia's friends, all of them old people awaiting evacuation from the island.

It soon becomes apparent in this novel that Rasputin, though a relatively young author (b. 1937), has little sympathy for modern, industrialized Soviet Russia, at least in its present forms, an inclination which serves to link him to the "ruralist" (*derevenshchik*) school of contemporary letters and to the broadly based "Russian national movement." The *sovkhoz* settlement where Pavel Pinigin and his wife now live has been set up "not in human fashion."[3] It is unsightly, squalid, and noisy, and its feeble soil is inappropriate for gardening. Even the director of the hydroelectric complex downstream is reported to have cursed when he saw what kind of settlement his project had fostered.

But Rasputin's indictment of Soviet modernity goes further than an exposé of its unaesthetic monotony and tawdriness. He also contests a number of the assumptions underpinning Soviet Prometheanism. Andrei Pinigin holds that "man is the tsar of nature" and that there is nothing which humanity cannot do with its wondrous machines.[4] Andrei's optimism and orientation toward the future are combined with an unquestioning fealty to the ruling hierarchy. If "they" say that a hydroelectric station is needed and that Matera, his birthplace, needs to be flooded, so be it. As for the meaning of life, Andrei's credo seems to be, "We live and that's all there is to it."[5]

Dar'ia, Rasputin's *porte-parole* in this essentially monophonic novel, counters her grandson's unreflective slogans at every turn. In contrast to Andrei's Promethean view of man, she sees human beings as small, weak, deserving of pity. Modern man, she believes, has grown proud, has sought to clamber out of his "human skin," has uprooted himself from the earth, from nature, and from God. He has become confused, not knowing "where right is, and where left," and has sown confusion around him.[6] Modern man is a "fumbler" (*putanik*), who has forgotten that he has a soul and a conscience.[7] As for modern cities, they remind her of the frenetic scurrying of ants and the swarming of midges.

Pavel, Dar'ia's son, is in the middle of the "debate" between his mother and son. Unlike Andrei, who wanders off into the woods to gather *kislitsa* when he is supposed to be helping with the harvest, Pavel has not lost an aptitude for hard physical work. He is drawn to the traditional rhythms of life on Matera and is disturbed by the changes brought about in his wife by life in an urban milieu, but he is also a member of the Party, a former *kolkhoz* brigadier, and, like Andrei, he unquestioningly accepts orders coming from above. *"Nado — znachit nado . . . ,"* sums up his stance toward the new industrial Siberia growing up around him. Pavel has no ideals and recognizes this as a serious lack.[8]

The author scrutinizes the slow passage of Matera's waning summer days with keen attention. The earth, which has been tilled with care for two hundred years, throws up one last abundant harvest and occasions a final outpouring of joy and yearning as the villagers gather together to sing their traditional harvest songs. But Rasputin reminds us that time moves on with the rapidity of the swiftly moving Angara ("the Angara flows, time flows . . .").[9] The threat of fire, like that of the approaching great flood, has been present from the novel's beginning when Dar'ia and her friends succeeded in driving off an "unclean power," workers ordered to burn down the village cemetery (future tourists who float down the Angara on pleasure craft, we are told, will not want to be greeted by crosses sticking up from below.)[10] But the "unclean power" cannot be held at bay for long. Soon the semi-demented village lad Petrukha burns down his hut, and its apocalyptic glow warns of conflagrations to come. Then shock workers, who are brought in to help with the harvest and who have no respect for the island's uniqueness, burn down the village mill and office. Fire, the ever swifter passage of time, and the specter of a final flood accompany the island's poignant last days. As the novel concludes, the *sovkhoz* director Vorontsov, Pavel, Petrukha, and a boat pilot are attempting to make their way through unusually dense, perhaps unprecedented, fog to take Dar'ia and a few remaining dwellers off the island. "We have to accomplish the task," Vorontsov shouts, but his exhortation is swallowed up by the thick fog.[11] The mood at the end of *Farewell to Matera* is one of acute apprehension and alarm, mirrored by the anxiety of a small animal, dubbed "the master" by Rasputin, whose movements about the island are several times reported in the novel.[12]

The bleak pessimism at the book's conclusion is somewhat mitigated on the symbolic level. The burners, whom the island dwellers call "arsonists," succeed in scorching everything on Matera with their terrible power, except one huge larch tree, which defies all their efforts. Neither fire, nor the ax, nor a power saw can affect this "tsar tree" (*tsar'-derevo*). "Two times two equals four," one of the "arsonists" repeats while performing his destructive work, giving expression to modern man's cocksure sense of mastery over nature,[13] but, as Dostoevskii's "underground man" discovered, mathematical formulae do not necessarily represent the last word. The *tsar'-derevo* carries the day, though a birch tree which has grown up next to the larch and has been protected by it is savagely destroyed by the burners.[14] The "tsar tree" thus gives cause for some hope, albeit faint, at the novel's end.

The flooding of Matera, a place name deriving from the root *mat'* (mother), will climax a process of national matricide. The very Russian earth, family cemeteries, venerable churches (Matera's church has been converted into a storehouse and its crosses knocked off) are being sacrificed for "electricity" and the specious cult of progress touted by Soviet Prometheans. It is not that Rasputin scorns the fruits of modern civilization and not, as many will probably allege, that he is obsessed with *byt* (mores), raising the samovar and Russian stove to the level of divinity. But modern Russia, he believes, must be rooted in the centuries-old wisdom of traditional Russia. If not, then fire and flood will inevitably ensue.

What are the values which the floodwaters will cover up, perhaps irretrievably? Neighborliness, a sense of community with those nearby; the physical and spiritual rewards of physical toil; the deep satisfaction of ownership — each peasant owns and cares for his own *izba* and cow, and cultivates his own plot of land; a closeness and intimacy with nature. But there is more: the village cemetery reminds one of links to one's ancestors, to the *rod*; this awareness induces a primal attachment to the Russian earth and to Russia herself. And life in accord with nature and the traditions of one's fathers brings one closer to God; like a number of *derevenshchiki*, Rasputin seems to be sympathetic to religious values. *Farewell to Matera,* let it be said in closing, is a well-crafted novel, which exhibits better control than Rasputin's previous works. The author's interweaving of the passage of time, the movement of the seasons, and the flow of the river sets up a pacific rhythm which contrasts with and is slowly undermined by a staccato rhythm of destruction initiated by man. The symbolic level of the work, which I have only broached, is subtle and richly allusive.[15] Rasputin appears to be maturing as a writer. I end with the words of a recent émigré, Viktor Nekrasov:

> With anxiety we follow the fate of the talented Valentin Rasputin, who has never once lied in his writings (and how unthinkably difficult that is in our country!). At his age, the lives of Vasilii Shukshin and Gennadii Shpalikov had been broken off; at his age, Aksenov, Voinovich, and Kopelev have chosen the difficult path of emigration. Will he be able to stand his ground, surrounded as he now is by honors and attention? Alas, they are not eternal. May God give him strength.[16]

Oberlin College

NOTES

1. Valentin Rasputin, "Proshchanie s Materoi. Povest'," *Nash sovremennik,* 1976, no. 10, p. 70. The novel appears in no. 10, pp. 3–71, and no. 11, pp. 17–64. It has also appeared in Valentin Rasputin, *Povesti* (Moscow: Molodaia gvardiia, 1976).
2. Rasputin termed his work a *povest'*. Other important novels which could be cited are: Iurii Trifonov, *Dom na naberezhnoi* (1976), Vasilii Belov, *Kanuny* (1972–1976), Evgenii Nosov, *Usviatskie shlemonostsy* (1977), and Rasputin's own *Zhivi i pomni* (1974).
3. No. 10, p. 43.
4. Ibid., p. 63.
5. Ibid., p. 69.
6. Ibid., p. 70.
7. Ibid.
8. Ibid., p. 43.
9. No. 11, p. 23.

10. No. 10, p. 10.

11. No. 11, p. 62.

12 This *zverek* presumably represents the "spirit of the place."

13. No. 11, pp. 42–43.

14. Ibid., pp. 41–42. The birch tree may be intended to represent Russia.

15. Alexis Klimoff of Vassar College believes that chapter 22 of the novel contains a reference to the myth of *Grad Kitezh*. Matera will live on, submerged in water and memory, as an ideal.

16. Viktor Nekrasov, "Chto zhe dal'she?" *Novoe russkoe slovo,* 25 May 1980, p. 2.

"ONE DROP OF POLITICS" ART AND IDEOLOGY IN SOVIET NOVELS OF SOCIAL INQUIRY

GEORGE GIBIAN

The purpose of this paper is neither to examine a single work of literature in depth, nor to tackle a hitherto neglected subject. It is rather to go once more down that most frequently travelled path in the study of Soviet literature — its political element.

The method is synoptic — a bird's eye view comparing aspects of several works. The originality of the attempt will have to be sought in two places: (1) in the fact that the overt statements of political or social ideas made in the work *are considered in relation to their balancing formal, expressive elements,* and (2) in the attempt to classify the resulting formulations according to the simplicity or complexity of the resulting skeletal structure.

The figure of a "drop of politics" in the title of this paper is borrowed from Aleksandr Blok's remarkable entry in his diary for April 1920, in which he disputes those who called his *The Twelve* a political poem, details the autobiographical circumstances of composing it, and concludes ". . . drops of politics remained in the poem. We shall see what time will do with it. It may be that all politics is so dirty that one drop of it mixes up and dissolves everything else; it may be that politics will not destroy the meaning of my poem; it may be, finally, who knows, that it will turn out to have been the leaven thanks to which *The Twelve* will be read at some future time beyond our own. I myself can talk about it only with irony. . . . "[1]

My assumption, which would have to be argued at great length and supported by detailed analyses of single texts, is, first, that explicit representations of political ideas in works of fiction are, in some works, multiple and variously divisible, and in others, single — unopposed on their own terms; and second, that in any work of literature in which they exist, elements are usually also present, on some other level, of what we might call the flesh, or the features. These poles can be antithetical or supportive—polar opposites or polar allies.

Again, in their turn, the features of the flesh side of the work can be either multiple or single.

The one or more political-social themes and the one or more formal or technical features form patterns. The "drops of politics" do not exist in a vacuum, but in a web of relationships, or, at the minimum, in a simple axial relationship. To isolate them is to wrench them and the work of literature out of shape.

It is my hope to suggest a possible scheme of comparing and contrasting the patterns of these relationships in six examples, all works of fiction in which social or political ideas are prominent. I sketch briefly what the results of such an examination as I suggest might be and set up a range of possible classes. The assertions about individual works which I put forward without full supporting details are of course highly arguable. Also I admit that some of my conclusions may merely confirm what we have already suspected to be the case. Others, however, may be novel, some even surprising. It is the method of inquiry and the suggested classifications which I particularly wish to put forward, for further development or refutation by others.

As our first example, let us take stories of a cycle, rather than a single novel — Isaak Babel''s *Red Cavalry*. They openly express not one set of political ideas, but four distinguishable categories of different attitudes towards the Bolshevik Revolution and its champions, the Red Cavalry engaged in war with Poland:

a) Highly idealistic support for the Revolutionary cause. This is exemplified in the protagonist of "My First Goose." He admires Lenin politically as well as aesthetically — for his direct rhetorical style; he wants to belong to the Red Cavalry because of the political cause for which it is fighting — the Bolshevik homeland; and finds joy in reading Lenin's speech in *Pravda* to his newly accepting companions.

b) "Pragmatic," "eyes-open" backing of the Revolution. The narrator in "Gedali" defends the use of violence. "We must cut their closed eyes open," he says, and regards the Revolution as the supreme value, accepting cruelty and destruction as necessary means to that end.

c) Belief in a supremely idealistic revolutionary scheme different from the Bolshevik one: Gedali's International of Men of Good Will. He advocates an uncompromising, pure ideal: his International must bring peace and brotherhood without any violence or destruction.

d) Revolution as revenge for personal grievances. Several characters regard the Revolution as a marvellous turn-about in personal power relations. After lifetimes of humiliation, they have come into their own and can give vent to their desires for personal vengeance.[2]

Babel''s cycle of stories, then, contains four openly stated pro-Revolutionary attitudes (three different pro-Bolshevik ones, one anti-Bolshevik, religiously Utopian one).

Are there elements in the stories serving as opposite poles to these four thematic categories? We find, first, a profusion of violent incidents. Brutal deeds and words, of such intensity and in such quantity that every reader of Babel' is keenly aware of them, form the matrix against which the four sets of revolutionary ideas act themselves out.

Secondly, there are recurrent islands of a quite different element: lyrical pathos, in purple patches. Each is very brief, and stands in strong contrast to the prose which surrounds it.

Thirdly, there is a chain of succinct, but prominent references to the sun, stars, and other celestial and natural phenomena — the eternal, non-human world which outlasts political causes as well as the brutalities committed by human beings.

The fourth category consists of items of the human cultural tradition: poetry of the past, ancient customs, religions, the Song of Songs, Maimonides. Strong emotions spring from this welter of ethnic Russian and Hebrew references.

The intense sensuous and emotional categories battle against the four powerful "drops of politics" we summarized above. The complex political ideas find worthy, equally powerful partners and opponents in violence and in the perennial human and natural legacies. Babel' does not bridge the chasm between them. The stories embody the continued coexistence of sharply opposed principles and qualities (only occasionally fused, as in the death of the Rabbi's Son). Four kinds of ideas are balanced by four kinds of features, which are all sources of intense emotionality.

When we turn to *Envy*, by Iuri Olesha, a few years later than Babel''s stories, and seek to define its political theme, we find a great contrast: very little, or nothing, which we could call political. The social inquiry consists of Olesha's pitting against one another two human types — historically rooted — as the men of the "New Age" conflict with those of the "Old." The space given to each side is about even, in contrast to Babel', where one side only, the Revolutionary, is presented almost exclusively (subdivided, it is true, into categories, and opposed in part by the advocates of the alternative vision of an International of Men of Good Will).

If *The Red Cavalry* is a tetraphony rather than a monophony, it is nevertheless a tetraphony all singing — or demonstrating — one side of the issue. In Olesha we have a very clear antiphony: Ivan Babichev and Kavalerov on one side, Babichev the sausage maker and Volodia on the other. Advocacy of feeling, art, Europe, the past, fantasy on one hand; practicality, liberation from drudgery, machine-like efficiency, health, sobriety, newness, on the other. Or we could simplify it into a conflict of art and utilitarianism.

What features of the novelette are prominent enough to stand against the central polarity of its social theme? The sensitivity and the vivid, original ways of perceiving of the characters on the "old" side; and the inventiveness and vividness of the language in which the work is written — whether from the point of view of, and dealing with, characters of one group or of the other.

Again, as in Babel''s stories, the two oppositions are left unresolved. The qualities attributed by Olesha to the characters on the two sides are mixed. Neither side has a monopoly on "positive" traits. The reader, according to his own scale of values, may be attracted to the men of feeling and poetry, but he will have to admit that they abound in despicable qualities — jealousy, malice, envy, and many others. The practical "New Men," with their stolid unimaginativeness, are unattractive to most readers;

nevertheless, they are reliable, altruistic, useful.

Although Olesha's work is included in most discussions of civic ideas in Soviet literature around 1930, yet when we seek stated, truly political themes, we find remarkably little. The surprise yielded by our kind of approach is that the ideological scheme of *Envy* is very simple, whereas the experience of reading the work is complex. In the world of the novel, both sets of counterpoised characters exist against, and within, elements of linguistic and rhetorical variety. The richness comes not from the complexity of ideas, but from the texture of the work — the linguistic imaginativeness, originality of perception, startling imagery, newly pointed out connections.

As our third example, let us take that widely read work of Nikolai Ostrovskii, *How the Steel Was Tempered*, written between 1930 and 1933. This work not only appears simple, and is remembered as such; when it is re-examined from our point of view, it remains utterly simple. When we try to find in the book elements serving as foils, or militating against, the political theme (which is itself unilinear and uncomplicated), the search is vain. We find no other major theme, no parallel or contrasting feature. There is only the one overriding, uncontested, idea: the repeated assertion that the Bolsheviks' cause is a most worthy ideal.

The text abounds in unequivocal teaching. There are obstacles: not only the Whites and the Poles, but also errors within Bolshevik ranks represent dangers. It is necessary to learn to avoid mistakes; purify one's outlook; steel and perfect oneself. But these are diversions — not amounting to a full scale antithetical theme. They are not a separate opposing voice, but rather steps on the climb upwards within the main theme. The opponents — the Whites and the Poles — are presented in such a dark light that no reader could feel moved to side with them. The Reds' ideas have the book, if not the battlefield, all to themselves, unopposed in the sympathies of the reader.

The pathos of the narration, the dialogue, and the dramatized action all merge, pointing in one direction.[3]

How the Steel Was Tempered is the *non plus ultra* of a propagandistic novel. Unlike other outstandingly didactic novels, for example, Chernyshevskii's *What is To Be Done,* it is devoid of either latent or overt contrasting elements.

When we seek "flesh" features other than the didactic skeletal ones, we do find one. The action itself is so vivid and powerful as to put it close to the level of intensity of the political assertion. There are dangers, beatings, rapes, plotting, killing, from cover to cover. These have made the book readable for millions of boys and girls. Deeds loom large beside the didactic element. The ideological compass needle of the action, however, points in the same direction as the political lessons; the plot supports and parallels the preaching.

There is utter simplicity in the pattern of relationships of the political elements to the non-political: complete overlap, perfect harmony.

Serafimovich's *Iron Flood,* on the contrary, while also utterly simple in some respects, is more complex than Ostrovskii's novel. As the title suggests and the text repeatedly reminds us, the book describes the march along the Caspian shores of a ragamuffin multinational horde, into, and through, a series of obstacles — human (Cossacks, Greeks, Georgians; German warships) and natural (mountains, sun, hunger, thirst). Disparate people combine into one organism, one flood.[4]

The author creates kaleidoscopic images. He displays list after list of powerfully presented items of striking variety, creating impressive difficulties and dangers. The "flood" of the pro-Red mass must overcome them; learn to control them; organize them.

In addition to these two elements (the "flood" of people, and the multifarious obstacles before them), there is one leader, one effective man of obviously superior courage, determination, and judgment. A strong antithesis is set up between this single, although popularly supported hero (he offers to resign, is persuaded by the masses to remain as commander) and the elemental force which is repeatedly compared to water and streams.

Serafimovich merges remarkably successfully various other component elements. The cruelty of the Whites is similar to that of most of the people within the "flood"; so are the harsh effects of the sun, hunger, mountains. The reader is given a sense of commonness among them all. Hardness recurs as a shared element on otherwise various levels.

Serafimovich's writing is recalcitrant in its diction as well as in the action and the piled up lists of people and objects. Ukrainian, Cossack, and similarly exotic diction is hard to penetrate. The rough thickets of resistant words are themselves a noticeable feature of the book. The difficulties of incidents of the plot combine with these difficulties of the linguistic medium. (Roads and paths are choked; a mother's nipples are clotted with milk; most actions in this book have to be performed against obstacles. Getting through with great effort is the dominant image.)

The "drop of politics" is a flooded human mass making its laborious way towards a Bolshevik country; and it is enriched and supported by several features, in the "flesh" of the book.

There is still greater contrast between Ostrovskii's novel and our two remaining examples. In Andrei Platonov's *Chevengur* the political theme consists of a simplified Bolshevism. The men in control of the little town are utterly dedicated to the ideal of building Communism in it. They refer to its chief tenets, to the names of leaders of the Communist movement, with pious devotion (even if Rosa Luxemburg is a horse). They struggle with the bourgeoisie and try to move into a proletarian dictatorship and a classless Communist future.

This political idea, however, is distorted by the way in which they grotesquely misapply it. There is no refutation of the Communist theory by a character or the narrator, no counter-statement. But the form which the Communist ideas take in action is in fact a parody on them. The ideal is undercut by the naïve practitioners of it. Those rural Russian extremists apply Bolshevism with the literalness and immediacy of the hero's father, who dies when he seeks to understand death, and hence looks for it by walking into a pond.

The results are bizarre: a mixture of humor and horror. The counter-theme is this *iurodivaia* population: a corner of rural Russia, inhabited by a touchingly naïve country people who have taken hold of a few Marxist-Bolshevik ideas and practice them after their light. In the context of *Chevengur,* perhaps we ought to translate the term *iurodivye* not Fools-in-Christ, but Fools-in-Lenin. The actions which result from the ideas include moving populations of towns, sending women and children across the river, murdering all bourgeois men.

The abstractable political ideals are utterly simple, streamlined, highly selective. Complexities enter through the presentation: the language.— distorted, almost impenetrable, rendered unusual and skewed in several ways through oddities of individual phrasing.

An entirely different set of relations is found in *Doctor Zhivago*. Here there is first of all a bifurcation of explicit statements of political ideas: different views are expressed in the early parts of the book, before the Revolution; and afterwards, when Bolshevik authority is established. In the early parts support is expressed for change and for the Revolution. Later, in the remainder of the book, different ideas are stated. Marxism and its Bolshevik application, and the resulting institutions and doctrines of the Soviet state are attacked. Beyond that, an entirely opposite philosophical, anti-political set of views is counterpoised. Ideas are presented at some length to the effect that the nature of human life is such that it cannot be shaped by social action. All attempt at political-social action is opposed. The "herdishness" of Communism, the distrust of one's own opinions, the lying due to the collectivization of agriculture, the rendering abstract of the human individual through dedication to an overriding cause, all these and other ramifications of Communist and all other group actions are argued against. The ideal of supreme individualism, of love, of the creation of beauty (poetry, for example) and of perceiving of beauty (by responding to artistic creations and nature) — these are all argued as well as repeatedly exemplified — as antitheses to any kind of "drop of politics."

Thus a multitude of philosophical ideas is presented. There are political discussions, and more numerous, metaphysical interrogations of destiny, and suggestions about the overcoming of death. In addition, numerous, impressive, particular oppositions are presented (the loves of Lara, Tania, and Zhivago; poetry; nature). Still another element is the lyricism of the narrator's own sentences.

We have, then, in *Doctor Zhivago* ramified confrontations of antitheses, ranging from the general to the specific. For all their complexity, however, they are one-sided: the general statements, in all their diversity, and the other, specific features of the book, point in one direction — they support one another and have no worthy adversary. The book is multiple in its construction, but as unidirectional as Ostrovskii's *How the Steel Was Tempered*. The antitheses are ramified; the orientation is monistic.

In conclusion: it might be possible to set up categories, with tabulations of logically imaginable combinations of explicit political statements (simple or multiple); opposed or otherwise deviating political statements on the same level (none; simple; multiple); antithetical elements in what we have called the "flesh" side of the work (again, simple or multiple); pointing either in the same direction as, or opposite to, the positive political statement. Our six examples would not fill all the possible categories; we should have empty sets. But of more interest are other things: exactly in what particular relationship the overt political statements and their polar partners stand (of tension, collaboration, amalgamation); how they are changed, colored by such partnerships.

One finding which our exercise yields is that the sense of richness of a work is not necessarily derived from, or an accompaniment of, the complexity of the political statement. Other, more powerful means create the effects of richness.

Still another conclusion is that neither pro-Soviet nor anti-Soviet ideologies have a monopoly on a particular kind of structural pattern. The same abstractable scheme of construction can accomodate works of different political orientations. There is no such thing as the structure of one or another kind of political orientation. In a structural analysis of our sort, Pasternak and Serafimovich, Ostrovskii and Solzhenitsyn might find themselves in the same grouping.

Finally, perhaps of the most interest is the nature of those features on the "flesh" side of the work which are frequent and important in twentieth-century Russian works — which Russian authors have deemed powerful enough to set up in a partnership, positive or negative, with the central political and social themes of this century. There are striking recurrences of subjects favored by them for these roles: violence and brutality; attitudes of the Great Russian Folksy Naïve; traditional modes of feeling; originality of artistic perception and expression; the recalcitrance of the milieu — nature, usually. Here, we might have put our fingers on significant differences from comparable works in countries other than Russia.

Cornell University

NOTES

1. «Я смотрел на радугу, когда писал „Двенадцать"; оттого в поэме осталась капля политики. Посмотрим, что сделает с этим время. Может быть, всякая политика так грязна, что одна капля ее замутит и разложит все остальное; может быть, она не убьет смысла моей поэмы; может быть, наконец, — кто знает! — она окажется бродилом, благодаря которому „Двенадцать" прочтут когданибудь в не наши времена. Сам я теперь могу говорить об этом только с иронией; но — не будем сейчас брать на себя решительного суда». Aleksandr Blok, *Sochineniia v 2 t.* (Moscow, 1955), vol. 1, p. 774.

2. The best examples are "Prishchepa" and "Zhizneopisanie Pavlichenki, Matveia Rodionycha." Matvei apostrophizes the year of Civil War victories in folklore diction appropriate to a lover's appeal to a girl: "Five lost years I lost, till the year eighteen came along to visit me, lost as I was. It came along on lively stallions, on its Kabardin horses, bringing along a big train of wagons and all sorts of songs. Oh you little year eighteen, my sweetheart! (*liuba ty moia*). Can it be that we shan't walk out with you one more time, my own little drop of blood (*krovinochka*), my year eighteen? We squandered your songs, drank up your wine, set up your justice (*pravdu*), but now only the pencil-pushers [clerks: *pisaria*] are left from your times." I. Babel', *Detstvo i drugie rasskazy* (Israel: Biblioteka Aliia, 1979), p. 155.

3. For example, the pathos in "People of a new sort appeared in the Leszczinski house. The word 'comrade,' for which only yesterday people had paid with their life, was now heard on all sides. That indescribably moving word, 'comrade'!" (p. 142). Or Pavel to Tonia: "I am not now the Pavlusha I was before. And I shall be a poor husband if you think I should belong first to you and then to the Party. For I'll belong to the Party first, and then to you and the other loved ones." (p. 190) Nikolai Ostrovskii, *Sobranie sochinenii* (Moscow, 1955), vol. 1.

4. "The carts and wagons creaked . . . . Kozhukh was drowning in the incessantly flowing stream." (p. 40) "In this wildly roaring stream (*potoke*) demobilized men from the Tsarist Army walk and walk." (p. 41) "From the town came another stream (*potok*) of loaded carts which began to flow (*stal vlivat'sia*) into this unending stream with crashes and obscene curses by voices salted with seawinds." (p. 49) Aleksandr Serafimovich, *Zheleznyi potik* (Moscow, 1957).

INNOVATORY FEATURES OF TSVETAEVA'S
LYRICAL VERSE

ROBIN KEMBALL

The past fifteen years or so have witnessed the publication of a number of studies devoted to various aspects of Tsvetaeva's poetic technique in general and her versification in particular. Most of these have been concerned either with statistical analysis (mainly of preferential meters or meter patterns)[1] or with general examination of a particular *poema*.[2] While the potential usefulness of the statistical method is not in doubt, interpretation of the results it yields calls for considerable caution, especially in the case of a poet such as Tsvetaeva, whose restless mind, sensitive ear, and unusually fertile imagination would frequently lead her abruptly from one genre to another, with the result that her creative impulse was in constant movement, not only as *between* one cycle and the next, but often *within* one and the same cycle (or *sbornik*). Moreover, her selection of material for inclusion in a given cycle was at times arbitrary,[3] and was in any case determined by content rather than metrical affinity, with the result that even cycles chronologically parallel may yield widely differing statistical results. For these and other reasons, statistical analysis alone, unless applied within clearly defined limits and subject to strict safeguards, may easily prove misleading. Conversely, studies of individual *poemy,* while interesting in themselves, are by definition too circumscribed and often too disparate in nature to provide any reliable overall picture of certain features common to Tsvetaeva's verse (more particularly her lyrical verse) as a whole. It is an examination of just such features (at any rate, the more important of them) that represents the primary object of the present study, which in this sense might be regarded as a continuation of the general studies already cited than as a variation on the theme originally presented by Karlinsky in the second part of his monograph devoted to Tsvetaeva's life and poetic technique.[4] It also represents an extension (in the sense of being based on a wider range of material) of our own study of certain metrical aspects of the poems of *Lebedinyi stan*.[5]

It should be emphasized from the outset that few of the features to be examined here are novel in themselves — the vast majority of them have been discussed and illustrated before, either in relation to Tsvetaeva herself or as applied to other modern Russian poets. Nor (again, with rare exceptions) are they features that could fairly be regarded as *specific* to Tsvetaeva. Taken in *isolation*, then, their novel character is by no means always apparent. On the other hand, taken *together,* they add up to create a very different impression; by their variety, their frequency, their sheer weight of numbers, they ultimately contribute in a significant manner to that "portrait" of Tsvetaeva's poetic technique which it is the aim of the present study to establish.[6]

*

Free rhyme. One of the first features to strike the observant *reader* of her verse is Tsvetaeva's fearless — even nonchalant — use of "free" rhymes, ranging from "approximate," through "inexact," to cases where there is little more than the barest assonance, if that. The poet's attitude in this connection is but one aspect of that "innocent audacity" to which we referred in an earlier study of her poetic technique:[7] audacious when set beside most of her Russian contemporaries; "innocent," in the sense that there is in it no trace of artifice or ostentaion, no seeking after sensationalism, but simply a "natural," unquestioning acceptance of the free rhyme as perfectly sufficient unto its purpose, its role as one unobtrusive binding element in the structure of the poem. It is also one element (among several) that reflects a more general feature of Tsvetaeva's poetic apprehension — the priority she accorded to the *auditory* element in verse, as opposed to the *visual,* in the form of the printed page; this in its turn was doubtless, in part at least, a by-product of her native feel for, and rooted attachment to, the popular, folk, element in Russian poetry. The real importance of free rhyme lies less in the metrical field as such than in the fact that its consistent application automatically opens up a vast new world of lexical potential — no less vast, say, than that of Maiakovskii. There seems to be literally no end to the lexical possibilities inherent in this device, when seized upon and exploited to the full by an ear as imaginative and as sensitive as Tsvetaeva's; certainly, we are a long way from the days when Pushkin could complain that *krov'* was the only rhyme available for *liubov'*!

Examples of free rhyme — of every shape and size, texture, and grammatical make-up — can be culled from almost any page of Tsvetaeva's verse, and it is impossible, but also quite unnecessary, to list more than a few examples here. It is in the nature of things that the most striking and most frequent examples usually occur in *dactylic endings* (where exact rhyme would demand the full concordance of three syllables) and, *a fortiori,* in *hyperdactylic endings,* which, though rarer, are by no means absent (e.g. in stanzas 3, 5, 7, 10, and 21 of "Poloterskaia" [*PR,* pp. 140–43] — naviázchivye, naváshchivaem, vzákhivaia, vymákhivaem; iásenevy, namáslivaem, nalásnivaem; mrámornaia, Lámanovoi, nalámyvaem, etc.). Characteristic dactylic rhymes include:

> dítiatka : výtkannoi — mal'chënochka : sólnyshka (*V-I,* pp. 48–49)
>
> výkresti : Antíkhristu (*LS,* no. 34)
>
> zapákhnutyi : shákhmatnykh — ospárivai : rozárium —
>
> mal'chísheskikh : rassýpavshis' (*PR,* pp. 48–51)

Even an entire poem may consist of free dactylic rhymes, as in *LS,* no. 42[8] (vzeléiali : lébedi — výtsvelo : rýtsari — vorótitsia : Bogoróditsa). A further extension of free rhyme occurs when the "rhymed" endings are *anisosyllabic.* In *V-I* we find rhyme between dactylic and hyperdactylic endings: blagoslovénnye : serébrianye (p. 17); zaméshkalis' : Dokréshivaiutsia (p. 27). In *LS* no. 5, we find the following combinations, the last of which includes rhyme between *three* different types of ending:

> F : D : F   svetáet : sbegáetsia : stáei
>
> F : M : M   polumráke : koe-kák : d'iak
>
> F : D : H   Bózhii : ostrózhnye : otlózhennye[9]

The examples given so far occur in haphazard fashion, reflecting in the event the generally free structure of the poem in question.

On other occasions, however, we encounter something far more sophisticated — the systematic and regular rhyming of anisosyllabic endings according to one of a number of set patterns: MFMD/abab (*V-I*, p. 45, where the F : D rhymes are — kolokól'ni : semikhólmie — Bogoslóva : zlatogolóvye — obédne : sosédnego — khlystóvskii : moskóvskoiu. DMFM/abab FMDM/cdcd etc. etc. (*V-I*, p. 102 — fýrkaly : kírke — pástva : pástora — serébrianom : shchédroi — príbyl : Bíbliiu).

In the poem "Popytka revnosti" (*PR*, pp. 134–36), there is no anisosyllabic rhyme as such, but F and D endings alternate regularly with M endings throughout the twelve stanzas of the poem, according to the pattern: FMFM/abab DMDM/cdcd FMFM/efef etc. The systematic (and technically irreproachable) use of these mixed endings is clear proof of the fact, not only that Tsvetaeva was keenly aware of the syllabic differences, but also that she could harness them and mold them to her own purposes with an unfailingly sure touch when she chose to do so. In such cases we are dealing with an essentially deliberate and conscious *literary* (rather than "popular") device.

Not infrequently, one of two D-rhymes (occasionally, both) is in the form of *compound rhyme*. Examples include:

V-I. výmoiu : s golový moei (p. 19) — Derevtsó moe : Nevesómoe (p. 36) — Budet tvói chered : Tozhe — dócheri . . . (p. 37) *LS.* znáiushchii : napomináesh' mne (no. 46) *PR.* mal'chísheskii : iz týsiachi (p. 50) — schástlivy? : Tiázhche li (p. 136) — zástitsia : ná serdtse (p. 153).

While the chances of compound rhyme occurring in F-rhymes are obviously reduced, cases exist (e.g. Kréml' moi! — : zémliu [*V-I*, p. 103] — sná net : pámiat' [*PR*, p. 19]). The poem "Klinok" (*PR*, pp. 110–11) alone contains 4 striking examples in 7 stanzas: prímes' : khraní nas — pronzái nas : kráinost' — sryváias' : Ostrová est' — rána! : dvá my.

Strange as it may seem, compound rhyme can even occur in M-endings, as two examples from *PR* help to demonstrate — krap : kogdá b (p. 79); slysh' : l'stí zh (p. 109).

In D-endings the effect of compound rhyme is usually to add weight to the final syllable of the clausula, which thus becomes more akin to the cretic ending ($\stackrel{\prime}{-} - \stackrel{\prime}{-}$) that is a familiar feature

of the Russian *bylina*. The poem beginning "Kanun Blagove-
shchen'ia" (*V-I*, pp. 25-28), written very much in *bylina* style,
and with a rhyme sequence that is not always easy to follow,
closes with a striking example of two cretic endings, the "popular" effect of which is further enhanced by the choice of words
(Moskva-reka) and by the absence at this point of any recogniz-
able rhyme:

> Begu k Moskvá-reké
> Smotret', kak lëd idët. [10]

*

Endings and ending-patterns. In examining Tsvetaeva's rhymes,
we have inevitably touched on her use of endings and even (in
connection with anisosyllabic rhymes) of ending-patterns. An
attentive study of the various cycles and/or *sborniki* reveals the
existence of what might be termed synchronistic "waves of predilection" for a particular type of ending or combination of endings (ending-pattern). In our study of *LS*, we called attention to
the presence there of a series of (more or less "central") poems,
all composed between september 1918 and the autumn of 1919
and all containing D-endings, either in part or in whole, to the
tune of 80% (64 D-endings in 80 lines of verse).[11] In the first
half of *V-I*, D-endings are likewise very much to the fore and,
again, a particularly intense "wave" may be detected in the series
of poems composed between 23 March and 28 April 1916 (pp.
23-62 incl.). The intensity of this wave seems to build up as it
proceeds; taking the poems written from 1 April to 28 April (pp.
48-62 incl.), we find a total of 110 D-endings in the course of
153 lines of verse, which represents an incidence of 72%. (In fact,
only one poem in this series — that on p. 60 — has less than 50%
D-endings.) On the other hand, the early poems of *PR* are marked
by a clear predominance of M-endings. The first eight poems
have exclusively M-endings and a count of the first ten (pp. 7-
15) reveals a total of 201 such endings in the space of 209 lines
(96%). These poems were composed between 11 and 25 June 1922.
This time, the intensity of the wave subsequently decreases, but
for some while to come this decrease is only relative. If we ex-
tend the analysis to include the following eleven poems, i.e. twenty-

one poems in all, covering the period 11 June to 31 July 1922, we still find an incidence of over 81% (312 M-endings in 384 lines). While, therefore, the existence of such "waves of predilection" can hardly be doubted, and while several other examples could be quoted, the instances cited here are nonetheless *isolated* phenomena in the sense that they do not permit of any general conclusions concerning the incidence of this or that type of ending in a given cycle. Thus, in *LS,* for instance, despite the "dactylic wave" referred to, statistical analysis shows that the total endings of this cycle (some 10% of which are nonrhyming) are, in round figures, 50% feminine, 40% masculine, and only 10% dactylic.[12] So far as we are aware, no corresponding figures exist for the other cycles of Tsvetaeva, though comparisons might prove extremely interesting, and perhaps surprising.

*

Enjambement. In assessing Tsvetaeva's technique of enjambement (as, indeed, that of other poets), one should at once distinguish between two types which, while they may well occur concurrently, yet differ considerably both in their nature and in the effect they produce upon the reader (or listener). If the Russian term for enjambement, *perenos*, be taken in its widest, literal, sense, then virtually every instance of "carry-over" from one line of verse to another would qualify for consideration. According to Zhirmunskii, *perenos* occurs "when(ever) the metrical segmentation (*chlenenie*) does not coincide with the syntactical. . ." — a definition which might well be held to include all such cases. A few lines later, however, the same author insists that "the most characteristic sign of *perenos* is the presence within a line of a *syntactical pause* (that is) more marked than (that) at the beginning or the end of that line."[13] Now, if *this* be taken as the ultimate criterion, it is obvious that mere "carry-over" does not of itself qualify as enjambement. Such simple "carry-over," without a significant pause in the following (or preceding) line, is particularly common in poems composed of short lines, where in fact all that often happens is that a sentence of some length is spread over several of these lines, its conclusion usually coinciding with the end of one of them. In most such cases, it would be perfectly possible to rearrange the poem into a smaller number of longer lines, though in Russian poetry the wealth of rhymed endings works against this tendency. Obvious examples of this type of *perenos* would be, say, Blok's poem beginning "Ta zhizn' proshla," (or that beginning "Poët, poët . . ." from the cycle *O chëm poët veter*)[14] — or any number of short-line poems by Fet. Tsvetaeva's earlier cycles likewise contain numerous examples, such as the celebrated poem on her birthday ("Krasnoiu kist'iu / Riabina zazhglas'." *V-I*, p. 47) or the one beginning: "Ruki liubliu / Tselovat' i liubliu / Imena razdavat' / I eshchë — raskryvat' / Dveri! (*V-I*, p. 74). Some of the early poems of *LS,* though less "fluid" in style, would also come under this heading (e.g. *LS* nos. 3, 5, & 9); likewise the first and third parts of "Plach Iaroslavny" (*LS* nos. 59 & 61), though here we occasionally encounter the "more marked" pause in mid-line, e.g. (from no. 59):

> — Igor' moi! Kniaz'
> Igor' moi! Kniaz'
> Igor'!
>
> Voron, ne sglaz'
> Glaz moikh — pust'
> Plachut!

In fact, Tsvetaeva handles this type of "carry-over" at least as well as any other Russian poet, but it is hard to discern anything specifically Tsvetaevan about it. Only towards the end of *V-I* do we find examples of more marked enjambement (with instances of mid-stichic pause), as in the poems beginning "I ne placha zria" (p. 109) or "Kazhdyi den' vsë kazhetsia mne: subbota!" (p.113) Here, the conflict between "metrical and syntactical segmentation" is unmistakable, and it is the more striking for being closely preceded and followed by two other poems with "carry-over" of the simpler, earlier, type (*V-I*, p. 107 & pp. 116–17). While *LS* contains other, more marked, cases of enjambement, very few of them, as we remarked elsewhere, "would be considered 'bold,' or in any way unusual, even by the canons of Russian usage" and the cycle as a whole "is not noticeably original" in this respect.[15] Even the examples cited there from no. 49 do

not particularly strike the reader for, despite the undoubted presence of a more marked mid-line pause, the accents of the words
immediately preceding these pauses coincide in both cases with
the metrical accent, which thus "houses" them quite comfortably:

> Nichego ne mozhem darom
> *Vziát'*—skoree goru dvinem!

> Budet nash otvet u vkhoda
> *V Rái,* pod derevtsem mindal'nym. . .

Discussing, in an earlier study, the role of enjambement in
Blok's verse, we remarked that, *"ceteris paribus,* enjambement
will be least marked . . . where the ending of the first line and
the opening of the second . . . are such that the basic meter flows
on without pause or interruption."[16] Put in more positive form,
one might say that enjambement will be *most* marked where there
is *maximum* pause or interruption. In other words the *(a)catalec-
tic factor* is clearly a further important element in determining
the "force" (or degree of ostentation) of enjambement, and this,
as we showed in our study of Blok, depends on the type of meter
and the system of ending-pattern used in each particular case.
But there is, at least with Tsvetaeva (which there was not with
Blok), a third element, whose role is at least as important as the
mid-line pause or the acatalectic factor. This is what might be
termed the "syncopation factor," which comes into play when
certain words involved in the carry-over process do *not* coincide
with the metrical scheme (as they *did* coincide in the examples
taken from *LS* no. 49), but are in evident conflict with that scheme.
In a sense, then, there is again conflict between "metrical and
syntactical segmentation," but it is of a very different nature
from that envisaged by Zhirmunskii, or at the very least it represents a very *particular manifestation* of the latter. This type of
enjambement sets in very early in *PR*, and several examples will
be found in the poems on pages 16–23 inclusive. However, closer
examination shows that, here again, individual cases are by no
means equal in their interruptive effect. Thus, in the second stanza
of the poem beginning "Nochnogo gostia ne zastanesh'. . ."(p.17):

> No esli — ne sochti, chto draznit
> *Slukh!* — *liu*biashchaia — chut'

Otklonitsia, no esli navzryd
*Noch' i kifa*roi — grud' . . .

there is obviously more "disturbance" (or "surprise") in the spondaic opening of the second line (Slúkh! — liúbiashchaia . . .) than in the last line, where the choriambic opening (Nóch' i kifároi) makes for easier accentuation of the word *Noch'*. In the poem beginning "Svetlo-serebrianaia tsvel' " (pp. 20–21), the third stanza opens with an even more "disturbing" case of syncopational enjambement, where the opening syllable (Spi!), apart from being in a nonstressed position, is then separated from the next accentuated syllable by no less than four unaccented ones ($\acute{-} - - - - \acute{-} - \acute{-} - -$):

Ibo ne védaiushchim let
— Spí! — golovokruzhén'e nrávitsia.

It is no mere coincidence that all these examples should be drawn from what are *basically iambic* poems. Where the basic meter is trochaic, the presence of a first metrically accentuated syllable in each line renders the "carry-over" far less problematical, and this is undoubtedly one of the reasons for the relative smoothness of the enjambement in the examples from *LS* no. 49 cited earlier, or of the far bolder and more widespread enjambement (some of it interstanzaic) that we find in, say, "Popytka revnosti" (*PR*, pp. 134–36). The same applies *mutatis mutandis* where there is a *constant* choriambic opening. Thus, in the poem beginning "Lety slepotekushchii vskhlip" (*PR*, pp. 22–23), there is bold enjambement almost everywhere, but the presence of a first metrically accented syllable ($\acute{-} - - - \acute{-}$) leaves nothing remotely like the interruptive effect of the stressed monosyllable at the beginning of a truly iambic line, i.e. in a metrically unstressed position. Here, for once, it seems legitimate to speak of a device *specific* to Tsvetaeva, or at least of one that bears her "signature," as we termed it in an earlier study,[17] in which we illustrated the device with two of the most striking examples of all, taken respectively from the poems "Rodina" and "Toska po rodine" (*IPBP*, no. 335 and no. 344). The second of these examples includes an instance — if not specific to, at any rate characteristic of, Tsvetaeva — of enjambement carried over from one stanza

to the next. The later Tsvetaeva makes use of this device as freely
and boldly as any Russian poet we know (*PR* abounds with examples, as do some poems of the 1930s) — but again, the phenomenon (while interesting and important *in itself*) varies widely
in the degree of its interruptive effect, and for the same reasons
as before. In this sense, the interstanzaic enjambement encountered in the trochaic "Popytka revnosti," in the *regular* iambic
"Minuta" (*PR,* pp. 109–10), or even in the *otherwise* "irregu-
lar" "Chas dushi – 3" (*PR,* p. 104), has nothing like the same
interruptive force as that which occurs, say, between the first
and second stanzas of "Toska po rodine" or, in a different way,
between the last two stanzas of the amphibrachic "Kust" (*IPBP,*
no. 345) or the final stanzas of *IPBP* no. 354, with its basically
anapestic opening.

    There remains one last type of enjambement which, though
extremely rare, may likewise fairly be considered as specific of
Tsvetaeva's technique. This is when a single *word* is split into
two parts between the end of one stich and the beginning of another. The best known examples are the two from the poem beginning "Nekotorym — ne zakon" (*PR,* p. 15), one of them cited
long ago by Karlinsky:[18]

> Vsmatryvaiutsia — i v skrý-
> tneishem lepestke: ne ty!
>
> Vpytyvaiutsia — i stí-
> snutym kulakom — v peski!

Occasionally this device is dictated by the meter alone, i.e. even
in the absence of rhyme, as in these lines from the poem beginning "Vkradchivostiiu volos" (*PR,* pp. 21–22):

> Zhalko mne tvoei upór-
> stvuiushchei ladoni: v losk
> Volosy, — vot-vot uzh cherez
>
> Krai — glaza . . . .

All the examples cited so far date from the summer of 1922 (June–
July). In a much later example (November, 1935: "Chitateli ga-
zet," *IPBP* no. 357), Tsvetaeva reintroduces a similar device which
virtually qualifies as interstanzaic enjambement as well (inasmuch

as the last "line" is set out separately from the preceding quatrain):

> Stoiu pered litsom
> — Pustee mesta — net! —
> Tak znachit — *nelitsom*
> Redaktora gazét-
>
> noi nechisti.

*

The time factor and the tiret. Tsvetaeva's bold use of enjambement is but one more reflection of that priority of the auditory factor mentioned earlier in connection with her free rhymes. A corollary of this general attitude is another priority, that accorded to the *time element* in her verse, rather than to the strictly *syllabic* one. Of course, Russian poetry also knows pure tonic, or accentual, verse (some of it popular, some of it literary, like the *dol'-niki* of the Symbolists and Acmeists) but by and large the time basis plays a less conspicuous role in Russian verse than, say, in its German or English counterparts. The simplest and most obvious examples often being the best, one could do worse at this stage than cite a typically English example from A. A. Milne's book of verse for children entitled *When We Were Very Young.* The poem "Disobedience" is built up on a meter that is *potentially* dactylic (two 2-foot lines followed by a 3-foot line catalectic), but with frequent omission of one or both unstressed syllables, the only "full" dactylic line in the opening stanza being the second:

> James ᴗ ᴗ James ᴗ ᴗ
> Morrison Morrison
> Weatherby George ᴗ Dupree
> Took ᴗ ᴗ great ᴗ ᴗ
> Care of his Mother, ᴗ
> Though he was only ᴗ three.

The *final* stanza of the poem repeats the "text" of the opening one, in humorously abbreviated fashion, *while retaining exactly the same time values* for its basic rhythm:

> J. J.
> M. M.

W. G. Du P.
Took great
C/o his M*****
Though he was only 3. [19]

This is an example of "time equivalence" at its most obvious.
Turning back to Tsvetaeva (and to more serious verse!), we find
an illustration of the same *principle* (albeit reduced to its very
simplest form) in *LS* no. 29, the opening stanza of which reads:

Bog —
Tleniem trav,
Sukhost'iu rek,
Voplem kalek,

In point of fact, all twelve lines of the poem follow the "choriambic pattern ´ – – ´ with the *one exception of the first line*, in
which the place of the two central unstressed syllables is "covered" by the dash (or *tiret*). This brings us to yet another *specific*
of Tsvetaeva's verse, the dash. Her poetry (as indeed all her writings) is liberally sprinkled with dashes, but these dashes do not
by any means always perform the same function. Leaving aside
her use of the dash to enclose direct speech (a normal part of
Russian poetic usage) or as a purely punctuative device, Tsvetaeva's "metrical dash" may take one of basically two forms.
One is the dash (as in the first line of *LS* no. 29 above) which
sometimes (though by no means consistently) takes the place of
syllables which exist potentially in a strictly syllabotonic context.
An interesting illustration in this connection is *LS* no. 42, a short
poem consisting of three couplets, the basic meter of which is
six-foot trochaic with D-endings: ´ – ´ – ´ – ´ – ´ – ´ – –. The
text (cf. *Appendix,* RT/1) contains in lines 2, 4, 5, and 6. However, whereas the dashes in the first two cases are purely punctuative, those in lines 5 and 6 are *also* metrical, to the extent that
they "cover" the position of the eighth syllable of the line (i.e.
the thesis of the fourth trochaic foot) which is here *absent:*

I nikto iz vas, synki! — ne vorotitsia.
A vedët vashi polki — Bogoroditsa!

Another example is the poem from *V-I* (p. 92), the basic scheme of which is five-foot iambic, but without the thesis of the final foot (i.e. the potential ninth syllable of the line): - ´ - ´ - - ´ - ´ (-) ´. Out of a total of sixteen lines, dashes occur (singly) in eleven of them, and all but one "cover" the missing ninth syllable of the line, as, for instance, in the opening two lines:

> V ogromnom gorode moëm — noch'.
> Iz doma sonnogo idu — proch' . . . .

The one exception is line 11, which reads:

> I shag vot etot — nikomu vsled,[20]

Sometimes the dash alone does not seem sufficient, and Tsvetaeva would deem it advisable to explain her understanding of the required rhythm in a footnote adressed to the reader. Two examples from *PR* (p. 11 and p. 18) illustrate this point.

The other type of "metrical dash" (or is it a hyphen — despite Tsvetaeva's own use of the word *tire* in this connection?) is that used (by analogy with the internal dashes in printed music which she recalled from the songbooks of her childhood) to mark what Karlinsky has termed "hyperprosodic stresses" — a device, incidentally, which he regarded, along with Tsvetaeva's canonization of the "choriamb," as representing "revolutionary developments in the history of Rusian versification."[21] Unlike the "compensatory dash," which "covers" the missing syllables required by a strictly syllabotonic scheme, the "internal dash," to quote Karlinsky once more, has the effect of providing certain words "with more syllables than they would normally have, as imitation of either a slow drawling diction, or . . . of shouting . . . ."[22] Several examples of this type of "dash" may be found in the poem "Provoda-1" (*PR*, pp. 65–66), e.g.:

> . . . Po alee
> Vzdokhov — provolokoi k stolbu —
> Telegrafnoe: Liu—iu—bliu . . .

> . . . Vdol' svai
> Telegrafnoe: pro—o—shchai . . .

> Cherez nasypi — i — rvy
> Evridikino: u—u—vy, . . .

or in this quatrain ("Slova i smysly-2," *PR*, p. 80):

> La—don' v ladon':
> — Za—chem rozhdën?
> — Ne—zhal': izvol':
> Dlit' — dal' — i bol'.

These poems are from March–April 1923. Long before this, however, Tsvetaeva had introduced the same device to reproduce the "shouting" of military commands, in *LS* no. 9:

> Slusha—ai! Nà—kra—ul!

and, in a different, but still military, context, in *LS* no. 58:

> — Kto ty? — belyi? — ne poimu! — privstan'!
> Al' u krasnykh propadal? — Ria—azan'.

Commenting, in her article "Mat' i muzyka," on the reception that greeted her introduction of those "completely legal dashes," Tsvetaeva remarked that "everyone scolded me for this for years on end, while a very few praised [me] (in both cases, on account of [my] modernism). ..."[23] Karlinsky himself, citing the comments, all of them negative, of various scholars, critics, and poets (Nikolai Kul'man, Iurii Terapiano, Aleksandr Bakhrakh), concluded, with understandable chagrin: "These are all the comments I could find on Cvetaeva's metrical system and they are truly amazing: the commentators clearly begrudge the poet her attempt to fix on paper the rhythmic and metrical structure of her work."[24]

*

Syncope and syllabism. While, then, as often as not, it is the time factor that lies at the basis of Tsvetaeva's verse and enables her to "carry it off" in the face of a (by Russian standards) unorthodox type of asyllabism or anisosyllabism, one occasionally encounters instances of the *reverse phenomenon,* passages where, for instance, the syncope and/or the enjambement is so audacious that the overall rhythm is "saved" precisely by the strictness of the syllabic framework in which it is set. One of the most striking examples of this is provided by the opening stanzas of the third part of "Chas dushi" (*PR*, p. 104). As we explained in an earlier study,[25] two "disintegrating" factors are here at work simultaneously, one of them (the less forceful of the two) being the enjambement, the other (and infinitely the more important) being the "off-beat" position suddenly and quite unexpectedly assigned to the key word *chas* in the second line and the beginning of the third line of the opening stanza. At this point, the word occurs three times in succession in a metrically unstressed position (odd syllables, the meter being iambic); moreover, on the third occasion, the word, carried over from the end of the second line, is immediately followed by itself — but this time, of course, in metrically stressed position (arsis), which with one minor exception then remains the case for the remainder of the poem (in which the word *chas* occurs seventeen times in all):

> Est' chás Dushi, kak chás Luny,
> Sovy — *chas*, mgly — *chas*, t'my —
> *chas*... Chás Dushi — kak chás struny
> Davidovoi skvoz' sny
>
> Saulovy... V tot chás drozhi, ...

It will be noted that there is also enjambement *between* the first and second stanzas, but, despite its bold *position,* its nature, for once, is that of a perfectly smooth "carry-over," since there is no interruption whatsoever of the basic iambic rhythm (partly due to the masculine ending *sny* in the key fourth line).

Before leaving Tsvetaeva's meters, it is worth calling attention to two poems from *V-I*, composed on successive days (2 and 3 July 1916) and each presenting a "freak" line out of keeping with the rest of the poem. The poems appear on pp. 90 and 91 respectively. The former is composed of two quatrains, the latter of four quatrains. In both cases, the basic meter is one of five-foot dactyls with alternating F- and M-endings:[26]

$$\acute{-} - - \acute{-} - - \acute{-} - - \acute{-} - - \acute{-} -$$
$$\acute{-} - - \acute{-} - - \acute{-} - - \acute{-} - - \acute{-}$$

Some would call this meter "dactylic pentameter." The freak line in each poem (line 2 and line 10 respectively) also corresponds to what is often known as a "pentameter," but it is the so-called classical pentameter of elegiac verse, with central caesura, which some regard as being in fact a special type of *hexameter* in which the third and sixth feet are monosyllabic:

$$\acute{-} - - \mid \acute{-} - - \mid \acute{-} \wedge \parallel \acute{-} - - \mid \acute{-} - - \mid \acute{-} \wedge$$

Whatever the terminology adopted, it is a fact that this type of line contains *six* (and not five) "long" (or stressed) syllables.[27] Equally certainly, in the two cases in point, the lines of this type produce a completely different impression from that of the straightforward five-foot dactyls of which the rest of both poems are composed, as the opening lines of the poem on p. 90 are sufficient to show:

> Ruki dany mne — protiagivat' kazhdomu obe,
> Ne uderzhat' ni odnoi, ‖ guby — davat' imena,
> Ochi — ne videt', vysokie brovi nad nimi —
> Nezhno divit'sia liubvi i — nezhnei — neliubvi.

The isolated introduction of the caesural "classical pentameter" is totally unexpected, and it is hard to say whether Tsvetaeva was herself aware of the deviation she was introducing. Knowing her instinctive ear, one is inclined to think that the regular dactylic lilt of the other lines — although mere pentameters, and not hexameters — struck a chord which reminded her of the classical "prototype," *including* the caesural pentameter so often associated with it. By contrast, in the case of "Chas dushi-3" cited earlier, the devices (syncope and enjambement) are evidently conscious, and it is one more tribute to Tsvetaeva's professionalism that she was as deft at handling the strict syllabotonic scheme as the best of them.

Tsvetaeva's preference for "playing it by ear" is betrayed in at least one other feature of her verse, which would not appear to have been remarked upon previously: her occasional habit of scanning monosyllabic nouns ending with the soft sign as disyllabic ones.[28] In this she was not entirely alone. She had before her the example of Lermontov, who scanned *zhizn'* in this way in his anapestic poem beginning:

> Potseluiami prezhde schital
> Ia schastlivuiu *zhizn'* ✗ *svoiu*, . . .

and we find something broadly similar in Blok's lines:

> S nei *zhizn'* ✗ vol'na,
> S nei smert' ne strashna, . . .

With Tsvetaeva, we occasionally (but not consistently) find the same treatment accorded to words of similar construction, e.g. *vikhr'*, as in *LS* no. 50:

> Ia etu knigu, kak butylku v volny,
> Kidaiu v *vikhr'* ✗ vóin.

or *vopl'* (*IPBP* no. 173):

> O *vopl'* ✗ zhenshchin vsekh vremën:
> "Moi milyi, chtò tebe ia sdelala?"

One is tempted to think that Tsvetaeva, whose passionate attachment to the old orthography is proverbial, even applied the same principle on occasion to the final *hard sign* (which, after all, was once at least a semi-vowel). In *LS* there are two successive poems (nos. 13 and 14), each containing a reference to *Pëtr''-Tsar'*. Each poem is, otherwise, in strict syllabotonic meter: no. 13 in five-foot iambics, no. 14 in five-foot trochaics. Yet, in each of the lines in which *Pëtr''-Tsar'* appears, there is an unstressed syllable missing somewhere, and in both cases the most "likely" place to situate it is together with the final hard sign of the word *Pëtr''*. This is especially the case in no. 14, where the parallelism of the first two lines is patent:

> Grishka-Vor'' tebia ne opoliachil'',
> Pëtr''-Tsar' tebia ne onemechil''.

*

Summary and Conclusions. A complete analysis of Tsvetaeva's poetic technique would require at least some examination of her use of *alliteration*. To judge by the results of our investigation into the alliteration of *LS*, the material would be so vast as to require at least another article in itself, if not a book.[29] Closely linked with the alliterative device are Tsvetaeva's parallelisms, her anaphora, and, of course, her widespread use of paranomasia. A study of these aspects would likewise lead us well beyond the limits set to the present article. If there be *one* example that calls for special mention, it is, in our view, the truly astonishing parallelism, the unsuspected sym-metry and sym-phony, of the two "innocent"-looking lines that close the introductory poem to *LS* (no. 1):

*Ia v*olosy go*niu po* vetru,
Ia v larchike khra*niu po*gony.

These lines read so naturally, so unostentatiously, that one is in
no way on the look-out for such technical perfection, which is
only revealed to the conscious mind by a far closer, *ad hoc*, examination of their make-up. Nothing, in our view, better demonstrates that totally genuine, instinctive mastery of poetic technique, bereft, *pace* so many of her detractors, of the very slightest
searching for effect, that places Tsvetaeva among the greatest
poets of any country and any age.

In the course of this article, we have endeavored to examine
certain isolated aspects of Tsvetaeva's technique. Many of them,
as we warned at the outset, are neither new in themselves, nor
necessarily specific (though others may be). It is rather the *sum*
of them all — and the exceptionally bold *nature* of so many of
them — which help to explain this sense of mastery which we, in
our turn, instinctively feel, but have difficulty in accounting for.
Ultimately, Tsvetaeva's originality lies less in her use of any isolated device, or sum of devices, than in her *overall attitude to
verse* — that uncanny "feel" for all the essentials of Russian verse
that enabled her to ride roughshod over most of the generally
accepted norms of Russian metrical practice, and this with scarcely
a fumble or a stumble. No one, it seems, understood this better
than Pasternak, and no more pertinent words have been written
concerning Tsvetaeva's artistry than those that appear in his
"Essay in Autobiography."[30] But there are other words of Pasternak concerning Tsvetaeva and poetry, and it is these, perhaps,
that form the most fitting conclusion to the present study. Speaking of her in the course of a conversation with Aleksandr Gladkov, a few months after her death, Pasternak said: "Of course,
she was more Russian than any of us, not only in her blood, but in
the rhythms that inhabited her soul, in her tremendous, uniquely
powerful language . . . She lived an heroic life. She accomplished
prodigies every day. They were prodigies of loyalty to the only
land whose citizen she was — [the land of] poetry."[31]

University of Lausanne

NOTES

1. General (mostly statistical) studies of recent years include (in chronological order): M.L. Gasparov, "Russkii trekhudarnyi dol'nik XX v.," in *Teoriia stikha,* ed. V.M. Zhirmunskii, D.S. Likhachev, V.E. Kolshevnikov (Leningrad: Nauka, 1968), pp. 59–106; Iu. Lotman, *Analiz poeticheskogo teksta. Struktura stikha* (Leningrad: Prosveshchenie, 1972); M.L. Gasparov, *Sovremennyi russkii stikh. Metrika i ritmika* (Moscow: Nauka, 1974), occasional references, mainly in statistical tables; G.S. Smith, "Logaoedic Metres in the Lyric Poetry of Marina Tsvetayeva," *Slavonic and East European Review* (hereafter cited as *SEER*). vol. 53, no. 132 (1975), pp. 330–54; G.S. Smith, "The Versification of Marina Tsvetayeva's Lyric Poetry, 1922–1923," *Essays in Poetics,* vol. 1, no. 2 (1976), pp. 21–50; G.S. Smith, "The Versification of Russian Émigré Poetry, 1920–1940," *SEER,* vol. 56, no. 1 (1978), pp. 32–46.

2. Studies devoted to specific *poemy* (and occasionally lyrical poems) include: V.V. Ivanov, "Metr i ritm v 'Poeme kontsa' M. Tsvetaevoi," in *Teoriia stikha,* 1968, pp. 168–201; A.N. Kolmogorov, "Primer izucheniia metra i ego ritmicheskikh variantov," in *Teoriia stikha,* 1968, pp. 145–67 (on "Stol" and "Poema kontsa"); G.I. Sedykh, "Zvuk i smysl (o funktsiiakh fonem v poeticheskom tekste)," in *Materialy 26-i nauchnoi studencheskoi konferentsii. Literaturovedenie. Lingvistika,* ed. P.A. Radnev and P.S. Sigalov (Tartu: Tartuskii universitet, 1971), pp. 87–89 (on "Psikheia"); G.I. Sedykh, "Zvuk i smysl. O funktsiiakh fonem v poeticheskom tekste. (Na primere analiza stikhotvoreniia M. Tsvetaevoi 'Psikheia')," *Filologicheskie nauki,* no. 1 (1973), pp. 41–50; L.N. Dediukhina, "Opyt analiza stikhotvornogo teksta. (Na materiale stikhotvoreniia M. Tsvetaevoi 'Toska po rodine! Davno...'),'' in *Semantiko-stilisticheskie funktsii iazykovykh edinits* (Sverdlovsk, 1974), pp. 24–37; G.S. Smith, "Versification and Composition in Marina Cvetaeva's *Pereuločki*," *International Journal of Slavic Linguistics and Poetics* (hereafter cited as *IJSLP*), vol. 20 (1975), pp. 61–92; Robin Kemball, "La poétique de Tsvetaeva: son audace — et son innocence," *Etudes de Lettres* (Lausanne), vol. 10, no. 1 (1977), pp. 38–43 (examples from the poems: "Kto utselel — umret, kto mertv — vosprianet" [1918]; "Chas dushi" [1923]; "Kto — m y? Potonul v medvediakh" [1926]; "Rodina" [1932]; and "Toska po rodine" [1934]); G.S. Smith, "Marina Cvetaeva's *Poèma gory*: An Analysis," in *Russian Literature* (The Hague: forthcoming).

There is also a word-frequency analysis and glossary of the *poema Krysolov*: Günther Wytrzens, "Zum Wortschatz des 'Krysolov' der Marina Cvetaeva," *Wiener Slawistischer Almanach,* no. 1 (1978), pp. 109–34, and no. 2 (1978), pp. 145–76.

3. See Tsvetaeva's own note concerning the contents of the cycle *Lebedinyi Stan*: "My *Lebedinyi Stan* ends here. Of course — I could have included in it the whole of *Razluka,* the whole of *Georgii* and altogether a good quarter of *Remeslo* — and very probably more besides — but — at the time I did not do so, finishing my *Lebedinyi Stan* at this point." Translated from the Russian original in the Manuscripts Division of the Basle University Library; cited in *Marina Tsvetaeva, The Demesne of the Swans / Lebedinyi Stan,* edited and translated by Robin Kemball (Ann Arbor: Ardis, 1980), p. 194.

4. Simon Karlinsky, *Marina Cvetaeva: Her Life and Art* (Berkeley and Los Angeles: University of California Press, 1966), esp. pp. 123–70 (Ch. VI. "Technical Aspects: Language, Versification, Poetic Devices"). Karlinsky's study, based on his doctoral thesis bearing the same title (University of California at Berkeley, 1964) is still the only *general* survey of Tsvetaeva's poetic technique.

5. *Marina Tsvetaeva, The Demesne of the Swans / Lebedinyi Stan,* edited and translated by Robin Kemball (Ann Arbor: Ardis, 1980), pp. 165–94 (Notes and Commentaries) and pp. 195–209 (Translator's Note). (N.B. This edition is henceforth referred to as *Demesne of the Swans.*)

6. The present study is confined to an examination of Tsvetaeva's *lyric* verse (by which is understood the shorter poems, leaving aside the *poemy,* whether examined elsewhere or not). Moreover, while the findings are based on a study of Tsvetaeva's lyric production as a whole, most of the examples cited have, for simplicity's sake, been drawn from a limited number of cycles (or *sborniki*), synchronistically spaced and sufficiently typical to fulfil their illustrative role. These cycles include primarily: a) *Versty I* (1916); b) *Lebedinyi Stan* (1917–1921); c) *Posle Rossii* (1922–1925); d) a few poems from the 1930s. N.B. The years in parenthesis refer to the dates of *composition.* The corresponding dates of *first publiaction* (often misleading in view of the circumstances surrounding Tsvetaeva's life) are: a) 1922; b) 1957 (!); c) 1928. The poems from the 1930s are taken from Marina Tsvetaeva, *Izbrannye proizvedeniia* (Moscow and Leningrad: Sovetskii pisatel', 1965, in the series *Biblioteka poeta, Bol'shaia seriia*). These four sources are henceforth referred to by the following abbreviated titles: a) *V-I;* b) *LS;* c) *IPBP.*

7. "La poétique de Tsvetaeva: son audace — et son innocence." See note 2 supra.

8. Poems from *LS* are referred to by the serial numbers given in *Demesne of the Swans,* as are poems from *IPBP.* Poems from *V-I* and *PR,*

in the absence of any such numeration, are normally identified by the page number(s), occasionally by the title or first line in addition.

9. Endings are henceforward referred to by the customary English abbreviations, M = Masculine; F = Feminine; D = Dactylic; H = Hyperdactylic.

10. The best and most frequent examples of cretic endings of this type occur, naturally enough, in the "folk" *poemy,* which lie outside the scope of the present study. A few examples taken at random from a part of the *poema (skazka) Tsar'-Devitsa (IPBP,* pp. 408 ff.) follow: boléznyi moi : brézgovat' — gúsel'nyi : chút' li ne — vósk daët : velikopóstnaia — vósku dve : slëzki dve.

11. See *Demesne of the Swans,* p. 186, note to no. 41. The poems in question are nos. 41, 42, 43, 46, and 48, after which no further dactylic endings occur in the cycle in the form of a regular ending-pattern.

12. See *Demesne of the Swans,* p. 199 and Table III on p. 208.

13. V. Zhirmunskii, *Vvedenie v metriku. Teoriia skikha* (Leningrad: Academia, 1925), pp. 173, 174.

14. See *Aleksandr Blok, Sobranie sochinenii* (8 vols; Moscow and Leningrad, 1960), vol. 3, p. 220 and pp. 284–85 respectively.

15. *Demesne of the Swans,* p. 198.

16. In *Alexander Blok — A Study in Rhythm and Metre* (The Hague: Mouton, 1965), p. 316.

17. "La poétique de Tsvetaeva: son audace — et son innocence," p. 39.

18. *Marina Cvetaeva: Her Life and Art,* p. 166. In a footnote on the same page, Karlinsky refers the reader to a discussion of Tsvetaeva's enjambement in an article by K. Taranovski, "Some Problems of Enjambment in Slavic and Western European Verse," *IJSLP,* no. 7 (1963), pp. 80–87.

19. A.A. Milne, *When We Were Very Young,* 35th ed. (London: Methuen, 1942), pp. 30–33.

20. This poem also figures in *IPBP,* as "Bessonnitsa–3" (no. 42), where four additional dashes are introduced in various positions in lines 3, 5, 11, and 13. The dash in line five covers the missing ninth syllable, as does the *new* dash in line 11, which here contains two dashes, one on either side of the word *nikomu.*

21. *Marina Cvetaeva: Her Life and Art,* p. 164. (The Tsvetaevan "dash" is discussed on pp. 161–65 incl.)

22. Ibid., p. 163.

23. See Mariva Tsvetaeva, *Izbrannaia proza v dvukh tomakh 1917–1937* (New York: Russica Publishers, 1979), vol. 2, p. 182.

24. *Marina Cvetaeva: Her Life and Art*, p. 164

25. "La poétique de Tsvetaeva: son audace—et son innocence," pp. 39–40.

26. The poem on p. 90 is unrhymed; that on p. 91 has the rhyme scheme *abab*.

27. For more detailed examination of the nature of the classical "pentameter," see *Alexander Blok—A Study in Rhythm and Metre*, pp. 334–35.

28. A *rough* equivalent in English usage would be the suffix -ism, which is theoretically monosyllabic, but is in practice pronounced by almost everyone in two syllables (-izz-um).

29. See *Demesne of the Swans*, pp. 200–204.

30. See Boris Pasternak, "Avtobiograficheskii ocherk," in *Proza 1915–1958. Povesti, rasskazy, avtobiograficheskie proizvedeniia,* ed. G.P. Struve and B.A. Filippov (Ann Arbor: University of Michigan Press, 1961), pp. 1–52, esp. pp. 45–48.

31. See Aleksandr Gladkov, *Vstrechi s Pasternakom* (Paris: YMCA-Press, 1973), pp. 52–53.

THE CHILD NARRATOR IN THE NOVELLAS

OF CHINGIZ AITMATOV

NINA KOLESNIKOFF

Any reader familiar with the novellas of Chingiz Aitmatov is aware of the important role children play in his writing. Children are not only the protagonists of many of his novellas, but often become the narrators: they not only tell the story but evaluate everything and everyone in it. Perhaps the clearest example of the child narrator appears in "Dzhamilia," which is told in the first person by the fifteen-year-old Seit; he witnesses the story of the growing fascination between his sister-in-law Dzhamilia, whose husband is at war, and Daniiar, a demobilized soldier.[1] Seit reports only what he can see and hear, or what he can guess, and is unable to penetrate the innermost feelings of the lovers. The advantage of this method is an unusual freshness and poetic beauty in the depiction of the love story, reflecting Seit's lack of prejudice and his innocent perception of the world.

Moreover, the choice of Seit as a narrator allows Aitmatov to introduce the other theme of the novella — that of the importance of art. Under the influence of Daniiar, Seit responds to the beauty of nature and experiences a strong desire to paint it. He leaves his native village to go to a city to study art. In the frame which opens and closes the novella, Seit is already a recognized painter, reminiscing about the events that made him an artist.

The frame establishes a dual temporal perspective, that in which Seit talks about his painting, and that in which he enacts his childhood experience. The past perspective predominates in the novella, and most of the story is filtered through the consciousness of the young Seit. But at the same time the narrative constantly

reflects the point of view of the mature Seit, who comments on
the events. Thus "Dzhamilia" offers a dual point of view which
is perfectly reasonable, and which allows Aitmatov to transcend
the limits of the innocence of his hero and to present values very
close to his own.

By comparison with the clear first-person narration in "Dzhamilia," the narration in Aitmatov's latest novellas about young
protagonists is not as easy to define.[2] Written in the third person,
they seem at first to employ an omniscient narrator who presents
the story, comments on the events, and sketches the characters.
But a closer look at the narrative reveals that the predominant
point of view in these novellas is not that of the omniscient author,
but that of the young hero. While retaining the third-person narration, the narrator identifies himself with his young protagonists
and reproduces their perception of the world around them.[3]

The most consistent use of the child narrator occurs in "Rannie zhuravli" ("The Early Cranes") written almost entirely from
the point of view of a fourteen-year-old youth experiencing the
hardships of war in a distant Kirghiz village. Like his predecessor
Seit, Sultanmurat is forced to leave school in order to help the
kolkhoz with farming. Together with his four friends, he forms
"a landing force," responsible for the plowing and sowing of the
spring crops in the Aksai steppe.

From the beginning of the novella the narrative transmits the
point of view of Sultanmurat as he reflects on the harsh life in
the village, the self-sacrificing work of women and children, and
on his own responsibility as head of his family. As a contrast to
these pictures of the difficult life on the homefront appear Sultanmurat's recollections of the happy days before the war; he
remembers his father, their trip to the city, and their stay over-
night in the steppe.

The two temporal planes of the present and the past are art-
fully interwoven in the novella, but there is also a third dimension — that of the future. Basically a daydreamer, Sultanmurat
often escapes into fantasies, imagining the return of his father
from the front and a happy life after the war. At the end of the
novella, however, his dreams are crushed when he pursues horse
thieves, loses his horse, and faces an uneven fight with a hungry
wolf.

The child narrator also predominates in "Belyi parokhod" ("The White Steamship"), which renders the point of view of a seven-year-old boy deserted by his parents and living with his relatives in a mountain forest preserve. Through the eyes of the child the reader sees the cordon itself, its inhabitants, and events that lead to his tragic death. In the course of the novella the reader learns the innermost feelings of the boy, who feels rejected by everyone except his grandfather Momun. To escape this cruel reality he creates a tale in which he becomes a fish and swims to the white ship on which his father is working. He has another favorite tale told to him by his grandfather. That tale depicts the fate of the legendary Horned Deer Mother, who once had helped the Kirghiz people but had had to escape with its offspring when people began hunting for its horns. In the boy's childish perception there are no strict boundaries between the real world of the cordon and the world of fairy tales, and when a deer and family appear in the preserve, he mistakes her for the legendary Deer Mother. The killing of the deer is a blow to the boy's dream, and he decides to turn into a fish and swim away. As in "Rannie zhuravli," the beautiful world of the child is crushed by the brute forces of real life.

By comparison with these two previously discussed novellas, the role of the child narrator diminishes in Aitmatov's latest work, "Pegii pes, begushchii kraem moria" ("The Skewbald Dog running along the Seashore"), in which the voice of the young protagonist is combined with the voices of other characters, as well as with the voice of the omniscient narrator. But even here the child narrator outshines the others. The initial pages register the excitement of eleven-year-old Kirisk, going for his first sea hunt. The boy recalls his preparation for the hunt and imagines the celebration that will follow his happy return home. It is through the eyes of Kirisk that the reader sees the sea, calm and serene at first, but later raging and powerful. Through the boy's eyes the reader watches the desperate struggle of the three men in a tiny boat against the sea. Miraculously the men survive the storm, but are unable to find their way home in the thick fog that follows it. Faced with a shortage of food and drink, the men throw themselves one by one into the sea, hoping to prolong the life of the boy even for several days. The final pages of the novella transmit the despair of Kirisk, alone in the boat, delirious and raving for fresh water. But the novella ends on an optimistic note — after several days of ordeal the boy spots the familiar silhouette of his native bay with its snowy mound resembling a skewbald dog running along the seashore.

Despite the differences in the narrative technique, itself, and the degree to which the narrative is filtered through the consciousness of a young hero, all the above novellas testify to Aitmatov's predilection for the child narrator. Why is the writer so attached to this method of narration?

One of the most obvious advantages of the child narrator is an unusual vividness of description. A child sees the world in a unique way, not influenced by any habits or misconceptions. Using the arguments of Victor Shklovskii we can say that a child sees the old and the habitual as if it were new and unusual.[4] A writer reproducing the child's vision defamiliarizes ordinary things and makes the reader see them instead of merely recognizing them. This is exactly what happens in the following passage in "Belyi parokhod":

> The lad ran quickly, hopping over bushes and around the boulders he wasn't able to jump. He didn't dally anywhere, even for a second — not near the high grass, nor near the rocks, although he knew that they were far from ordinary. They could feel insulted and even trip people. "The motor-market's arrived. I'll come back later," he tossed off while rushing past "lying camel," as he called a ginger, hunch-backed piece of granite sunk into the earth up to its chest.
>
> Ordinarily, the lad wouldn't pass without patting his "camel" on its hump. He patted him in the manner of an animal's master, like grandfather his short-tailed gelding — just a casual, off-handed tap as if to say, "You wait around, I'm off to take care of something nearby." He had a boulder called "saddle" — half white and half black, a skewbald rock with a saddle-like hollow on which you could mount, as on a horse. There was also a "wolf" rock which looked very much like a real wolf — tawnyish and flecked with gray, with powerful withers and weighty brows. He would steal up to him on all fours and take aim. But his favorite rock was the "tank," an indestructible boulder on the very bank of the

river, which was hollowed away by the current. Any second now the "tank" would charge from the bank and plunge on, and the river would seethe, boiling with whitecaps.[5]

The familiarization is motivated here by the age and character of the protagonist. The only child in the cordon, not spoiled by any toys, he had learned how to play and communicate with natural objects: rocks, plants and grasses. His closest "friends" are his binoculars, through which he can see the white ship in the distant Issik'kul Lake, and his briefcase to which he can confide all his injuries and worries.

Like all Aitmatov's other children, the boy is very close to nature. He knows a lot about the trees and animals in the forest, and through the teaching of his grandfather, respects all living things. Such an attitude towards nature is of great importance to Aitmatov, who stressed that by writing "Belyi parokhod" he wanted to make people aware of the need to establish a harmonious relationship with nature, "to preserve the wealth and beauty of the world around us."[6] The boy in the novella expresses perfectly this idea, without any additional authorial comments or generalizations.

In a similar way, the child narrator allows Aitmatov to convey in his novellas the idea of the necessity to preserve the link between tradition and the new way of life. In all these novellas the young protagonists have a close relationship with their real or surrogate grandfathers, who pass on to them the old traditions. Grandfather Momun in "Belyi parokhod," the old man Organ in "Pegii pes," the team leader Chekish — all these old and wise men tell the youngsters about life in the past and by their own example teach them how to live.

Throughout all these novellas the colorful details of the local customs are transmitted not in authorial descriptions, but through the eyes of the young protagonists. Thus the local color does not burden the narrative, but adds to its vividness. As in descriptions of nature, Aitmatov often defamiliarizes local customs by filtering them through the consciousness of his young heroes, who do not understand the true meaning of what they witness:

We walk home and hear: somebody starts singing a song. A young

shepherd probably, or maybe an old one. Grandfather stops me.
"Listen. You can't always hear those songs." We stand still and
listen. Grandfather sighs. The song makes him nod his head.

Grandfather says that long ago one khan had another khan
prisoner. And this khan said to the captive khan: "If you want
to you can live as my slave. Otherwise I'll fulfil your most cher-
ished wish and then kill you." The other one thought before an-
swering: "I do not wish to live as a slave. I'd rather you kill me,
but before this, summon the first shepherd you meet from my
homeland." "Why do you want him?" "Before my death, I
want to hear him sing." Grandfather says that these people give
their lives for their native songs. Who are these people? I'd like
to see them. I guess they live in big cities?[7]

It is important to note that local color as used by Aitmatov is
devoid of the usual exotic flavor: it reproduces realistically the
setting, customs, and way of thinking of the Kirghiz people.
Moreover, this local color is not mere decoration, but an essential
element of the structure, strengthening the characterization and
revealing truths about human nature.

The child narrator is used by Aitmatov not only as a means to
describe the settings vividly, but also as a vehicle for his ideas.
In an interview given to *Literaturnaia gazeta* the writer stressed
that as his creative goals had become more complex, he was looking for heroes that could express his ideas naturally, by their own
essence. He had found such heroes in children:

At the very essence of man's inner self lies the full value of childhood. The unity between adults and children, the selfless love of
a mother, father, sister, and a grandmother, creates the impression
of a loving, good world. Hence, the child's capacity to experience
someone else's grief, his belief in truth . . . But the integral child's
nature is confronted in life with lies, egoism and compromises.
And a young person is not capable of sophistry. Here an artist can
find the dramatic material and the sharp conflicts. By looking at
the events with the eyes of youth, he can reveal the drama of life
in a new, ingenious way.[8]

The dramatic conflict between the child's innocent vision and
the cruelty of the real world is the underlying principle of Aitmatov's recent novellas. In all of them he portrays extremely dra-

matic situations which reveal the true character of the protagonists. Depicted at the moment of their first serious trial, Aitmatov's young heroes prove themselves not only idealistic, but strong
enough to defend their principles.

Faced with the killing of the deer, the boy in "Belyi parokhod"
decides to swim away from the cruel people. He prefers to die
rather than to live in the immoral and hypocritical world of adults.
The boy dies, but the moral victory is his.[9]

A similar effect is achieved by the tragic ending of "Rannie
zhuravli," portraying Sultanmurat in the pursuit of the horse
thieves. The boy loses his horse and has to face an uneven fight
with a wolf. Although he is likely to lose this fight, his death
symbolizes his willingness to die to defend his principles.[10]

The confrontation depicted in "Pegii pes," unlike that in the
other two novellas, is not between the idealistic world of the young
and the immoral world of the adults, but between men and nature. The sea represents here the cruel force that crushes the boy's
dream of a successful hunt which would initiate him into the
world of adults. The adults, on the other hand, exemplify the
highest moral standards possible — they sacrifice their own lives
in order to save the boy. At the time of the events Kirisk does
not comprehend the full meaning of their action, but eventually
he will grasp the value of their self-sacrifice.

The change of the dramatic collision in "Pegii pes" forced
Aitmatov to change the narrative method. In order to reveal the
full meaning of the sacrifice of the adults, he could not rely exclusively on the perception of his young hero. Therefore, Aitmatov introduced into the novella the points of view of the other
characters as well, primarily of Organ, an old man who is sum-
ming up his life while preparing for death, and of Emraiin, Kirisk's
father, who, before dying, contemplates his responsibility towards
his son.

Moreover, Aitmatov combined the concealed narrator with an
omniscient one who describes the setting, introduces characters,
and comments on the uneven struggle between the four men and
the sea. In addition, the narrator renders the myths and legends
which help to endow the concrete events described in the novella
with cosmic dimensions. Because of the presence of the omniscient

narrator "Pegii pes" reads like a philosophical tale about the
meaning of life and the responsibilities of people towards each
other.[11]

In the other two novellas the author is more consistent in the
use of the child narrator, but even here he occasionally introduces
other points of view. In "Belyi parokhod" he renders the thoughts
of Momun, the boy's grandfather and protector, and of Orozkul,
the forest warden and the virtual ruler of the three families in the
cordon. The character of Orozkul is univocal — he is the symbol
of the hypocrisy and immorality of the adults, which shatter the
boy's dreams of beauty and goodness. The character of Momun
is more complex — he represents the good forces in life, but because of his inability to defend his principles he becomes an un-
willing instrument in the death of his grandson. The convincing
psychological portrayals of Momun and Orozkul throw into relief
the opposing forces in the conflict and prepare the reader for the
tragic ending of the novella.

The superficial treatment of minor characters, on the other
hand, weakens the artistic impact of "Rannie zhuravli," where
the figures of the horse thieves are depicted one-sidedly, without
a trace of psychological substance. They are brought into the
novella suddenly, without any prehistory, simply to illustrate the
evil forces that destroy the beautiful dreams of youngsters.

In addition to using the points of view of several characters,
Aitmatov also introduces the voice of a narrator, very close to
himself, who occasionally comments on the events and reveals
their importance. In "Rannie zhuravli" the narrator draws a
parallel between his young protagonists and the brave warriors
of Manas, legendary heroes of the Kirghiz epos, thus emphasizing
the heroic aspect of the boys' hard labor. In "Belyi parokhod"
the narrator takes over the story after the death of the boy. In a
peculiar epilogue, the narrator reiterates the moral message of
the novella:

> I can only say one thing now: you rejected what your child's
> heart could not reconcile itself to. And that's my consolation. You
> lived like a bolt of lightning which once — and only once — flashed
> and expired. But lightning strikes from the sky. And the sky is
> eternal. This too is my consolation. And that a child's conscience

in a person is like an embryo in a particle of grain: the grain won't grow without the embryo. That whatever awaits us on earth, truth will endure forever, as long as people are born and die.[12]

The narrator concludes by repeating the words of the boy, addressed to the white steamship, thus suggesting that he had fulfilled the dreams of his hero by reaching the ship and telling it about the boy's short life, about his indestructible belief in the Deer Mother, and the principles of beauty and justice.

Nowhere do the voice of the narrator or the voices of other characters outweigh the voices of the protagonists. In all the novellas discussed, the child narrator remains the chief storyteller, describing the main events and forwarding the action. Moreover, the child narrator performs an important ideological function — through the child's innocent vision the writer penetrates the essence of life's complexities and contradictions. In order to make these contradictions more apparent, Aitmatov supplements the voice of the child narrator with the voices of other characters.

The role of the authorial narrator, on the other hand, is to strengthen the ideological message by transplanting the ordinary events depicted in the novellas into the philosophical framework. All three novellas force the reader to think about such eternal questions as the meaning of life and the responsibilities of men towards nature and towards each other. And the position of Aitmatov is very clear — he believes that good will trimuph over evil, and that truth will endure forever.

McMaster University

NOTES

1. Ch. Aitmatov, "Dzhamilia," *Novyi mir,* 1958, no. 8, p. 3–31.

2. The novellas in question are: "Belyi parokhod," *Novyi mir,* 1970, no. 1, pp. 31–100; "Rannie zhuravli," *Novyi mir,* 1975, no. 9, pp. 37–94; "Pegii pes, begushchii kraem moria," *Znamia,* 1977, no. 4, pp. 4–55.

3. Among the numerous studies on Aitmatov in Russian, only a very few touch upon the question of the narrative technique in general, and the child narrator in particular. The most revealing remarks on the child

narrator can be found in N. Gei and V. Piskunov, "Natsional'noe svoe-obrazie literatury," *Zvezda,* 1970, no. 9, pp. 186–96; V. Voronov, *Chingiz Aitmatov: Ocherk tvorchestva* (Moscow: Sovetskii pisatel', 1976); V. Novikov, "Khudozhestvennye poiski: Zametki o tvorchestve Chingiza Aitmatova," *Novyi mir,* 1978, no. 12, pp. 254–63. The question of Aitmatov's narrative technique is also ignored by his Western critics; see T. and G. Feifer, Afterword, in Ch. Aitmatov, *The White Steamship* (London: Hodder & Stoughton, 1972), pp. 167–88; N.N. Shneidman, "Soviet Literature at the Crossroads: The Controversial Prose of Chingiz Aitmatov," *Russian Literature Triquarterly,* 16 (1979), pp. 244–64.

4. V. Shklovskii, "Iskusstvo kak priem," *Poetika: Sborniki po teorii poeticheskogo iazyka* (Petrograd, 1919), pp. 101–14.

5. Ch. Aitmatov, *The White Steamship,* tr. by T. and G. Feifer (London: Hodder & Stoughton, 1972), p. 9.

6. Ch. Aitmatov, "Neobkhodimye utochneniia," *Literaturnaia gazeta,* 29 July 1970, p. 4.

7. *The White Steamship,* pp. 45–46.

8. Ch. Aitmatov, "Vozvrashchenie legendy," *Literaturnaia gazeta,* 12 May 1976, p. 6.

9. The ending of the novella generated a heated controversy among Soviet readers and critics alike. Some of them criticized Aitmatov for awarding a victory to pessimism, and questioned the novella's facts and logic; see D. Starikov, "Ne skazkoi edinoi," *Literaturnaia gazeta,* 1 July 1970, p. 5; S. Saitov, "A esli sootnesti s zhizn'iu," *Literaturnaia gazeta,* 22 July 1970, p. 6. But many others agreed with Aitmatov that the tragic ending aroused in the reader feelings of compassion and protest against evil; see V. Soloukhin, "Skazki pishut dlia khrabrykh," *Literaturnaia gazeta,* 22 July 1970, p. 6; F. Kuznetsov, "Kak cheloveku byt' chelove-kom," *Iunost',* 1973, no. 5, pp. 66–71.

10. The reviewers of "Rannie zhuravli" were unanimous in their praise of the novella; see V. Bykov, "Vitiazi aksaiskoi stepi," *Literaturnaia gazeta,* 15 October 1975, p. 4; N. Krymova, "Tol'ko by vernulsia otets," *Druzhba narodov,* 1976, no. 2, pp. 266–69; I. Andreev, "Aksaiskii de-dant," *Oktiabr',* 1976, no. 5, pp. 214–16.

11. The philosophical aspect of the novella was stressed by all the reviewers, see V. Turbin, "Za drugi svoia," *Novyi mir,* 1977, no. 8, pp. 250–53; R. Levchenko, "Chetvero v okeane vechnosti," *Literaturnaia gazeta,* 18 May 1977, p. 4; M. Auezov, "Ostaetsia podlinnaia zhizn'," *Literaturnaia gazeta,* 4 June 1978, p. 4.

12. *The White Steamship,* p. 164.

FLIGHT OF FANCY: ALEKSANDR GRIN'S NOVEL
THE SHINING WORLD (BLISTAIUSHCHII MIR, 1923)

NICHOLAS LUKER

Though recognized today as one of Grin's finest works, his short novel *The Shining World* (*Blistaiushchii mir*) provoked virtually no critical response when it first appeared, in serialized form, in 1923.[1] Only one extremely negative, brief review by an anonymous commentator is known to have greeted its appearance.[2] After making the customary reference to Grin's close resemblance to foreign authors, the critic wrote disparagingly that in this new work the author had departed from his usual technique of imitating the "foreign novel in translation" to produce a piece which was "hopelessly tedious."[3] As was invariably the case during the 1920s and 1930s, the ethical significance of Grin's work seems to have completely escaped the critic. This paper aims to examine that significance and to show that *The Shining World* is crucial to an understanding of Grin's weltanschauung.

The novel was written only during the last decade of Grin's life — between November 14, 1921 and March 28, 1923[4] — but its genesis is to be found much earlier in his career. His first wife, Vera Pavlovna Kalitskaia, recalls that the Aviation Week in Petersburg from April 25 to May 2, 1910 made Grin sullen and gloomy. "When I began to talk with delight about the flights," she writes, "he replied angrily that all this enthusiasm of mine was absurd: the aircraft were unwieldy and ugly, while the pilots were just like car drivers."[5] It was not long before Grin expressed his distaste for flying machines in print, first in his story *The Heavy Air* (*Tiazhelyi vozdukh*, 1912)[6] (originally entitled *The Flier Kirshin* (*Letchik Kirshin*),[7] and then in the mordant tale *The Competition in Liss* (*Sostiazanie v Lisse*),[8] which Vera Pavlovna says was written soon after the Aviation Week but apparently not published until 1921.[9] It is in the latter that the predecessor of Drood (in direct transliteration *Drud*), the flying hero of *The Shining World,* first appears. Drood's criticism in the novel of artificial flying machines echoes that voiced by the anonymous hero of the tale, who describes the airplane as "a fragile, ugly structure in the sweaty exhalations of the brain which has devised its suspect construction. . . . Its wings are lifeless. It is matter crucified in air; on it sits a man thinking about petrol, the roaring of the propeller, and the strength of bolts and wire, and even before he has taken off, he thinks he has crashed to the ground."[10] To the hero of *The Competition in Liss* with his radiant face and intense eyes, the air is just as natural an environment as it is to his literary descendant in *The Shining World*. Like Drood he flies through the air with a nonchalant ease which makes man-made flying machines seem ludicrously cumbersome: "He hurtled along in the position of someone lying on his side, with his head propped on his arm."[11] But while the theme of the tale is the contrast between the machine and the power of the human will, and the infinite superiority of the latter, in the novel which followed it this concern is only secondary.

Though structurally less finished than Grin's first novella, *Scarlet Sails* (*Alye parusa*), *The Shining World* is thematically far more complex. In the earlier work Grin made no attempt to ameliorate the unsympathetic environment of Kaperna or to inspire its people with poetic values; instead he created an aesthetic and spiritual vacuum in which his exclusive heroes could find happiness together.[12] In *The Shining World,* however, he attempts to bring his special hero and the ordinary people together in an effort to inspire the latter. Herein lies an important difference between Grin's first two major works and it points to a development not only of technique but also of attitude. Whereas in *Scarlet Sails* fantasy was a means of escape from a hostile reality, in *The Shining World* Grin attempts — despite overwhelming odds — to bring fantasy to the attention of the real world and to make it an organic part of real life.

Set in Grin's imagined subcontinent of *Grinlandia,*[13] the work tells how Drood, a man possessing the miraculous gift of flight, is persecuted by the State because of it and jailed. His escape is engineered by Runa Beguem, an influential and wealthy young woman who wishes to make selfish use of his ability and with him gain supreme power over the world. But when Drood rejects her designs, she becomes his implacable enemy. After enjoying short-lived happiness with Tavi Tum, a girl whose purity of heart enables her to share his selfless purpose, the hero is destroyed at the very end of the novel when, for no apparent reason, he suddenly crashes to the ground.[14]

Grin's choice of a hero who is able to fly without the assistance of artificial aids derives directly from his convictions about flight. Mikhail Slonimskii recalls a discussion he had with Grin about an early draft of what eventually became *The Shining World,* and during it he realized Grin believed that man could once fly. For that reason, he writes, Grin saw nothing unusual in Drood's feat:

> He saw the doubt on my face and began to demonstrate that there was nothing improbable after all about a man taking off and flying into the air. He explained to me that at one time man undoubtedly could and did fly. He said that people used to be different and would again be different from what they were now. . . . He spoke of dolmens as proof of the existence of giants on earth in ancient times. And if people were not giants now, he said, then they would become giants again one day.
>
> He referred to dreams in which the sleeper flies as proof that man could once fly, and he saw those dreams — which are familiar to everyone — as man's recollection of his now atrophied capability. He maintained that the development of aviation depended upon man's urge to regain this lost ability to fly.
>
> "And one day man will fly by himself, without a machine!" he asserted.[15]

Grin's conviction explains why he makes no attempt to render his hero's gift of flight more credible to the reader by attempting to *explain* it. Drood's peculiar ability is not something he has acquired in a conscious manner; instead he finds it perfectly natural, even commonplace. Furthermore, never does Grin suggest that to the observer, Drood's flight is an illusion, a trick of the eye. So substantial is Grin's fantasy that he has no need to reinforce it by explanatory references to reality. Drood's extraordinary ability belongs securely in the realm of the miraculous, and as such is essentially inexplicable. As Elizabeth Beaujour points out, however, his gift of flight is never treated as a mode of *negative* escape from the pressures of reality. Instead it is a profoundly *positive* phenomenon, while the hero himself is "an affirmation of the potentiality of the human spirit, of the communion of pure hearts, indeed a symbol of a whole potential system of human relations."[16]

The supremely exclusive quality of Drood's gift is underlined by Grin's insistence on his hero's virtually complete isolation from his fellowmen. A curiously insubstantial figure who is just as much at home in the ether as on terra firma, he has no apparent means of existence, no profession, and almost no acquaintances. Indeed, before he meets Tavi, his only friend is Stebbs, the Liss lighthouse keeper. Were he not rendered more human by his association with Tavi and Stebbs, he would remain a totally symbolic figure amounting to little more that a "pure abstraction."[17]

As was the case in *Scarlet Sails,* the characters of *The Shining World* (and, implicitly, the whole of mankind) fall into two unequal camps on the basis of their receptivity or hostility to fantasy. The extremely small minority possess an imaginative nature which enables them to believe unconditionally in Drood's ability and to appreciate what it symbolizes — limitless human potential. But the overwhelming majority are profoundly insensitive, and their soullessness and lack of imagination (what Grin often ironically called "common sense" (*zdravyi smysl*) make them infinitely suspicious of the flying man. Indeed, they see him as nothing more than a confidence-trickster and charlatan. Fantasy and the purity of heart on which it depends, Grin implies, are granted only to the happy few.

Though both Grin's early major pieces examine the creative potential of fantasy, the ethical implications of *The Shining World* are far greater than those of its predecessor. After the localized village setting used in the novella, Grin makes his stage a global one. While Assol' was scorned by fellow villagers unable to understand her, Drood is systematically hounded by a reactionary State which considers his gift nothing but a threat to its own exis-

tence. As a miraculous figure attesting to vistas of boundless possibility, he is seen as "dangerous to all the entrenched structures
of the status quo."[18] Behind the schematism of Grin's plot, therefore, we glimpse the collision between the highly creative individual and the iron apparatus of repressive orthodoxy.

Drood's flying is very much more than the phenomenon of a
human being accomplishing what only winged creatures are designed to do. His flight is a poetic symbol, the physical manifestation of a creative "soaring of the spirit" (*parenie dukha*) as
Grin once described it to Iurii Olesha,[19] and it is this extraordinarily creative principle which he tries to communicate to those
who watch him fly. Both his flights are not so much demonstra-
tions of his ability to a sceptical crowd as attempts to unite the
miracle of his gift with the witnessed reality of it, and to make
the spectators aware of the vast potential present in the human
soul. But so suspicious and prejudiced are his fellowmen that
both his flights, witnessed though they are by hundreds of people,
arouse only the most minute response. Even when they see him
soaring into the air, the spectators simply refuse to believe that
it is anything but an illusion.

Drood's flight in the circus causes panic[20] and brings an order
from the government minister, Daugovet, for his arrest. Only
upon Runa Beguem does his display have the effect he had hoped
for:

> His only consolation was the sight of an unknown woman lift-
> ing up her arms with a cry of triumph; and he recalled a flock of
> domestic geese cackling on catching sight of their wild brothers
> flying beneath the clouds: one goose, stretching out its neck and
> frantically flapping its wings, tried desperately to fly upwards too,
> but its fat prevented it from taking to the air (80).

His second flight is a further attempt to make the public aware
of the creative principle which he represents. On this occasion,
though, his technique is more involved, for in response to the
"scientific" requirements of the Liss aeronautic club he uses an
elaborate, silk-covered flying machine with four thousand tiny
tinkling bells attached to it. The bells, however, play no part in
the flight at all, and he can fly perfectly well without them. Moreover, as he explains, their number is completely immaterial. The

entire apparatus thus represents a deliberate compromise on the hero's part. The bells (and the machine too, for that matter) are simply palpable tokens of a spiritual gift in which he wishes the spectators to believe; they therefore serve merely as tangible pointers to an intangible purpose.

Just as earlier Runa was the sole individual to respond to Drood in the way that he wished, so his second appearance produces just one positive reaction. Only Tavi is convinced that he will fly before he actually takes to the air, and only she is prepared to state that conviction despite ridicule from the crowd. Her acknowledgment of Drood's gift suggests that she is sympathetic towards what he is attempting to do, and indeed, further developments in the novel reveal that she is the only person on a spiritual par with the hero. Runa, by contrast, immensely talented and sensitive though she is, proves too egocentric to participate in his humanitarian purpose.

Like so many of Grin's characters, Runa is fascinated by the extraordinary. Just as rare books attract her bibliophile uncle, she says, so "everything extraordinary attracts me" (101). Intelligent and cultured but proud and cold, she confidently awaits an exclusive destiny and an exclusive love. As she explains to her unlucky suitor, Gall': "I would look upon love as a misfortune if it were to come to me *without the agency of destiny* [Grin's italics] . . . I mean an exceptional destiny . . . I want this destiny to be *special*" (73). When Drood, his smile "full of hidden promise" (76), walks into the ring and flies above the audience, it is as though her lifelong anticipation of the extraordinary has finally been rewarded: "the spectacle exceeded the bounds of a trick and became a miracle, something we secretly wait for all our lives . . ." (78). After Drood's appearance Runa becomes aware of his immense potential and at the same time discovers hitherto unsuspected reserves of strength within herself. Suddenly, she feels, what she has always desired seems within reach. "So it is," Grin remarks, "that often through ignorance a person stands for a long time with his back to what he secretly longs for . . ." (102). At first, Runa appears to appreciate Drood's gift exactly as he would wish. Indeed, he himself is initially mistaken about her — he is glad that this one goose attempts to emulate its wild kin by

trying to take to the air. Even during her visit to him in prison
he is unable to detect her selfish intentions, and it is not until
they talk after his escape that her true purpose becomes clear.
The meeting between Runa and Drood in Chapter XV of Part I
of the novel is pivotal to the work, for during it Grin contrasts
their respective poetic and nonpoetic weltanschauungen. But behind them, more significantly, he points to the wider contrast
between humane and inhumane outlooks in the world at large,
a contrast which lies at the heart of his romantic writing. As Runa
proposes how Drood should utilize his extraordinary ability, it
becomes clear that her outlook is diametrically opposed to his.
While she wishes him to employ his gift in a profoundly antisocial
way, Drood's intentions are purely humanitarian. She would have
the flying man become king of the world:

> "If this is not yet your aim, then sooner or later it will be; . . .
> not in the circus or on other occasions which are the product of
> whim, but in full awareness of your great . . . aim, you will an-
> nounce yourself by a long journey through the air, designed to
> astound and enthrall mankind. What happened in the circus will
> happen everywhere. America will awake from her dreams of
> gold . . . ; Europe will become young again; Asia will howl in
> frenzy; and wild tribes will light sacred bonfires and pay homage
> to the unknown" (118).

After two or three months, she goes on, the government will no
longer try to destroy Drood because society will spring to his defense. He must have a vast castle equipped to receive the count-
less faithful who will flock to worship him,

> ". . . people of all lands, races and nationalities. The name
> 'Drood' will ring like 'air' and 'breath.' Wanderers, seekers of
> the 'meaning' of life, dreamers of every kind, those who are secre-
> tive by nature, those who are disillusioned, those who suffer from
> spleen or melancholy, potential suicides, the unbalanced and the
> partially insane, gentle . . . scholars . . . and adventurers, inven-
> tors and schemers, cadgers and beggars, — and women, legions of
> women . . . This will be your great army" (119).

Runa even visualises a book written by Drood and printed in so
many copies that every family on earth can have one. In it — and
her idea suggests a surrogate Bible — Drood will reveal where the

secret of happiness lies: "You will write about yourself, explaining that the . . . conditions of happiness lie in . . . your hands —
something that all will believe, for by happiness they understand
the unrealizable (*nesbytochnoe*)" (119). The miraculous, embodied
in the messianic figure of Drood and manifested in his superhu-
man gift of flight, will swiftly become the irresistible catalyst for
an unprecedented transformation of the world. This is Runa's
vision and hope — the uncontested omnipotence of the flying man
and his dominion over all the earth:

> "Then . . . the regular, constant awareness of this sensible
> miracle — witnessed in your person — will make [governmental]
> power so precarious that the very first time the choice is clearly
> expressed: 'I or they?' the earth will answer: 'You!' Nothing will
> stop her. She will believe that she is gaining possession of brilliant
> wings" (120).

Drood's response to Runa's impassioned tirade is an abrupt
refusal. Though fully aware of his potential, he finds her proposal repugnant. "Without any doubt," he declares, "I could
enslave the whole of mankind, but that object is detestable to
me. It would interfere with life" (120). Instead, he says, he has
eyes only for what is naturally beautiful and quietly poetic in the
world:

> "I have no ambition. What takes its place for me? you will ask.
> A smile. But I am passionately fond, too, of flowers, the sea,
> journeys, animals and birds; of beautiful fabrics, marble, music
> and caprice. I move with the speed of the wind, but I also love
> to wander slowly down picturesque little paths" (120).

As Drood points out, in proposing that he put his gift only to
selfish use, Runa has rejected the opportunity to see the beautiful
and poetic in his company: "You could have looked down on the
world like the little cup of a flower, but instead you only want
to be a stubborn caterpillar!" (121). His unequivocal rejection
of her aggressive philosophy of "It's all or nothing. . . . I want
power!" (122), shows the humane way in which he believes his
special ability should be used. Through the contrast between flying miracle man and earthbound caterpillar, Grin points to the
gulf separating the individual of genius from the common herd,
and indicates the insurmountable resistance often encountered

by the creative artist in bringing his gift to his fellowmen.

The conversation between Runa and Drood shows that she is incapable of seeing in him anything but an unparalleled opportunity for self-aggrandizement. But while the personal differences between them are of limited importance, the danger he is seen to represent to society is far more significant. Through both Daugovet and the "Leader" — who personify repression and persecution respectively — Grin not only illustrates that supposed danger (which is in fact nonexistent), but also indicts the kind of collective which persecutes the extraordinarily talented individual simply because of his gift.

The authoritarian machine controlled by Daugovet — "its might effective from time immemorial through menace and the pen" (82) —moves obediently into action as soon as the minister sees Drood fly in the circus, and sends out a secret order forbidding the press to mention him. As Daugovet explains to Runa, Drood's gift puts him totally beyond the control of authority and therefore cannot be tolerated:

> "Who he is, we do not know. His aims are unknown to us. But his potential *is* known to us. In your imagination glance down on everything which we are accustomed to see in horizontal projection. You will discover the interior of forts, docks, harbors, barracks and artillery works — all of them barriers erected by the State . . . there are no safeguards or secrets left any more. . . . In addition . . . there is no protection for anyone or anything any longer; the elusive Someone [i.e. Drood] can command the life, property and destiny of everyone without exception. . . . This phenomenon requires ruthless control, and perhaps even — destruction" (99–100).

But, Daugovet continues, Drood represents an even greater threat: because of its miraculous quality, his gift of flight has the power to bring about a revival of religious fervor or even of fanaticism, in a society where the established view is that "nonbelief is life" (100):

> "Let us imagine what will happen if into the tensely expectant void of the contemporary soul there bursts this image, this stupendous marvel: a man who flies over towns in defiance of all the laws of nature. . . . No explanation will destroy the supernatural,

picturesque quality of the spectacle. It will create an easily inflam-
mable atmosphere of thoughts and feelings similar to the ecstatic
mood prevalent at the time of the Crusades. Religious speculation
is possible here on a gigantic scale" (100).

Daugovet foresees the catastrophic effect such a revival would
have upon social order, an effect which would be tantamount to
rebellion: "Sects will spring up . . . ; men's passion for the fantastic will open the floodgates of unbridled fantasy of every kind;
legends, superstitions, rumors, predictions and prophecies will
shuffle all the cards in the State's game of patience — a game
whose name is Stability" (100–01). The minister's attitude to
Drood epitomizes that of society as a whole. Suspicious from the
outset, it is based on the assumption that the hero will put his
gift of flight to evil use: "I see . . . an evil intention here," says
Daugovet, "since a good one cannot be proved" (99).

For his part, the "Leader" financed by Runa to track Drood
down is adamant that the flying man must be destroyed: "His
existence is intolerable. He is interfering in the laws of nature and
is himself an outright denial of them" (209). Unlike Daugovet,
however, he sees in Drood primarily not a threat to state security
or the danger of a religious revival, but an immensely powerful
agent of social discontent. Drood's miraculous gift, he maintains,
brings equally miraculous radiance into the drab lives of the un-
derprivileged, allowing them a dazzling glimpse of hitherto unsuspected happiness: "There are lives doomed by stern law to endless
poverty and suffering; a hard crust of chill ice covers their inau-
dible stream, and he smashes that ice, allowing the sun to penetrate
the gloomy depths" (209).

The Shining World is the first of Grin's major works in which
he creates two female characters — Runa and Tavi — to represent
completely opposite spiritual standpoints. He was to use this simple
device later in both *The Golden Chain* (*Zolotaia tsep'*, 1925) and
She Who Runs on the Waves (*Begushchaia po volnam*, 1928), but
applied it to greatest effect in *Jessy and Morgiana* (*Dzhessi i Morgiana*, 1929), where the two sisters come into fatal collision. Like
Assol' before her, Tavi is the willing pawn of a benevolent destiny
in which coincidence (or "engineered chance") plays the principal
role. Hearing of the debauched Torp's death just as she reaches

his house, Tavi is struck by the extraordinarily opportune nature of an event which spares her the unsavory experience of working for him. Moreover, only a few hours earlier, coincidence brought Drood and her together in a square in Liss, and when by chance she meets him again at the aeronautic club (with the flying apparatus which she happened to see going by on a cart shortly before), Grin describes her as "standing at the crossroads of destiny" (154). The alliance between hero and heroine is thus as delightfully inevitable as that in *Scarlet Sails*. As Drood explains to Stebbs after rescuing Tavi from the police: "You'll think that it was I who saved her . . . no — she carried her salvation in her own breast. We were both walking down one and the same road. I caught up with her and she turned round, so now we'll walk on together" (203). Like her biography — "she could remember neither her father nor her mother" (177) — Tavi's outlook is as disarmingly simple as Runa's is dauntingly complex: "She belonged to those few truly happy people for whom everything in the world is just as uncomplicated as their gentle placidity; an airplane and a butterfly hardly differed in her opinion, except for the fact that a butterfly has no propeller" (178).[21] Tavi's poetic temperament not only brings her to an understanding of Drood's purpose; it also makes her aware of the gulf separating him from the vast majority of his fellowmen who fail to see how his gift can bring them spiritual benefit. Sensible of his unique position among those who are unable to understand him, she asks: "Is it not tedious, not hard for you amidst ungifted dolts?" (199).

What is vitally important about Tavi's faith in Drood is its spontaneous, ingenuously childlike quality. This above all, Grin implies, enables her to *believe*. Not for nothing is it a *child* who is the first to shout in the circus that Drood is flying (77). Though much of the novel suggests otherwise, however, this childlike characteristic — while extremely developed — is not peculiar to the heroine; it lies quiescent and perhaps virtually forgotten in all of us, silently awaiting a favorable opportunity to reveal itself. It stirs, for example, in the gray-haired *littérateur,* and in a subconscious response to the words uttered by Tavi high in the air, he feels an unaccountable urge to write down a fleeting childhood poem which begins: *"Esli ty ne zabudesh', / Kak volnu zabyvaet volna . . ."* (204). And as Grin tells us in the closing sentence of his novel, the selfsame words communicate themselves even to Runa and are recalled at pensive moments as she gazes at birds high in the sky. They are words heard many years ago — in her childhood (214).

If Tavi is intuitively sure of the hero's ability before she sees it demonstrated, then Stebbs has been convinced of it by witnessing it many times in the past. Once Drood's childhood companion — an intriguing detail on which, rather annoying, Grin does not enlarge — and now his faithful friend, the lighthouse keeper is an interesting but relatively undeveloped character. Though unable fully to share the poetic outlook of hero and heroine, he longs for literary fame and writes mediocre verse about the shadowy kingdom of demons awaiting man beyond the grave.[22] But his feeble lines are the product of a mind almost devoid of talent — "in his little soul poetry lay face downwards, for there was no room for it to turn round" (124). As Drood explains to him that his verses lack penetration, we catch a glimpse of Grin's own view of literary creativity: "Your poetry is like a blunt saw: it snatches at the soul but does not divide it in two. To create is to . . . *divide,* introducing *one's own* into the mass of another's soul" (126) [Grin's italics]. Ironically, Stebbs's splendid homemade "xylophone" of hanging bottles on which he is able to play such items as "It's a long way to Tipperary," gives Drood far more pleasure than his poetry and in a humorous way indicates that its inventor is more talented than his verses suggest. For Drood, whom he nicknames "Mountain" (*Gora*), Stebbs has boundless affection, and is even prepared to burn all his poems if only his friend will stay another day. The master-disciple nature of their relationship is clear, a fact which underlines the portrayal of Drood as a quasi-religious figure with a message for all mankind. It is difficult, however, to see exactly what Grin intended in creating Stebbs, unless it was an amusing foil to the hero. Perhaps he represents the untalented man who, unlike the vast majority of his fellow human beings, is nevertheless curiously receptive to inspiration and beauty — be they in poetry or music.[23]

However exalted Drood's purpose may be in the ethical sense,

Grin treats it in an immediate way, so avoiding the philosophical complexities to which he could so easily have fallen prey. Since it involves people — first Runa, then Tavi — and because it depends upon them for our insight into the hero's attitudes, Drood's mission is stated in poetic, personal terms rather than philosophical, general ones. Furthermore, however symbolic of the creative principle Drood becomes as the novel progresses, Grin never allows us to forget that his hero is meant to be a human being living and moving among his fellowmen. Thus Drood takes off from the lighthouse but then returns because he has forgotten his matches! (129). For his part, though, the hero is always acutely aware of the unique nature of his gift: "Only . . . I was fated to know neither distance nor height" (201). Moreover, he realizes that his exclusiveness brings with it great loneliness in a world which fails to understand him. Tavi's company, however, will make his difficult task easier, as he explains to her:

> "We are solitary amid the many people who [apparently] resemble us, for we live according to different laws. . . . I invite you, my girl, my kindred spirit, to go with me into a world which is perhaps inaccessible to anyone else. It is dazzlingly bright and peaceful there, but it is difficult for a single soul to reflect that brilliance, as it is like the brilliance of ice. Will you help me melt that ice?" (201).[24]

Grin's treatment of the relationship between Tavi and Drood reminds us that *The Shining World* is a short novel whereas its predecessor, *Scarlet Sails,* was a novella. While the union of hero and heroine in *Scarlet Sails* represented the logical outcome of their mutual spiritual quest and gave the work a natural and fitting conclusion, that of Tavi and Drood is designed to herald a new and more effective phase in the hero's altruistic mission.

What makes *The Shining World* unique beside Grin's other major works is that its hero is portrayed as divine. While emphasizing Drood's exclusiveness in this way, Grin stresses the enormous significance of his philosophy. In semi-hagiographical fashion, he paints a series of facial portraits of his hero — each more precise than its predecessor — which amount to what Kovskii terms "a kind of astonishing icon painting."[25] Though the critic's comparison of Drood's monologues about creative inspiration with Ser-

mons on the Mount is rather fanciful,[26] he has unerringly detected the god-like aura with which Grin surrounds his hero.
There are in addition several textual reminders that Drood is a
religious figure. He walks into the circus ring "as erect as a candle flame" (75) with his forehead "as radiant as a cupola" (76);
when he sings high above the audience the word "clergy" (*klir*)
(79) is distinctly audible in his unfamiliar song; the hotel maid,
Betsy, declares that he is "as beautiful and meek as an angel"
(88); there is "something more important" (108) than life, the
hero tells Runa; and as he snatches Tavi from from the clutches
of the police and lifts her high into the air, he says to her: "Be
patient and have faith" (197). Moreover, Drood's intuition and
prescience are as supernatural as his gift of flight. When he sees
Tavi for the first time in Liss, he immediately knows that she is
a creature of destiny for whom danger is imminent: "before him
was a person who, without knowing it, had stepped into a per-
ilous, closed circle. Above the crystal glass hung poised a hammer" (133). Not long afterwards Tavi is astonished to hear that
Drood is already aware of Torp's death that morning, while when
she is arrested he immediately knows of it and quickly rescues
her. Finally, towards the end of the novel, he reveals that he singled Tavi out as an exceptional human being long before they
ever met: "I could always see you," he tells her, "until I actually
found you" (201).

It is during the scene set in the empty church in Liss in Chapter XI of Part II that the portrayal of Drood as a divine figure
reaches its climax.[27] Kneeling before a painting of the Virgin and
Child, Runa Beguem prays for release from her inner torment.
But her prayers are not answered in the way she expects. Instead,
she sees the hero appear from the picture, dressed like one of the
disciples in poor fisherman's clothes:

> Through the golden haze of the alter, . . . Drood stepped out
> of the frame and sat down at the feet of the infant Christ. . . .
> The child smiled at him with the contented smile of a little boy
> seeing an amusing uncle, while She looked kindly on. The new-
> comer picked up a sharp seashell with its edge furled inwards and
> put it to his ear. "That's the sea murmuring," he said softly.
> "Sea . . . murmuring," whispered the echo in the corners of the

church. And he handed the shell to Christ so that the child could hear how the sea murmurs in men's souls (175).

Drood's closeness to the infant Christ serves to emphasize the spiritual gulf between Runa and himself. (Exhausted, she returns home, wondering whether after this experience it is even possible to go on living.) At the same time, Drood's communion with Christ indicates the sacrosanct nature not only of his person, but also of the gift of flight and of the creativity which it represents. Anticipating Pasternak's *Dr. Zhivago,* Grin affirms the link between human creativity and the divine principle from which it derives its strength and inspiration..

As the novel draws to its close, Drood's star seems to be in the ascendant. He has escaped persecution at the hands of the State and found spiritual happiness with Tavi. Moreover, the scene in the church suggests that he enjoys a measure of divine protection. For these reasons his sudden death on the penultimate page of the work comes as a total surprise. What is particularly disturbing about the manner of his death, however, is that it is apparently caused by a sudden failure of his gift of flight. Only two days earlier, Grin tells us, Drood had escaped for good the clutches of the "Leader" and his six anonymous henchmen — "laughing, he crossed the limits laid down by his dread pursuers" (211). The unexpected denouement adds a disturbing new dimension to the work and abruptly changes its mood, for goodness manifestly fails and evil triumphs. Drood's selfless appeal to his fellowmen has fallen on deaf ears, and the collective which he sought to inspire has all but crucified him in the name of sterile orthodoxy. Seeing his body lying in a pool of blood on the street, Runa cries jubilantly: "Here he is — my enemy. The earth is more powerful than he is; he is dead, yes, dead, and I shall live again as I used to live before" (213).

The volte-face of the work's conclusion is hard to explain. It has been suggested that it was occasioned by the disillusionment Grin felt at measures introduced under the New Economic Policy in 1921. There is, however, no evidence that he was sufficiently devoted to the ideals of the 1917 Revolution to be disturbed by NEP policies which Russians more committed to the cause saw

as a shameful retreat from socialist positions. Perhaps, as Slonimskii has suggested, a sense of creative fatigue led Grin to show
the "shattered dream" of Drood's death as the inevitable result
of the collision between fantasy and reality.[28] This suggestion
derives, however, from the critic's view that *The Shining World*
reflects Grin's own passivity and pessimism, a view which indicates that Slonimskii has failed to detect the profoundly life-
assertive significance of the hero's gift. Kovskii's odd suggestion
that Drood's death is a deliberate corrective "inevitably introduced into the dream of human perfection by Grin's philosophy
of history"[29] (i.e. as the result of his disenchantment with the
SR Party) seems most improbable, if only because of the considerable time that elapsed between Grin's SR days and the writing of the novel in the early 1920s. (Furthermore, were Kovskii's
suggestion correct, it is strange that *Scarlet Sails,* written much
earlier, appears to contain no such corrective.) Perhaps it might
be truer to say that Grin regards the struggle between creative
fantasy and sterile reality as an extremely unequal one (*Scarlet
Sails* offered proof enough of that); and that in view of the intense pressure under which fantasy finds itself in *The Shining
World,* it is far less likely to emerge victorious in the way that
it did in the preceding work. Whatever the real reasons for the
novel's perplexing conclusion, its mood resembles that of only
one other major work by Grin — his last, which bears the significant title of *The Road to Nowhere* (*Doroga nikuda,* 1930).

The altruistic way in which Drood chooses to use his gift represents a highly significant advance upon the attitudes of earlier
Grinian heroes. Given his unique ability, for example, the egocentric and isolationist Tart of *Reno Island* (*Ostrov Reno,* 1909)[30]
would have opted unhesitatingly for an environment in which he
could have escaped the rest of mankind. Blium, on the other
hand, the victorious and cruel hero of *The Tragedy of Suan Pla-
teau* (*Tragediia ploskogor'ia Suan,* 1912),[31] would have used his
gift to subjugate the world. But Drood refuses to put his ability
to either inhumane or selfish use, and by offering it for the benefit of his fellowmen, does his best to offset the social and spiritual exclusiveness which it inevitably bestows on him.

It is perhaps unfortunate that the startlingly tragic ending of the novel makes it all too easy to miss Grin's point. The work is optimistic, not pessimistic, its hero active, not passive, and its affirmation of the primacy of creative fantasy assures it a central place in Grin's romantic writing. It is the attempt Drood makes to jolt his fellowmen out of their torpid complacency by demonstrating the boundlessly creative potential of inspiration that is of prime importance in the novel, not his lack of success or his enigmatic death. There can be little doubt that *The Shining World* is thematically the most significant of Grin's novels, even though its conclusion is less satisfying than those of major works with which it belongs. It is his most persuasive treatment of the spiritual regeneration which all men can derive from inspiration, and of the unenviable lot of the talented, sensitive human being in a society too bigoted to acknowledge his gifts. Though Grin may never have intended it, his *Shining World* is uncannily relevant to the plight in which the highly creative and unorthodox individual finds himself in the Soviet Union today.

University of Nottingham

NOTES

1. In *Krasnaia niva,* nos. 20–30. The novel was published in book form by *Zemlia i fabrika* in 1924.

2. See *"Blistaiushchii mir.* Roman," *Kniga o knigakh,* 1924, nos. 7–8, pp. 64–65.

3. Ibid., p. 64.

4. See A.S. Grin, *Sobranie sochinenii v shesti tomakh* (Moscow: Pravda, 1965), vol. III, p. 214. All quotations from the novel derive from vol. III of this edition, and page numbers are given henceforth in the text.

5. See note, Ibid., p. 440.

6. See *Sobranie sochinenii,* II, pp. 170–76.

7. In *Ves' mir,* 1912, no. 26, p. 9.

8. See *Sobranie sochinenii,* III, pp. 432–37.

9. In *Krasnyi militsioner,* 1921, nos. 2–3, pp. 27–30. See note, *Sobranie sochinenii,* III, p. 446.

10. Ibid, p. 435.

11. Ibid., p. 436.

12. For a brief examination of *Scarlet Sails* (*Sobranie sochinenii,* III,

pp. 3–65), see N.J.L. Luker, *Alexander Grin* (Letchworth, England, 1973), pp. 73–80. An informative recent article is Barry Scherr, "Aleksandr Grin's 'Scarlet Sails' and the Fairy Tale," *Slavic and East European Journal,* vol. 20, no. 4 (1976), pp. 387–99.

13. Though it is set in *Grinlandia,* unlike the major works which followed it, *The Shining World* contains few references to specific places within that setting. Liss, Gvinkel' and San-Riol' are the only towns mentioned: both the circus and the flying club are in Liss; Runa retreats into rural isolation at Gvinkel'; and Tavi lives in San-Riol'. Though we are told that the hero's lighthouse is in Liss, the locations of his numerous other refuges are not specified.

14. As if dissatisfied with the work's ending, in the fragment *Meetings and Conclusions* (*Vstrechi i zakliucheniia,* first published in 1960), Grin himself later referred to the obscure manner of Drood's death and suggested that he might still be alive after all. See A.S. Grin, *Dzhessi i Morgiana. Povest', novelly, roman* (Leningrad: Lenizdat, 1966), pp. 492–94.

15. M. Slonimskii, "A.S. Grin," introductory essay to A. Grin, *Zolotaia tsep': Avtobiograficheskaia povest'* (Moscow: Sovetskii pisatel', 1939), p. 32.

16. Elizabeth K. Beaujour, *The Invisible Land: A Study of the Artistic Imagination of Iurii Olesha* (New York and London: Columbia University Press, 1970), p. 171.

17. V. Kovskii, *Romanticheskii mir Aleksandra Grina* (Moscow: Nauka, 1969), p. 76.

18. Beaujour, p. 166.

19. Iu. Olesha, *Izbrannye sochineniia* (Moscow: Khudozhestvennaia literatura, 1956), p. 464. When Olesha congratulated Grin on his excellent choice of the flying man theme for use in a novel of fantasy, Grin retorted: "What do you mean, for a fantastic novel? It's a symbolic novel, not a fantastic one! It's not a man flying at all — it's the soaring of the spirit!" (Ibid.)

20. Apropos of the public reaction when Drood's appearance becomes generally known, Grin makes a very brief sociopolitical comment: "In the affair of Drood, the creativity of the masses — about which, apparently, an extraordinary amount of fuss is made nowadays — manifested itself with as much lack of restraint as a fit of hysterics" (82).

21. For his part Drood is said to be "as simple as a calf" (179).

22. Stebbs's poem with its amusing title of *The Telegraphist from the Underworld* (*Telegrafist iz preispodnei*), an excerpt from which he reads to Drood, is a skit by Grin on the literary manner of the Russian Decadents. It contains motifs typical of their work, ranging from the Devil

and Hell to sobbing lyres and candles made of human fat. "Everybody writes like that nowadays," says Stebbs to Drood in justification of his verses (125).

23. Vladimir Rossel's suggests that because Stebbs *has* something creative to offer, however unsophisticated it may be, his role in the novel is primarily sociological, "for his soul — the soul of the people — is the source of all creativity." See Vl. Rossel's, "A.S. Grin," *Istoriia russkoi sovetskoi literatury*, vol. 1, 1917–1929 (Moscow: Nauka, 1967), p. 378.

24. These lines have a strongly autobiographical ring. Already in the early 1920s Grin foresaw the isolation he was to suffer as a writer, and the last years of his life under the RAPP organization were to prove his worst fears correct. His second wife, Nina Grin, was without doubt his main source of encouragement and consolation during these lonely years.

25. Kovskii, p. 77.

26. Ibid., p. 78.

27. It is interesting that this section was omitted from all earlier editions of the novel and only restored in the 1965 six-volume collection of Grin's work. (See note 4.)

28. Slonimskii, pp. 32–33. Though it may not have been the case in 1923 when the novel was written, there is strong evidence to suggest that Grin's imagination was failing him towards the end of his life. He admitted as much in a conversation with the critic Dmitrevskii two years before his death, as they were walking along the Neva embankment in Leningrad on a white night in the summer of 1930. Gazing at a small steamer gathering speed on the river, Grin said: "It's just an ordinary little tug . . . though on a night like this it should really be a corvette under full sail. But I don't see those sails now. However hard I try, I just don't see them!" Vl. Dmitrevskii, "V chem volshebstvo Aleksandra Grina?", afterword to A. Grin, *Zolotaia tsep'; Doroga nikuda* (Leningrad: Detskaia literatura, 1957), p. 379. (Beaujour gives the quotation in her own translation on p. 164 [note 63], but her page reference to the Russian original is incorrect.)

29. Kovskii, p. 89.

30. See *Sobranie sochinenii*, I, pp. 250–71.

31. See Ibid., II, pp. 177–211.

TOWN AND COUNTRY IN THE WORK
OF VASILII BELOV

ARNOLD McMILLIN

Vasilii Belov is one of the most talented and versatile of the so-called *derevenshchiki* who came to prominence in Russian literature of the sixties. His earlier writings, particularly "Privychnoe delo" (1966), provoked extensive and varied critical discussion, but for one reason or another several of his later, in many ways more ambitious, prose works have been largely ignored by Soviet commentators. Particularly noticeable is the neglect of his novel *Kanuny* (1972), a major and many-sided achievement illustrating all the most important aspects of his writing as a whole.[1]

As is well known, Belov himself does not accept the existence of village prose as a separate category,[2] and his latest writing shows an increased tendency to thematic diversification, as well as an impressively developing range of stylistic and linguistic resources. At his best he is a powerfully realistic yet lyrical writer, with a distinctive individual voice, whose work is illuminated throughout by a strong love for his native Vologda region and its inhabitants.[3] The linkage of town and country has seemed to many critics to be of central importance in his writing.[4] Whilst it would be wrong to present this theme as the juxtaposition of antagonistic opposites, or to exaggerate Belov's hostility to the town, as Borisova did in an early review article,[5] the interrelation of urban and rural civilization raises numerous contrasts and parallels which reflect some of the most central issues in his work.

For Belov Soviet man's true *rodina* is his native countryside, whither he is constantly drawn by powerful ties which are to be broken only at his moral and spiritual peril. In *Na rodine* (1968) he writes:

> From this fortress of fir trees, from these amazing gates I once

set out into the big and threatening world, naïvely vowing never to return, but the further and faster I went away the more fiercely I felt drawn back again.[6]

This characteristic passage reflects deep emotional dependence as well as simple local patriotism, though Belov can also portray such feelings with a lighter touch, as in an amusing passage from *Kanuny* when the village priest and his friend, having just arrived in Moscow, tell a curious taxi driver, "Yesterday evening we were Vologda region people, but now we are both Soviet."[7] V. Gusev has described the world created by Belov's writing as a dream, a utopia, although not a dream to be emulated,[8] and his town dwellers do frequently look back to or dream of their native places, which are contrasted in their naturalness and simplicity with the noise and bustle of urban life. "Kolokolena" is typical in that the recollection of the countryside (in this case mainly represented by a talkative old village woman) comes to a young man kept awake by the constant din of heavy traffic outside his hostel window.[9] "Vospitanie po doktoru Spoku" (1974), a mordantly comic description of corrupted urban attitudes to education, marriage, and work, begins with the hung-over young father waking to harsh reality from a dream of sunlit forests.[10] Quite different is another story published at the same time, "Moia zhizn'" (1974), the, untypically for Belov, wholly tragic account of the first forty years in the life of a woman born in 1932: time and again country happiness is contrasted with the misery of town life, associated as it is for the autobiographical narrator with immorality and vulgarity of such intensity as, seemingly, to threaten her sanity.

In "Moia zhizn'" the gap between town and country is naturally related to that between adulthood and childhood, a recurrent idea which is reflected more obliquely in another interesting story, "Tezki" (1965), where the garden of a consumptive social outcast, befriended only by a child who plays in it, possesses the wild and magnificent disorder of nature, thus pointing up the contrast between the naturalness of rural childhood on the one hand and the inhumanity of urban "maturity" on the other.[12] This often cruel generation gap is vividly depicted in "Na vokzale," where the interests and, indeed, language of an old coun-

trywoman and more sophisticated youth hardly touch as he en-
gages her in condescending and desultory conversation;[13] in "Di-
alog" a grandmother tells of the ill-treatment she receives from
her avaricious and inhumane town-dwelling sons.[14] Childhood,
on the other hand, is described with affection and sensitive understanding in such short stories as "Mal'chiki," "Skvortsy,"[15]
and "Dania,"[16] as well as in the broader context of *Kanuny*, and
in "Privychnoe delo" where Ivan Afrikanovich is described by his
wife as the tenth child of the family.[17] As L. Antopol'skii has noted,
the frequent appearance of children in Belov's stories helps to provide an additional, often clearer, perspective on what he is describing.[18] In "Vospitanie po doktoru Spoku" the young child also provides a focus on adult *mores*, but her purely urban upbringing is
made miserable by the neglect of her quarrelsome and selfish parents who expect gratitude for the immense trouble they have had getting her into a kindergarten, despite their deplorable lack of parental care, and obsessive preoccupation with their own difficulties.

  The town can sometimes be a corrupting influence for countryfolk: in "Manikiur" a rustic visitor to the capital is turned into a
grotesque painted doll by her Muscovite brother,[19] whilst in *Plotnitskie rasskazy* (1968) the townified Anfeia cuts a coarse and ridic-
ulous figure with her mincing attempts to speak with *akan'e*, Mos-
cow-style.[20] In "Privychnoe delo," as Geoffrey Hosking has remarked, Ivan Afrikanovich undergoes an abrupt character change
when faced with the prospect of moving to town.[21] In the event, the
abortive attempt to abandon his roots for imagined urban pros-
perity brings not only disorientation but tragedy. More usually,
however, when Belov's countryfolk make excursions to town, as
in the delightfully comic *Tseluiutsia zori* (1968–73),[22] they retain
all their rustic habits regardless of the environment, not infrequently immunizing themselves with drink. In *Kanuny* the two
villagers, vainly attempting to obtain justice in Moscow through
personal contacts rather than formal letters, make few conces-
sions to their new surroundings, though at first timid; of the two
the redoubtable priest Nikolai feels the more at home, but it is
also he who is most aware of hidden dangers, discreetly nudging
his friend into silence as they ride through Moscow in a sledge.[23]
Both eventually depart with a feeling of relief, as, somewhat

later, does Petia Girin, a young man from the same village employed for a time in Kalinin's office, who escapes from Moscow after being asked to spy on his fellow-workers.[24]

The country people make no lasting impact upon the town, but when townspeople visit the countryside they are often portrayed as positively harmful in their disastrous lack of sympathy with it. The vulgar campers in "Chok-poluchok," for example, spend their time amidst inimitable natural surroundings breaking bottles, quarrelling, getting drunk, and playing silly "sophisticated" games. In *Kanuny* this lack of sympathy and understanding is epitomized by a small but significant incident during the official roundup of "kulak" and other doubtful elements during the Kazanskaia holiday (one of the many traditional celebrations which Belov describes with tremendous enthusiasm and detail in this novel), when the authorities show total ignorance of the holiday's meaning for the villagers.[25] But whereas vandalism and insensitivity, though lamentable, have few long-term consequences, the town authorities' complete lack of sympathy with village life symbolizes the misapprehensions which, canonized as Party policy, were to have disastrous consequences in the enforced transformation of the village through collectivization.

Kanuny chronicles in rich social and ethnographical detail life in a north Russian village during a brief by crucially significant period at the end of the twenties, showing how the ground was laid for the impending tragedy of collectivization. The agent for much of the tragedy to follow is the wretched but sinister Ignatsii Sopronov, a despised and despicable pariah during his youth, who returns to revenge himself on his native village as the vindictive instrument of blind and divisive official policies. Belov's portrait is a major piece of realistic characterization, showing him by turns hectoring and downtrodden, ignorant and cunning, driven not so much by political idealism or even fanaticism as by a bitter sense of humiliation and inferiority. The full significance of the damage done by Sopronov in fostering artificial social divisions is illustrated by the tragedy of the Orlov family's enforced deracination — an unparalleled misfortune in the eyes of the other villagers, used as they were to natural disasters, and also for Belov himself with his immense commitment to the preservation of native roots.[26] Sopronov is entirely divorced from the sympathy and interests of the people, but he has a measure of power: as one of the villagers remarks about the proposal to build a windmill, "The people propose, but Sopronov disposes."[27] Although the second part of *Kanuny* ends with Nosopyr', the simple-minded village pauper whose wanderings had opened the novel, as Sopronov's only ally, the still only incipient process of *raskulachivanie* has not only begun to destroy enterprise and success, but also to show who, indeed, was to inherit the earth under Stalin's dispensation. Sopronov is a villain, portrayed dramatically, even melodramatically in places, as when he suddenly appears in church to disrupt a wedding ceremony,[28] or bursts in upon a private conversation with bullying threats,[29] but the most destructive element in the book is not an individual, but rather the urban-based Party which, in its ignorance of village traditions and reality, intrudes with a series of directives and orders; irrelevant to village life, they are also in the long run its corruption and virtual destruction.

Belov has sometimes been accused of excessive nostalgia for the past, and of idealizing traditional values, be it through his hostility to certain aspects of modern life, or through his portraits of rustic characters.[30] His stories do indeed contain a series of excellent portraits of country dwellers, many of whom possess admirable qualities,[31] although none is imbued with the near mystical significance of, for instance, Solzhenitsyn's Matrena; indeed, the émigré critic Grigorii Svirskii is right to contrast Belov's dry-eyed view of his characters with the tendency of another major *derevenshchik,* Valentin Rasputin, to invest great moral capital in his old country people.[32] Though concise and often understated, Belov's realistic details in works like *Kanuny* and *Plotnitskie rasskazy* give the reader a clear picture of past injustices, and make impossible any serious suggestion of idealization.

Realism, political, psychological, and linguistic, is, in fact, the principal feature of the majority of Belov's works, linking him with not only Soviet but also classical Russian literary tradition. In an important passage in "Bobrishnyi ugor" Belov stresses the strong spiritual affinity he feels for Tolstoi, reflected above all in their mutual closeness to nature,[33] and many commentators have observed links between his lyricism and that of Bunin and Prishvin, on both of whom he has written,[34] whilst George Gibian, speculating on the social and anthropological causes of the national nostalgia for village life in the sixties and seventies, takes Belov's antecedents back to writers like Grigorovich and Turgenev.[35]

So far Belov's only really important digression from realistic techniques has been in the magnificent collection of satirical miniatures in *Bukhtiny vologodskie* (1969) which, written at a particularly difficult moment in Soviet literary life, combine stylistic virtuosity with sardonic humor in their topsy-turvy presentation of rural reality. Here it is plainly circumstances that make the genre of *bukhtina* appropriate: as the narrator declares at the start of the eighth section, "What are people coming to nowadays! You tell them nonsense stories [*bukhtiny*] and they listen open-mouthed. They believe you. But if you start telling the truth, no one listens."[36] Elsewhere Belov has shown himself bold in the realism he brings to, for example, the various meetings between the authorities and peasants in *Kanuny,* where the latter's blunt comments and replies recall such earlier village stories as Abramov's outspoken "Vokrug da okolo."[37] What the authorities call the peasants' *kulatskie repliki*[38] have an urban equivalent in the political meeting at Pet'ka Girin's factory when he has to rescue the slogan-mouthing Party orator from an indignant workers' meeting.[39] In other works, too, Belov's characters behave in a convincingly realistic way, particularly in the area of relations between bosses and lesser mortals; in "Za tremia volokami," for instance, the brigade leader, having discovered that the major he meets is, despite his "good clothes," not "some boss or other," explains how he runs for cover when he sees officials from the town coming, hiding in a special place in the hay barn, or, if caught in the fields, diving into one of the bushes.[40] A different kind of realism is shown in the depiction of the villagers' bawdy games in *Kanuny,*[41] or in Ivan Nikitich's remark to his teenage daughter and her friends, "You should at least cross yourselves. As soon as you've got tits to shake all you want is to get out of the house."[42] Although not directly relevant to the theme of town and country, it may be mentioned here that Belov's language as a whole is notable for its realism and variety, particularly in what may loosely be called *skaz* techniques, comically Aesopian in *Bukhtiny vologodskie,* but often entirely serious, and used in town and country stories alike, though more frequently in the latter.[43] *Kanuny,* for instance, combines a remarkable variety of styles and narrative viewpoints without ever seeming to strive after novelty or effect. Here, as in the stories, Belov's ear is remarkably faithful to subtle nuances of language, as the novel ranges from political letters and documents (literate and illiterate) to the hollow jargon of politicians, the clerical intonations of Father Nikolai, and the strongly dialectal speech of his mainly peasant characters. In this connection it is interesting to note that in 1967 he linked the "democratization" of the literary language with what he perceived as the tendency of Soviet literature "to become ideologically and artistically more truthful."[44] In other theoretical statements Belov has consistently called for the preservation of dialectal words and expressions, which he sees as an essential counter to the growing tendency towards unnecessary foreign borrowings, carelessness, and the corruption by bureaucratic jargon of the modern literary language.[45]

Belov's desire to preserve and enrich Russia's linguistic heritage through dialect reflects a wider conservatism. Thus, the frequently humorous attacks on superfluous loan words he makes from time to time in articles and stories ("Dnevnik narkologa," for example) have an implied parallel in the ironic title of "Vospitanie po doktoru Spoku." A more general cultural conservatism is felt in stories like "Beskul'tur'e" (1968), where the narrator is appalled to find modern dancing and a blaring radiogram at the opening of a kolkhoz House of Culture.[46] In "Prosvetlenie (Rasskaz babushki)", a masterly example of *skaz,* Belov makes even the coming to the village of mains electricity seem a mixed blessing in a world where cows will no longer sleep without light, and where people "have not time to say good morning, let alone to describe their dreams."[47] Many of Belov's characters are spiritually close to the animal world ("Privychnoe delo," for instance, opens with Ivan Afrikanovich holding a drunken conversation with his horse), and clearly Belov prefers the natural world of animals to that of machines: in the humorous sketch of "U pereezda" (1973) a drayhorse triumphs over an exhaust-belching motorcycle by chewing a piece out of its rider's jacket;[48] in "Koni" (1964) a shepherd's quiet love of horses is contrasted favorably with the flashy behavior of his chauffeur friend who tries to persuade him to adapt himself to the (noisy, smelly, unnatural) world of the future;[49] animals and their care play an important part in Belov's writing, and he abhors all cruelty, often heightening our apprehension by showing animals' pain through the eyes of children.[50] What, in fact, infuses everything he writes, thematically, psychologically, and stylistically, is a deep regard for all that is natural rather than artificial, in harmony with nature, and attuned to its preservation rather than destruction.[51] In this sense Sergei Zalygin is entirely right when he describes Belov as "deeply, organically, and consistently traditional."[52]

It is not difficult to indicate points of conflict between town and country in Belov's prose. To take two extreme examples, unmitigated hostility may be seen in the early story "Kaleriinaia bulochka," where a young man, recalling the near starvation of his childhood years in a village, watches with loathing a vulgar townswoman in a restaurant using a bun to clean her fingers;[53] and more recently the play *Nad svetloi vodoi* (1973) was heavily criticized for exaggeration and even schematism in its contrasting of consistently sincere village people with their less moral urban counterparts.[54] But hardly less important in Belov's writing than this opposition are the features which the two share, be they negative aspects of life common to town and country, or, on the other hand, positive, moral links. Thus, for example, the casual violence of the urban teenagers who fell Konstantin Zorin from behind in "Vospitanie po doktoru Spoku"[55] has a rough equivalent in one of the many fights in *Kanuny* where Pashka is clubbed in the back by a gang of village youths,[56] although it should be noted that violence during village holidays in *Kanuny* is depicted as a basically unmalicious phenomenon: "if no one was killed and there were simply bruises and broken heads then all offence was forgotten."[57] Similarly, such unpleasant aspects of urban existence as slovenliness and bad service have their rural equivalents, as does the ubiquitous drunkenness, though the latter may come across as comic rather than offensive in, for instance, "Privych-

noe delo," as compared with "Vospitanie po doktoru Spoku"
or "Dnevnik narkologa." Sexual immorality, too, is a shared feature of modern life, highlighted in "Svad'ba" (1973) where an
old man describes to a companion a wedding he had seen at which
the heavily pregnant bride was barely able to stagger to the regis-
try office.[58] "Vospitanie" and "Dnevnik" do, however, indicate
two deep-rooted problems which seem particularly, though not
exclusively, characteristic of town life: in the former it is the
ubiquitous and chronic unwillingness to take responsibility which
affects even doctors,[59] whilst in the latter it is the reluctance of
people to undertake menial work (in this case cleaning hospital
staircases, which sometimes have to be swept by the nurses).[60]

Work is, in fact, one of the major positive linking themes in
Belov's writing. *Kanuny* contains powerful scenes of smelting in
the city factory, contrasted with infinitely less satisfying bureaucratic and political work, and elsewhere in the novel the building
of a new windmill, despite its fateful role as a symbol of kulak
aspirations, evokes descriptions rich in enthusiasm for hard physical toil and the satisfaction of creation.[61] In *Plotnitskie rasskazy*
a fundamental distinction is drawn between men of good conscience like the hardworking peasant Olesha and morally inferior
types such as the former party activist Aviner who are physically
lazy and, indeed, incapable of work.[62] Conscience is, characteristically, the quality that Belov prizes most highly in writers,[63] and
it is not only one of his own most striking features, but emerges
time and again as a key distinguishing element in a whole range
of his characters from town and country alike, people who, like
(to take a random example from *Kanuny*) Shilovskii and Daniil
Pachin, live a hardworking and natural, honest life whatever their
circumstances.

M. Gin is right to observe that Belov seeks to overcome the
polarization of town and country, to show links between the two,
and to create greater understanding, essential if village life and
agriculture are to survive,[64] but inevitably for Belov it is in the
village that traditional moral values are enshrined and there that
they are most likely to be perceived. In the last analysis, country life is more natural: as the philosophical ex-landowner Pro-

zorov observes in *Kanuny:* "In reality, everyone in the world is
at heart a ploughman. . . ."[65]

University of Liverpool

NOTES

1. The easy-going peasant hero of "Privychnoe delo," Ivan Afrikanovich Drynov, has received more critical attention than the rest of Belov's
characters together, ranging from, on the one hand, somewhat exaggerated adulation as a moral paragon to, on the other, condemnation
as a weak and irresponsible relic of the past with no relevance for the
development of Soviet society. A major example of the former was Efim
Dorosh's "Ivan Afrikanovich," *Novyi mir,* 1966, no. 8, pp. 257-61;
amongst the latter see V.Voronov, "Eshche raz o tsennostiakh istinnykh i
mnimykh," *Literaturnaia gazeta,* 13 March 1968, and I.Dedkov, "Strani-
tsy derevenskoi zhizni (Polemicheskie zametki)," *Novyi mir,* 1969, no. 3,
pp. 231-46, esp. 242-46; and for a general discussion of differing interpretations of this character see also A.Marchenko, "Iz knizhnogo raia,"
Voprosy literatury, 1969, no. 4, pp. 48-71, Iu. Seleznev, "Sovremennost' traditsii. Zametki o tvorchestve V. Belova," *Nash sovremennik,*
1974, no. 11, pp. 162-72, esp. 167-70, and G.A. Hosking, "Vasilii
Belov — Chronicler of the Russian Village," *Russian Review,* vol. 34,
no. 2 (1975), pp. 182-84. In stark contrast, Belov's major work to date,
Kanuny (Moscow, 1976), has been received in silence by most Soviet
critics, apart from L. Emel'ianov's cautiously commendatory "Razru-
shenie tishiny" (*Zvezda,* 1972, no. 11, pp. 217-20) for which he was
officially rebuked on ideological grounds by L. Novichenko, a secretary
on the board of the Writers' Union; see "Kriterii. Metodologiia. Mas-
terstvo," *Literaturnaia gazeta,* 6 February 1974. The novel was, however,
reprinted, again by "Sovremennik," in 1979. Recently, another hero
(or anti-hero), Kostia Zorin, who features in several of Belov's stories
including "Vospitanie po doktoru Spoku" (1974), "Chok-poluchok"
(1976) and, more tangentially, "Moia zhizn'" (1974) and *Plotnitskie rasskazy* (1968), has begun to arouse extensive critical comment and controversy somewhat analogous to that surrounding the character of Ivan Afrikanovich. See, for example, four articles which appeared in *Literaturnoe
obozrenie* in 1977: A.Strelianyi, " 'Perestavilsia' li svet?" no. 5, pp. 51-55;
L. Kuznetsova, "Semeinaia zhizn' Konstantina Zorina," no. 5, pp. 56-60;
G. Naan, "Emansipatsia, patriarkhat i 'voina polov'," no. 9, pp. 57-62;
and Vs. Surganov, "Konstantin Zorin—ego beda, liubov', zagadka,"
no. 10, pp. 49-55.

2. Vasilii Belov, "Derevenskaia tema obshchenatsional'na," *Druzhba narodov,* 1970, no. 9, p. 254.

3. It may be noted here that although Belov describes Russian urban and rural scenes with equal assurance he, like many other Russian writers past and present, loses much of his conviction in stories with a foreign setting. See, for example, two from *Kholmy,* Moscow, 1973: "Oko del'fina" (pp. 506-19), with an international background, and "Dama s gornostaem" (pp. 520-29), set in Cracow. For an analysis of this phenomenon see Seleznev, "Sovremennost' traditsii," pp. 171-72.

4. See, for instance, M. Gin, "Serdtse narodnoe," *Sever,* 1967, no. 6, pp. 116-21.

5. I.Borisova, "Den' za dnem," *Novyi mir,* 1964, no. 6, pp. 233-36.

6. *Plotnitskie rasskazy* (Arkhangel'sk, 1968), p. 125. See also "Bobrishnyi ugor" (1967) for the fullest philosophical analysis of the importance to man of his rural roots, now threatened by urbanization and change: "one by one before our eyes are dying the hearths of our rural native places *(derevenskaia rodina)* — the source of everything," *Gudiat provoda,* Moscow, 1978, p. 167. Other stories in which this strong sense of local patriotism is expressed range from the romantic "Za tremia volokami (1965) (*Gudiat provoda,* pp. 5-29, esp. 16) describing the search for a no longer existing native village, to the disillusioned account of a modern camping trip "Chok-poluchok" (*Druzhba narodov,* 1976, no. 10, pp. 102-17, esp. 104).

7. *Kanuny,* p. 47.

8. V. Gusev, "O proze, derevne i tsel'nykh liudiakh," *Literaturnaia gazeta,* 14 February 1968, p. 6.

9. *Gudiat provoda,* p. 33.

10. *Utrom v subbotu* (Vologda, 1976), p. 176.

11. *Utrom v subbotu,* pp. 152-75. Other stories depicting the hardships of wartime in a less tragic manner include "Mal'chiki" (*Nash sovremennik,* 1973, no. 7, pp. 116-21) and "V trudnye gody" (*Pod"em,* 1971, no. 2, pp. 44-57).

12. *Gudiat provoda,* pp. 55-61.

13. *Gudiat provoda,* pp. 135-37.

14. *Gudiat provoda,* pp. 138-40.

15. *Gudiat provoda,* pp. 93-100.

16. *Plotnitskie rasskazy,* pp. 119-24.

17. *Kholmy,* p. 253.

18. L. Antopol'skii, "Poznanie sovremennosti," *Iunost',* 1974, no. 8, pp. 69-70. Analogous further evidence of Belov's ability to handle different viewpoints imaginatively may be found in three stories about ado-

lescent feelings from the early *Rechnye izluki* collection (Moscow, 1964): "Devich'e leto" (pp. 70–84), "Ekho" (pp. 139–47), and "Klavdiia" (1962) (pp. 148–55).

Belov has also written for children. See, for example, *Katiushin dozhdik (Rasskazy)* (Voronezh, 1969); other collections appeared in 1972 and 1974.

19. *Gudiat provoda,* pp. 144–45.
20. *Plotnitskie rasskazy,* p. 32.
21. Hosking, "Vasilii Belov," p. 172.
22. *Tseluiutsia zori . . . (Iumoristicheskie rasskazy i povesti)* (Moscow, (1975), pp. 59–126. This extended anecdote has been made into a successful film.
23. *Kanuny,* p. 48. This lack of success is typical: in *Plotnitskie rasskazy* the narrator recalls how he three times walked the hundred and fifty or so miles to the city in search of the documentation needed for his full human rights, only to be told on the third occasion, "There is no record of you! None! Is that clear?" *Plotnitskie rasskazy,* p. 6.
24. There is, characteristically for Belov, a pronounced contrast between Girin's hasty departure from the city at the end of part 2, chapter 1 and the highly lyrical nature description with which the following chapter opens. *Kanuny,* p. 161.
25. *Kanuny,* p. 255. Presumably they were already in the late twenties more familiar with such formalized, often purely nominal, celebrations as the "Day of Workers in Trade," referred to ironically in a recent story "Dnevnik narkologa: vybrannye dni i mesta" (*Avrora,* 1979, no. 12, p. 17).
26. *Kanuny,* p. 321.
27. *Kanuny,* p. 89.
28. *Kanuny,* pp. 77–79.
29. *Kanuny,* p. 113.
30. See note 1.
31. Apart from Ivan Afrikanovich, there are many such portraits in, for example, *Kanuny, Plotnitskie rasskazy,* "Pod izvoz" (*Gudiat provoda,* pp. 118–34), "Na vokzale," "Koch" (1976) (Ibid., pp. 151–63), "Prosvetlenie" (1971) (Ibid., pp. 141–43), and "Grisha Funt" (Ibid., pp. 62–66), q.v.
32. For example, Dar'ia in *Proshchanie s Materoi.* See Grigorii Svirskii, *Na lobnom meste* (London, 1979), p. 591.
33. *Gudiat provoda,* p. 173.
34. N. P. Sedovoi (ed.), "Iz otzyvov sovetskikh pisatelei o Bunine (Vasilii Belov)," *Literaturnoe nasledstvo,* vol. 84, pt. 2 (1973), pp. 368–

69; Vasilii Belov, "Vesna, kotoraia vsegda s nami. K 100-letiiu so dnia rozhdeniia M.M. Prishvina," *Doshkol'noe vospitanie,* 1973, no. 4, pp. 88–95.

In a short contribution to a survey of writers' opinions on literature and language Belov has written of the distinctive qualities of prose writers who write or have written poetry (*Voprosy literatury,* 1967, no. 6, pp. 98–99) and it is worth noting that he himself began his literary career with verse (*Derevnia moia lesnaia,* Vologda, 1961), and has recently produced another slim volume of poetry, *Verby nad Khoprom* (Voronezh, 1976).

Iu. Seleznev emphasizes the lyrical aspects of Belov's work when he declares, "Belov is a poet in the broad sense of the word. He is not afraid to rise to solemn poeticality in the expression of feelings" ("Sovremennost' traditsii," p. 164). O. Voitinskaia also describes him as "a poet in prose": "Proza Vasiliia Belova," *Znamia,* 1967, no. 4, p. 244.

35. G. Gibian, "The Urban Theme in Recent Soviet Prose: Notes toward a Typology," *Slavic Review,* vol. 37, no. 1 (1978), p. 43. V. Bursov goes so far as to call Turgenev Belov's teacher: "Puti k khudozhestvennoi pravde," *Zvezda,* 1967, no. 1, pp. 210–11.

36. *Novyi mir,* 1969, no. 8, p. 167.

37. *Neva,* 1963, no. 1, pp. 109–37.

38. *Kanuny,* p. 261.

39. *Kanuny,* pp. 154–56.

40. *Gudiat provoda,* p. 15.

41. *Kanuny,* p. 166.

42. *Kanuny,* p. 71.

43. On this and other formal elements of Belov's writing see T. V. Krivoshchapova, "Skaz i rasskazchik v proze Vasiliia Belova," in A. M. Bulanov (ed.), *Problemy iazyka i stilia v literature* (Volgograd, 1978), pp. 94–101, and Id., "Rol' prozaicheskikh fol'klornykh zhanrov v proze Vasiliia Belova," *Vestnik MGU: Filologiia,* 1976, no. 4, pp. 33–44. See also Hosking, "Vasilii Belov," pp. 167–70, and S. Zalygin, "Rasskaz i rasskazchik (Zametki pisatelia)," *Literatura i sovremennost',* 1970–71, no. 11, pp. 319–35.

44. See *Voprosy literatury,* 1967, no. 6, p. 98.

45. See, for example, "Chistota, tolkaiushchaia k ubozhestvu (O dialektizmakh v russkom literaturnom iazyke)," *Russkaia rech',* 1969, no. 2, pp. 41–44, "Eshche raz o iazyke," *Molodaia gvardiia,* 1971, no. 6, pp. 270–72, and "Gruz zhiznennykh vpechatlenii," *Voprosy literatury,* 1977, no. 7, p. 200.

46. *Plotnitskie rasskazy,* pp. 144–48.

47. *Gudiat provoda,* p. 141.

48. *Tseluiutsia zori,* pp. 43-50.

49. *Gudiat provoda,* pp. 103-12.

50. See, for instance, several of the "Rasskazy o vsiakoi zhivnosti" (1974) (*Utrom v subbotu,* pp. 238-77), or the gelding scene in *Kanuny* (pp. 179-80). In this respect Belov may be compared to Ghingiz Aitmatov in "Belyi parokhod" (*Novyi mir,* 1970, no. 1, pp. 31-100).

51. In *Kanuny* Belov's Chekhovian feeling for the conservation of trees reaches the point of anthropomorphism (pp. 97-98).

52. Zalygin, "Rasskaz i rasskazchik," p. 321.

53. See Borisova, "Den' za dnem," pp. 235-36. A somewhat less categorical view of this opposition is taken by L. Anninskii who perceives in Belov's writing a move away from specifically village or town elements towards more general questions of morality ("Tochka opory. Eticheskie problemy sovremennoi prozy," *Don,* 1968, no. 7, p. 183), whilst M. Gin ("Serdtse narodnoe," pp. 118-20) finds him far from the traditional opposition of town and country.

54. See, for example, Sh. Galimov, "Konflikty i kharaktery," *Moskva,* 1973, no. 11, pp. 198-200, and I. Shaitanov, "Dve p'esy o derevne," *Teatr,* 1975, no. 1, p. 18.

55. *Utrom v subbotu,* p. 197.

56. *Kanuny,* p. 33.

57. *Kanuny,* p. 226.

58. *Tseluiutsia zori,* pp. 41-43.

59. *Utrom v subbotu,* p. 196.

60. *Avrora,* 1979, no. 12, p. 19.

61. See *Kanuny,* pp. 50-52, 69, and 152-53 on the one hand, and pp. 186-90 and 310-14 on the other. The Tolstoian link is self-evident.

62. See G. Hosking, *Beyond Socialist Realism: Soviet Fiction since "Ivan Denisovich"* (London, 1980), p. 65.

63. See *Voprosy literatury,* 1977, no. 7, p. 202.

64. Gin, "Serdtse narodnoe," p. 117.

65. *Kanuny,* p. 181.

WOMEN WRITERS IN RUSSIAN MODERNISM 1890–1910

TEMIRA PACHMUSS

"You are a sculptor, Socrates, and have made statues of our governors faultless in beauty," said Glaucon to Socrates. "Yes," replied the latter, "and of our governesses, too; for you must not suppose that what I have been saying applies to men only, and not to women." "There you are right," Glaucon agreed, "since we have made them to share in all things like the men."[1]

As early as the fifth century B.C., then, the great Greek philosopher insisted that women be allowed to play an equal role in society and be given the same recognition as men for their achievements. And yet Alexandra Kollantai, Soviet ambassador and feminist, deplores that in the twentieth century poets, novelists, and scholars have passed by "the shining images of the nascent 'new woman' . . . offered by the reality of Russian life in silence." She continues: "They neither perceived nor heard them, nor did they comprehend them to distinguish between them." Oblivious to this emerging self-awareness, men were not able, and did not wish, "to grasp this *novum* [the 'new woman'], to appropriate it and to stamp it upon [their] memory."[2]

Aleksandra Kollontai's charges appear to be well founded. Despite the fact that the important women writers of the Russian avant-garde were enthusiastic in welcoming, and even contributing to, the aesthetic revolution at the turn of the century, their names and literary works have been largely neglected by contemporary scholars. Yet they are no less deserving of attention than Valerii Briusov, Andrei Belyi and Aleksandr Blok, figures ordinarily associated with Modernism in Russia around 1900. The literary contributions of these female representatives of Russian letters belong to the history of Modernism no less than its more celebrated or sensational works.

Some of these women writers, among them Zinaida Hippius, Nadezhda Teffi, and Poliksena Soloveva, only too painfully aware of the reluctance of the male-dominated literary world to recognize the literary achievements of Russian women, often used masculine pseudonyms to disguise their true identities: Anton Krainii, Teffi, and *Allegro,* respectively. To avoid emphasizing their sex, Hippius and Soloveva used the masculine forms of verbs and personal pronouns corresponding to the term *chelovek* (a human being) in Russian. On more than one occasion Hippius insisted that she wished to write poetry not merely as a woman but as a human being: "*kak* chelovek, *a ne tol'ko kak zhenshchina.*" She wanted to be a poet, without any extra-literary considerations influencing the critical evaluation of her work. She demanded further that a woman be, above all, a person. Only after asserting herself as a human being could she insist on her womanhood. This paper is a tribute to those women writers of Russian Modernism who helped pave the way for the Silver Age in literature and actively sought to realize in their art a new personal, aesthetic, religious, and sociopolitical consciousness.

Russian *art nouveau* was part and parcel of the European avant-garde. In Europe, there was a strong desire to overcome the traditions of the past and the older generation's fixed and stagnant attitudes. The expressions New Humor, New Realism, New Drama, New Theater, New Art, New Woman were bandied about in Belgium, France, England, and Germany. Various concepts based on classical philosophies were formulated, such as New Paganism, New Hedonism, Neo-Christianity, a "new religious consciousness," New Voluptuousness, and a new vision of woman, as seen in Aubrey Beardsley's illustrations for *Morte d'Arthur* (1892) and *Salomé* (1893), as well as in Edvard Munch's women.

The new movement had a strong impact in Russia, where its partisans were cultured, extremely well-read, and "Western" in outlook. They were responsible for bringing about great changes in poetry, ballet, and the drama. The early Russian Modernist writers succeeded in revitalizing Russian verse and restored the standards of craftsmanship by creating new similes, bold images and metaphors, sophisticated rhymes, and "sound orchestration." They insisted that the artist should not depict life by merely presenting surface reality or mirroring "life as it is."

In prose, the Modernist writers sought to present basic psychological and intellectual dimensions instead of portraying characters through lengthy discussions of their social milieu, motivations, and interrelationships. They claimed that there is no stable, definable, socially determined man. Zinaida Hippius, Nadezhda Teffi, and Lidia Zinov'eva-Annibal presented man in the process of maturation; hence their concern with the psychology of children in the process of becoming and seeking. In refined prose, furthermore, they portrayed visions, dreams, unusual situations, and exotic or morbid sensations.

The movement in Russia may be likened to Western European *art nouveau* not only in certain mannerisms of form, but also in its haughty individualism and aristocratic aloofness. The Modernists' individualistic attitude frequently bordered on narcissism, since they themselves were most often the focus of their work. Individualism reached the Russian Modernists primarily through the works of Nietzsche; their amoralism originated in the works of Rimbaud. D.S. Merezhkovskii, Zinaida Hippius, Valerii Briusov, and Fedor Sologub, like the French Decadent poets, at times revealed an indifference toward ethical issues, refusing to choose between good and evil. Other Russian Modernists, such as Zinov'eva-Annibal or Mikhail Artsybashev, found their inspiration in eroticism. The Decadents' preoccupation with certain "extreme" subjects — sex, disease, calamity, and death — was one manifestation of their protest against the asceticism of the previous age. Vasilii Rozanov made the following important statement concerning eroticism in Modernist writing: "The god as old as Mother Nature, driven once and for all from the civic poetry of the 1850s–1870s, re-entered into the sphere that had always belonged to him."[3] These were, then, the diverse sources of Russian Modernism.

There were two periods of *art nouveau* in Russia. First came the aesthetes, or Decadents, who in the 1890s revolted against traditional concepts and reevaluated them in the light of their own artistic criteria. These literary aesthetes and early Decadents — individualists and rebels against the utilitarian ethic and radicalism of the preceding age — turned toward Western culture. However, the metaphysical, religious, and (subsequently) sociopolitical proclivities which had been lying dormant within them gradually gained primacy. At this time Russian Modernist writers began to advocate a more profound conception of the objective of art, together with a religious affirmation of life. Thus, the second period of Modernism began about 1901, when Hippius and Merezhkovskii opened their St. Petersburg salon to the contributors of the journal *Mir iskusstva* (The World of Art, 1898–1904) for religious discussions. At this point the Decadent movement evolved into Symbolism. Its representatives longed for a new religious consciousness, for a new, *inner* Church.[4] Now Western European Decadence lost its hold on the Russian artistic imagination, and the literary movement of Symbolism was soon transformed into a metaphysical and mystical philosophy. Writers began to insist on a bond between religion and literature. They wished to create a new metaphysical and social awareness, a new man, a new society, a new religion, a new (ecumenical) church, a new Russia, and even a new Europe. The individual representatives of Modernism were characterized by a diversity of allegiances, even though they had an essentially common point of departure: their opposition to any utilitarian function for literature. The Modernist writers turned to Pushkin, Gogol', Tolstoi, Dostoevskii, Tiutchev, and Fet in order to rediscover their ethics and aesthetics. They were also united by their tragic premonition of the approaching cataclysm.

The term "Modernism" is very complex. It resembles the reflection of diverse symmetrical patterns in the mirrors of a kaleidoscope — heathenism and neo-Christianity; apolitical attitudes and active political preoccupations; pornography and the nobility of the lonely, pensive, melancholic spirit; hopelessness and the sensation of trimuph; cosmopolitanism and nationalism; aristocratic alienation from the crowd and a "prophetic" tendency combined with a desire to "teach," as well as many other characteristic antinomies, found their expression within it. It produced many writers, each with a specific weltanschauung, poetic universe, and literary technique. For Zinaida Hippius, for example, literature was a profound spiritual experience. The central theme of her creative work is the spirit and its efforts to attain the ultimate restoration of a harmonious relationship between love and eternity, life and death, the real and the miraculous.[5] In her estimation, literature was the means of embodying for humanity the unity of the transcendental and the phenomenal. Challenging the social and ideological approach to creative art, Hippius insisted on paying more respect to universal culture and to the mystery of spiritual beauty and harmony. Her poetry and prose reflect an antipositivistic, dualistic view of a world divided into the realm of physical phenomena and a higher reality, eternal, indivisible, and intangible. Hippius' own law in art was formulated in an aphorism: "Art should materialize only the spiritual." Art reveals the divine spirit; in art the divine logos assumes a human image. She conceived of poetry as a path to the knowledge of ultimate mysteries and as an intuitive access to preternatural reality. Poetry, she insisted, should originate in the artist's spiritual and religious ecstasy. Her poetic universe appears as a horrifying vision, a Manichean world in which evil often gains the upper hand over good and the Devil overpowers God. These portrayals, however, are always counterbalanced by idealistic strivings and an ardent faith in God and His mercy. Hippius' poems are spiritual psalms, reminiscent of pious hymns or chants such as the "Gloria in Excelsis." A salient feature of Hippius' poetic temperament was her determination to serve humanity. Advocating an apocalyptic Christianity which awaited the Second Coming, she wished to participate in the creation of the new man, whose spirit would be enlightened and dignified and whose flesh would be transformed and ennobled.

In her prose, Hippius revealed interest in expressing both male and female views on the relationship between the sexes and the need for defining new roles for man and woman within (and outside) this relationship. She was equally adept at portraying the claustrophobia of women confined by outmoded views of male-female relations, and at expressing the confusion of men in these changing times. Religious divination, reflections on beauty and harmony, social concepts, and the preaching of Neo-Christianity and ecumenity (*sobornost'*) are concepts intrinsic in Hippius' stories. Her characters strive for an "enlightened love" of God, the elevation of the flesh, and the ability to achieve understanding and harmony among people. Mystical clairvoyance, spiritual contemplation, and an awareness of the beauty and mystery inherent in nature play an important role in her fiction too. The heroes and their idiosyncratic modes of thinking and speaking are drawn in sharp relief. Tension between the comic and the tragic is created in many of her stories, and her scenes and dialogues testify to her exquisite sense of humor and sophisticated craftsmanship. Hippius' emphasis on aesthetic, religious, and philosophical aspects in literary works helped set the stage for a new twentieth-century literary movement, Russian Symbolism. The critic E. Koltanovskaia admired Hippius' own and her heroes' intense search for the meaning of life, for its new forms, for new moral laws, and for new beauty.[6]

Zinaida Hippius' philosophy retains its validity even in the light of modern existentialism, for her works are surprisingly relevant in today's cultural climate. The central themes of her fiction (the search for God, a preoccupation with the problems of good and evil, the treatment of love, passion, marriage, parenthood, a sense of responsibility toward oneself and one's fellow man, the place of woman in society, and even homosexuality) are very relevant today. Hippius is indeed important today to the searching and troubled young generation, especially to young women.

Another woman writer of the period, Anastasia Verbitskaia, was interested in a new image for woman and her new association with man. In marriage, said Verbitskaia, woman is either dominated by man or dominates him; there can be no harmony or unity within the prevalent definition of marriage. This view of matrimony and woman's possible alternative role in society was radical for that time. Verbitskaia's protagonists also explored the entanglements of sex and free love, and they protested the false morals of Russian society and the position of woman within it. In correspondence with the Decadent moods of the period, Verbitskaia portrayed people trying to transcend the vulgarity and triviality of life. In her short stories, novels, and plays she posed questions which were extremely important for Russian youth of that time: what is truth? What does the future hold? What should man do now for the future of humanity?

Verbitskaia had a talent for selecting her protagonists from among average people and fathoming their particular problems — the family, occupation, ideals, or the "new consciousness." Some of the leading Russian writers — Kornei Chukovskii[7] and A. Bartenev,[8] for example — were alienated by her emphasis on the problems of women in Russian life, and were therefore critical of her writing. Her advocacy of equality, self-assertion, and material independence for women was indeed a new and highly controversial issue at that time and not welcomed by many men. On the other hand, her artistic presentation of woman's inadequate position and the latter's struggle for the realization of her ideals (for example, in Verbitskaia's play *Mirage,* 1913) elicited a profound response at the turn of the century, and the social problems treated in her works were of interest to many readers, both male and female.[9] The most successful character in *Mirage,* Variagin, a zealot of beauty and a confirmed individualist, guided in his actions by the selfish dictates of his Ego, appears to have been a prototype of Zinaida Hippius' Iuri Dolgorukii in her novel *The Devil's Doll* (1911) and of Mikhail Artsybashev's crude and instinctive Sanin (*Sanin,* 1907). As in the works of most Russian Modernist writers, Verbitskaia's novels and plays reveal contemporary restlessness, a social and individual fragmentation, an absence of faith, an anxious pursuit of personal happiness, as well as hope, despondency, and an attempt at adjustment or escape.

Lidiia Zinov'eva-Annibal was entirely submerged in the atmosphere of Modernism. In her works valid psychological observations alternate with scenes of a sensual and erotic nature. Together with other Modernist writers, she heralded a new concept of love designed to enable women to transcend the vulgarity and emptiness of immediate surroundings. And she, too, was preoccupied with the individual's private world of Beauty and Harmony. She, too, was engrossed in the psychology of the emerging, "liberated" woman and in the portrayal of such a woman's fulfilled life outside of a relationship with men. Zinov'eva-Annibal's play *The Rings: A Drama in Three Acts* (1904) was intended to transform this process, through a tragic perception of the world, into a mystery and thus return it to its original source, the liturgical ritual at the alter of the suffering God. There was, on the other hand, a great deal of sensuality and crude eroticism in the play, evident also in her story *Thirty-three Abominations* (1907). These two works were harshly censured by the leading critics of the time, such as A.V. Amfiteatrov,[10] A.A. Izmailov,[11] and Zinaida Hippius.[12] However, with all due esteem for Hippius and the other critics, it should be mentioned that Zinov'eva-Annibal did in fact argue that only by revering love more than any other value can man create his own private world of harmony and beauty. Beauty is the essence of the spiritual world of inspiration, the world of joy, happiness, and peace for Zinov'eva-Annibal's female protagonists. But beauty, she warned, can be easily corrupted through contact with the exterior world — as was the beauty of Vera's beloved (in *Thirty-three Abominations*), which was at the mercy of the thirty-three clumsy male artists. Zinov'eva-Annibal's metaphysical considerations form the aesthetic theme of the story; this feature distinguishes it from other works of the period written in response to a literary vogue that had, as its sole purpose, the portrayal of sexual love, as in some of the works of Boleslav Markevich, Ieronim Iasinskii (literary pseudonym Maksim Belinskii), Anatolii Kamenskii, Sergei Sergeev-Tsenskii, Mikhail Kuzmin, Leonid Andreev, Mikhail Artsybashev, and even Fedor Sologub.

The emotionally heightened style, impressionistic, colorful imagery, and erotic themes in Nadezhda Teffi's poetry, especially in *Seven Fires* (1910), likewise make her an integral part of Modernism. She, too, divided the universe into a multitude of polar opposites, of which the polarity of the "dead" empirical world versus a higher, spiritual reality was the most fundamental. Her treatment of erotic themes, especially her distinctly Eastern eroticism, is not offensive, however, since it is characterized by external decency and refinement of form.

In her short stories and one-act plays,[13] Teffi gave a negative view of marriage and suggested, as did Verbitskaia, that happiness for a woman cannot be achieved through union with a man. She portrayed with sad humor the bewilderment and alienation of woman in the modern world. Since there is no activity open for her in contemporary society, she is forced to look for personal fulfillment in matrimony. This proves a failure, however. On the whole, Teffi was interested mainly in the social position and psychology of woman. She presented the emotional entanglements between men and women almost invariably through the eyes of her heroines.

Imagery, poetic devices, and the flamboyant style of her *Seven Fires* all point to similarities between Teffi's serious poetry and the works of the Russian Symbolists. Her dualistic vision of the universe may also be identified with theirs. Earthly existence is void, meaningless, and dead; "true reality" lies elsewhere. Distant and unattainable, it exists only as a dim reflection on earth. The soul longs for this higher spiritual reality, yet it can never detach itself completely from the dead and mechanical world of finite experience. This perception of the world lies at the heart of Teffi's entire artistic work. Paradoxically, however, in her comic stories she maintains that this ideal, beautiful, spiritual world is merely a mirage, a sweet illusion. This world of illusion is nevertheless superior to a dead and banal existence on earth.

Mirra Lokhvitskaia, the "Russian Sappho," was a poet much admired by both critics and readers. Her poetry manifests her departure from the old devices practiced by poets contemporary to Pushkin, and it is striking in its sensual evocation of fragrances and its imaginative ingenuity. Her poems reveal the vitality of life, its elemental force, and the flame of passion. The singularity of Lokhvitskaia's poetic voice and vision is unparalleled in the history of Russian versification, for in her work the Hellenic cult of beauty is perfectly unified with Bacchanalian outbursts of passion. Since some of her verse is sensual and unabashedly erotic, her poetry was a source of perplexity for the Russian male reader brought up in the "civic" tradition of Russian literature. Lokhvitskaia urged women to express their individuality, to lay bare the passionate, erotic aspect of their emotions, to explore and portray elements of their nature which outmoded and stereotyped definitions of "female" and "feminity" had excluded. Her "song of love and sensuality" was of course alien to many Russian critics, and in Volume II of her verse (St. Petersburg, 1900) she gave this answer to them:

> I do not know why they reproach me
> For having too much fire in my poems,

> For striving to meet the lively sunbeam
> And refusing to heed the accusation of gloom.
>
> For shining like a tsarina in my elegant verses,
> With a diadem in my opulent hair,
> For weaving myself a necklace of rhymes,
> For singing of love, for singing of beauty.
> . . . . . .

Lokhvitskaia's sensuality was indicative of her search for extreme, extravagant, and feverish perceptions. Her interest in erotic passion, exotic flora, the mood of dreams and reveries, the cult of the ego, and her striving to escape the world of empirical reality — all these mannerisms and attitudes were typical of Decadent poetry in Russia. Like other Symbolist poets, Lokhvitskaia believed in a higher reality; it found expression in her works as those ethereal, eternal gardens permeated with spiritual significance. The same ambiguity is inherent in the poetry of Zinaida Hippius and Aleksandr Blok: the spirit and the flesh, the divine and the demonic, faith and disbelief, the bright sunrise and the gloomy sunset, ethereal gardens and the dark impulse of human passion on earth.

Poliksena Solov'eva glorified nature, solitude, weltschmerz, and death in her beautiful filigreed verse. Her poetry is one of contemplation — the persona sees no escape from the triviality and boredom of life. In her aesthetics, art is a means of salvation, of raising the soul from the temporal to the eternal. Solov'eva's realm of revery, beauty, harmony, and "correspondences" to "fragrances, flowers, and sounds" served as her abode on earth. Her "allegiance" to Modernism also found expression in her yearning for refinement, beauty, and delicacy, as well as in her belief in the forthcoming dawn of a new spiritual life for man. Solov'eva's poetry is a song of evening, of late autumn with nature dying; it is a hymn of death. Hers was a cult of tranquil negation, a rhythmical flow of splendor, calm, evil, and malaise. Her verse neither inveighed against Russian social conditions nor bewailed the unfortunate position of the Russian peasant, as was fashionable at the time. Rather, it revealed the poet's aspiration to the beautiful and unattainable, the world of lofty hopes and dreams. In keeping with the zeitgeist of the period, Solov'eva experimented with other literary genres — folktales, plays, short stories, hymns, a novella in verse, and so forth. Like the other poets of Modernism, she also created new images, poetic atmosphere, and poetic mood.

Cherubina de Gabriak was another Modernist poet in the first decade of the twentieth century. This was the literary pseudonym of Elizaveta Ivanovna Dmitrieva, a young schoolteacher in St. Petersburg. In her poetry, she tended toward the extreme by using magnificent colors and expressive imagery in her attempt to transcend the tedium and boredom of everyday life. Together with other Modernist poets, de Gabriak wished to establish a link between Beauty and the "essence of things," as mirrored in a work of art. Like other avant-garde women writers of her day, she was engrossed in specifically female feelings and passions, as well as in breaking away from the stereotyped view of woman (virtuous and dutiful toward her husband and family) that had generally dominated nineteenth-century Russian literature. De Gabriak boldly revealed the erotic curiosity and passion of contemporary woman. In her poems, she dealt with a daring, "emancipated" woman eager to enter into an intimate physical relationship with Jesus Christ. De Gabriak's poetry may be referred to as a *lai,* a medieval type of lyric verse composed of asymmetrical couplets each sung to its own melody. This form, revived in the seventeenth century in France, was skilfully adapted by the poet in the first decade of the nineteenth century, and this revival may serve as an example of de Gabriak's daring craftsmanship. She often availed herself of rarely used closed forms of ancient poetry — the rondeau, vilanelle, rondel, and various systems of interlacing and repeating lines, as seen in her long poem "The Golden Bough" (1909). Cherubina de Gabriak's poetic gift is evident throughout her poetry. It is unfortunate that the male-dominated literary group of *Apollon* — where she published her verses — headed by Sergei Makovskii and Nikolai Gumilev, crudely silenced the young poet. She ceased publishing entirely and was lost to her readers after Gumilev's spiteful behavior toward her in public, as reported by Marina Tsvetaeva in her book *Prose.*[14]

The poetry of Adelaida Gertsyk, the last Modernist writer selected for this presentation, is based on "sound instrumentation."

Gertsyk's verse depends on alliterations, assonances, and the "fleeting" nature of verbs and nouns, thus creating a strong evocative effect. She used Slavicisms and old Russian song rhythms, aspiring to an "artistic folklore" somewhat similar to the sectarian melodies of Aleksandr Dobroliubov (1876-1944?) and the poetry of Liubov' Stolitsa (1884-1934), Pimen Karpov (1884- ?), and Marina Tsvetaeva (1892-1941). Gertsyk's religious poems resemble those of Zinaida Hippius, being at once personal *méditations religieuses,* prayers, and hymns to God. In harmony with the zeitgeist, Gertsyk had been fascinated with new artistic forms, paying tribute to various poetic schools and literary movements. Her own poetic universe, however, is very original, even paradoxical. One of the leitmotifs is her strong desire to tempt — and subdue — suffering, even to play with it. Her attitude toward death is no less parodoxical — what is death? What is its poetic image? In her poetry, there is no clear demarcation between the two realms of life and death. People do not know how to live; they do not know how to die. Love, too, is as unstable and illusory as death. These poetic dialogues with the "self" are, of course, characteristic of the works of the Russian Symbolists.

Gertsyk's versification is unique — she was attracted by the elemental force in the Russian folksong, with its typical imagery, repetition, meter, color, and intonation. The early Russian Modernists, Hippius, Bal'mont, and Valerii Briusov, could not serve as examples in this genre, for the Russian folksong was not their forte. She had to find her own way, unaided by the contemporary *maîtres* of poetry. Her verse does not adhere to the artificial canons of versification. It contains funeral (or mourning) songs and laments, chants of exorcism and curses, love spells and lullaby songs. All of these elements reflect the traditional magic symbolism of ancient Russia. As Viacheslav Ivanov put it, Adelaida Gertsyk clothed the elemental force of myth in a poetic garment.[15] Her poetry is indeed a new artistic experience of the ancient folk heritage of the Russian past, couched in contemporary lyrics. Her vocabulary abounds in neologisms, old Russian idioms and invocations, dialectisms, archaisms, and rarely used words. Gertsyk carefully avoided poetic clichés in her epithets and comparisons, but she often used allegory. Her rhythm, language, imagery, and the emotional force of her verse are ingenious and novel in Russian poetry.

Taken as a whole, the works of Zinaida Hippius, Mirra Lokhvitskaia, Anastasiia Verbistkaia, Poliksena Solov'eva, Lidiia Zinov'eva-Annibal, Cherubina de Gabriak, Nadezhda Teffi, and Adalaida Gertsyk were part of nascent Modernism's expression of its new mystical, religious, ethical, and philosophical perceptions, the expression of a weltanschauung that protested and denied the social and civic obligations of the preceding generation in favor of complete freedom for the artist's spiritual and aesthetic aspirations. This attitude also included a denial or obliteration of any outmoded views of man or woman and the nature of their roles.

The very essence of Modernism in Russia, which involved the earnest search for an inner transfiguration and expression of man's unique individuality and spiritual worth, is not unfamiliar to the contemporary young generation. The aspirations of the avant-garde women writers to transcend the traditional role and function of women in society and the family, and to share an equal place with men, are of immediate concern in today's world. Moreover, their works, reflecting the immense aesthetic renaissance of the time, greatly enriched the Silver Age in Russian literature, and our own epoch, by the clarion call for craftsmanship, the aesthetic appreciation of art, and the unimpeded artistic self-expression of these writers.

University of Illinois
at Urbana-Champaign

NOTES

1. Plato, *The Republic,* Books VI and VII, Set Four (Chicago: Great Book Foundation, n.d.), pp. 77–78.

2. Alexandra Kollontai, *The Autobiography of a Sexually Emancipated Communist Woman,* edited with an afterword by Irving Fletscher; translated by Salvador Attanasio (New York: Herder and Herder, 1971), pp. 51–52.

3. V.V.Rozanov, "On Symbolists and Decadents," *Russian Literature Triquarterly,* no. 8 (Winter, 1974), p. 282.

4. N.A. Berdiaev, *Samopoznanie* (Paris: YMCA-Press, 1949), passim.

5. For more detail, read Temira Pachmuss, *Zinaida Hippius: An Intellectual Profile* (Carbondale: Southern Illinois University Press, 1971).

6. "Alyi mech. Rasskazy. Z.N. Gippius," *Obrazovanie,* no. 9 (1906), pp. 94–96.

7. See, for example, K. Chukovskii, *Kniga o sovremennykh pisateliakh* (St. Petersburg: Shipovnik, 1914), p. 14.

8. See A. Bartenev, "Parazity literatury (A. Verbitskaia)," *Zhatva,* Book I (1922), pp. 234–35.

9. Verbitskaia's reading audience was very large. Since she had always been interested in progressive ideas, she was especially popular with Russian students who read her works with enthusiasm. They were attracted by her plots and by her concern with various questions much in vogue at the turn of the century. She, too, strove to create "new ideals" and new people. This challenge, of course, had a strong appeal to the student population, also seeking fresh approaches for the continuing struggle with the traditions of the past.

10. See A.V. Amfiteatrov, *Protiv techeniia: zametki* (St. Petersburg: Prometei, 1908), pp. 147–50.

11. For more detail, read A.A. Izmailov, *Pomrachenie bozhkov i novye knigi: kniga o novykh veianiakh v literature* (Moscow: Sytin, 1910), pp. 111–15.

12. See Anton Krainii, "Bratskaia mogila," *Vesy,* 1907, no. 7, p. 61.

13. See, for example, her *Iumoristicheskie rasskazy* (2 vols.; St. Petersburg: Shipovnik, 1910–1912).

14. *Proza* (New York: Izdatel'stvo imeni Chekhova, 1953).

15. Viacheslav Ivanov, "Zametki o poezii," *Apollon,* 1910, no. 7, pp. 41–42.

A POETIC VISION IN CONFLICT:
CHINGIZ AITMATOV'S FICTION

CONSTANTIN V. PONOMAREFF

Poetic vision in conflict, as understood in this paper, is taken to occur whenever a conscious and *non-* or *anti-aesthetic* manipulation of fictional material interferes with the natural thematic flow of an author's poetic imagination, which may, as it does on occasion in Aitmatov's work, cause psychological lapses in the credibility of literary characters. To a sensitive reader these manipulations of theme and character can be recognized as a lessening of the tragic tension of the poetic whole.

Before proceeding further it will be useful to establish the essential nature and direction of Aitmatov's creative energy, that which holds his work together, the better to indicate later any conscious shifts away from his natural poetic vision. His major work, written between 1957 and 1970, offers the best examples.

As I have tried to show in my previous work on Aitmatov,[1] the essential poetic structure of Aitmatov's fiction is built by the presence and positive function of female figures and their children in human or animal guise. In his first significant novella "Litsom k litsu" (Face to Face, 1957), a vicious father figure stands in direct contrast to the mother and child configuration.[2] His love story *Dzhamilia* (1958), which brought him an international reputation, revolves about the morally and emotionally exceptional character of Dzhamilia, who left an unloving husband for a man who understood and appreciated her.[3] In his more tragic love story "Topolek moi v krasnoi kosynke" (My Little Poplar in the Red Kerchief, 1962), Asel took her child and left a young husband who lacked moral stamina for an older, but more selfless man.[4] In "Materinskoe pole" (Mother Field, 1963) the whole action revolves about the lot of women who lose their husbands and their sons to war.[5] Finally, in his major novels *Proshchai, Gul'sary!* (Farewell Gul'sary, 1966) and "Belyi parokhod" (The White Ship, 1970),[6] he metaphorized the female figure into animal forms, a device which gives his work a further mythical and symbolic dimension.

In each of these works woman as virgin, mistress, or mother is the creative focal point around which Aitmatov's fictionalized world turns. The men who are worthy figures are only those who remain in a positive relationship to the female figure at the center. Those who lose her love lose their humanity and become negative counter figures, a development which is not without significance for Aitmatov's creative process with its female orientation. The confrontation of a negative male with the feminine element is a formula valid in varying degrees for all of these major writings by Aitmatov. We see this most easily in his novellas "Face to Face," *Dzhamilia* and "My Little Poplar in the Red Kerchief." In "Mother Field" the men are away at war and thus do not have an immediate role to play. Curiously, an earlier tale, "Pervyi uchitel'" (The First Teacher, 1957), which had a man at the center, was not a deviation from Aitmatov's creative orientation, because Diuishen the village teacher actually functioned as a surrogate "mother" figure to all the schoolchildren. Though the female motif was muted in *Farewell, Gul'sary!* it explodes in full force in "The White Ship" where the central core of the novel is energized by a legend about the Horned Deer-Mother and her children.

It is perhaps not an accident that what I call Aitmatov's tampering with his poetic and lyrical art coincided with his official rise in the Soviet literary establishment, an ascent marked by his receiving the Lenin Prize in 1963 and the State Prize in 1966. It is also surprising how very few of the Soviet critics writing on Aitmatov in the last two decades have dealt with the problem of the conscious manipulation of literary material in his writing.[7]

Though one can find earlier instances of Aitmatov's conscious attempts to manipulate the psychology of his characters, as for example in "My Little Poplar in the Red Kerchief" the lack of credibility of the psychological motivation of the truck driver Il'ias,[8] it was not until his *Farewell, Gul'sary!* and especially his

"The White Ship" that the conscious interference with character and theme became more apparent. In this respect it is primarily women among Soviet critics who have been most perceptive of this aspect of Aitmatov's writing. Thus, V. Stanislavleva writing about Aitmatov's novel, *Farewell, Gul'sary!* was first to point to the crucial break in the psychology of Tanabai, the herdsman, at the point where he is expelled from the Party. Why, she asked, did Tanabai not protest his expulsion from the Party (which would have been more in keeping with his character), but instead became suddenly inert?[9] Stanislavleva's answer is that the reason for such a sudden psychological inertia in Tanabai lay in the fact that the literary character and the author had parted ways:

> And it was here [at the point of the expulsion and after] that the author violated the logic of the development of Tanabai's character, entrusting his favorite hero with too much of what he himself thought as author. Here, the dialectical way of portraying Tanabai's character gave way to the conclusions the author had set for himself, for whom his own subjective evaluations and ideas about events become more important than the true delineation of character (*pravda kharakterov*) and of circumstances. The artistic exploration of life was interrupted. And that is why everything subsequent to this in the novel turns out to be not shown but told by Ch. Aitmatov and, therefore, is not artistically convincing.[10]

This conscious reshaping of a character in greater consonance with what we might call Socialist Realist decorum and to the detriment of the artistic whole, suggests Aitmatov's capacity for the ideological manipulation of literary material. In this connection his "The White Ship" is a very interesting case in point showing how a gifted Soviet writer tried to correct the natural impact on his readers of what remains to date his greatest novel.

The original impact and ending of the novel as it appeared in the first issue of *Novyi mir* for 1970, when it was entitled "Belyi parokhod (Posle skazki)" (The White Ship [After the Fairy Tale]), was tragic and hopeless both for the boy, who committed suicide after the brutal slaying of the Horned Deer-Mother, and symbolically, for man in general. For a writer who had claimed (in 1967, in connection with *Farewell Gul'sary!*) that it is the function of modern Soviet literature to solve "the problem of creating the image of our contemporary . . . ,"[11] the ending and impact of "The White Ship" could only mean public embarrassment as a Socialist Realist writer. His attempt to exculpate himself in his "Neobkhodimye utochneniia" (Necessary Clarifications), which he published shortly afterward in the July issue of *Literaturnaia gazeta,* subtly though it was argued, could not do away with the tragic human import of the novel.

Aitmatov, for whom according to L. Lebedeva the development of the novel had in some sense come as a surprise[12] (no doubt a mark of its artistic authenticity), was clearly worried about the impact of this novel on the Soviet reader. He therefore came to a decision, hallowed by Soviet literary practice, to revise certain key sections leading up to and including the end of the novel. Taisa Napolova, who based her findings on the revised 1971 Kirghizstan edition of the novel — where Aitmatov even deemphasized the original title by inverting it to read *Posle skazki (Belyi Parokhod)* — showed the actual changes made by Aitmatov. In effect the changes were meant to weaken the Horned Deer-Mother theme by giving more resonance to Kulubek, who was a substitute father figure to the boy. As a result, Aitmatov undermined the tragic inevitability and artistic power of the original version of the novel.[13] It may also be interesting in this context to remind ourselves that a 1975 collection of important articles on Aitmatov's work included only those written between 1962 and 1967, thus leaving out any mention of "The White Ship" altogether.[14] Aitmatov's utter artistic failure (in our opinion) in "Early Cranes"[15] (1975) due to his trend toward the father figure and his forcing masculine motifs into the female mold of his poetic imagination,[16] only further destroyed the poetic unity of his work and made him regress to his groping beginnings of before 1957.

Indeed, if one looks back at Aitmatov's early writing before 1957, one becomes aware of the fact that it was during that time that his awakening creativity became defined by a tension between male and female figures. And that by the time he had written his first mature work in 1957, the female orientation of his poetic vision had finally overcome the initial male-centered tendency of his earliest stories.

Aitmatov's pre-1957 and artistically immature writing thus
gives us a preview of those thematic and structural ingredients
which were both to shape and, on occasion, to disrupt his future
creative development. Aitmatov's early stories already utilized
father and/or mother figures (and their children) in thematic
and structural terms. In "Sypaichi" (1954), for example, Aitmatov centered his fiction around a father and son relationship.
After a conflict between the proud and old-fashioned father and
his more modern-minded son over the best method for prevent-
ing river floods, the son triumphs and the two finally become
reconciled to one another. The son's victory reaffirmed the inherent idealization of the male in this story.[17] In "Belyi dozhd'"
(White Rain, 1954), however, the action had already shifted to
one between mother and daughter. But the mother's position
remained "inferior" to man's, both in the sense that her only
daughter, Saadat, left her to marry, but even more so because
it was left to the mother's brother, Tokoi-Ake, to justify Saadat's
action and to heal the break between mother and daughter.[18]

With "Soperniki," (The Rivals, 1955) Aitmatov was definitely
moving in the direction of his later, mature work. Though much
of the action had to do with the competitive conflict between
two men — the jealous Karatai and the much more responsible
Sabyrbek on how effectively to irrigate their respective Collective
State Farms — a new emphasis was placed on the tender and loving relationship of the mother (Karatai's wife) with her small
son,[19] as well as on the now somber and hostile father figure
Karatai. For example, at one point Karatai "coldly glanced at his
wife and son" while the mother, a forerunner of Seide in "Face
to Face," "stood stunned, pressing the child to her breast."[20]
Portrayed as repulsive and beast-like,[21] the father's hostility to
the mother is unmistakable: "With a face distorted by rage he
turned to this wife and stared at her with a ferocious look filled
with hate."[22] The climax of the story came when Karatai's wife,
Kanymgul, moved by love and compassion, physically struggled
with her husband and managed to overpower him.[23] In this story
it was she, a woman and not a man, who played the crucial role
in bringing Karatai and Sabyrbek together again.[24] Finally, in
"Na reke Baidamtal," (On the River Baidamtal, 1955)[25] Aitmatov

found his major theme: Woman. For here it is the young girl Asiia's moral strength that has an exemplary and formative influence on the selfishly irresponsible and, at first, cowardly, Nurbek.[26] Nurbek ultimately was able to overcome his weakness,[27] but this was only due to Asiia, to Woman, who is envisaged as a marvelous source of moral strength, love, knowledge and happiness.[28]

It remains for us to discuss Aitmatov's latest novella *Pegii pes, begushchii kraem moria* (The Skewbald Dog Running at the Edge of the Sea, 1977).[29] It provides us with an interesting confirmation of our view that not only is Aitmatov's poetic vision feminine in orientation, but that in order for him to avoid conflict within his creative process, he cannot *neglect* or abandon Woman who is at the very nerve center of his creative world.

This holds true in spite of the fact that *Skewbald Dog Running at the Edge of the Sea* seems at first sight to run counter to our view because Aitmatov here succeeds for the first time in his fiction in giving us a moving and *sustained* portrayal of a father and his son during a tragic sea hunting expedition where all, save the son, Kirisk, perish. But in our view, Aitmatov was able to draw this sustained relationship precisely because he did not try to abandon his Mother oriented universe (as he had attempted to do in the revised "The White Ship" and in "Early Cranes"). Though the immediate focus is on the father and son, there is essentially no shift away from his natural poetic perspective and therefore no possibility for poetic conflict. That Aitmatov had found a way back to the true poetic sources of his vision is suggested in several ways. For one, the frequent hostility in Aitmatov's fiction of the father to the mother is totally absent in this novella. Instead, a deep and loving bond unites Kirisk's parents whether they are together or apart. Even more significant is the fact — reminiscent of the Horned Deer-Mother — that the whole conception of the novella is bound up with the image of Fish-Woman who is the progenitor of Kirisk's tribe. As such she pervades the story from beginning to end. She is present symbolically and culturally in the waking thoughts of the protagonists and especially, figuratively, in the dreams of Kirisk's grandfather who is also in the boat. Her haunting and commanding presence therefore unifies the whole and creates a female world in which the characters live and die. More significant, still, is that the novella, metaphorically and creatively speaking, is actually about the *death* of the Father and the miraculous return of the Son to his Mother. Consequently, Aitmatov has, at least temporarily, healed the conflict within his creative vision which for a time threatened the future development of his art.

University of Toronto

NOTES

1. Constantin Ponomareff, *The Silenced Vision: An Essay in Modern European Fiction* (European University Papers: Series 18, Comparative Literature; vol. 20; Frankfurt am Main, 1979), pp. 26–38.

2. Chingiz Aitmatov, *Verbliuzhii glaz. Povesti i rasskazy* (Moscow, 1962), pp. 153–98. Henceforth cited as *Verbliuzhii glaz.*

3. Chingiz Aitmatov, *Dzhamilia. Povest'* (Moscow, 1959).

4. *Verbliuzhii glaz,* pp. 59–152.

5. Chingiz Aitmatov, *Povesti i rasskazy* (Moscow, 1963), pp. 114–211.

6. Chingiz Aitmatov, *Proshchai, Gul'sary!* (Moscow, 1967) and "Belyi parokhod (Posle skazki)," *Novyi mir,* no. 1, 1970, pp. 31–100.

7. See for instance the collection of articles and reviews written between 1962 and 1967, only one of which (by V. Stanislavleva) touches on the problem of poetic conflict in Aitmatov's work: K. Abdyldabekov, ed., *Chingiz Aitmatov (Stat'i i retsenzii o ego tvorchestve)* (Frunze, 1975). There is a host of other articles on Aitmatov, some of which make a positive contribution to an analysis of his work, but remain totally insensitive to the area of creative conflict. Some of the best of them are: G. Gachev, "V uskorennom dvizhenii literatury," *Voprosy literatury,* 1963, no. 3, pp. 78–93; B. Brainina, "Madonna v bomboubezhishche," *Druzhba narodov,* 1966, no. 3, pp. 246–56; I.M. Dubrovina, "Ideal khudozhnikov revoliutsii," *Filologicheskie nauki,* 1967, no. 5, pp. 47–57; R. Bikmukhametov, "Roman i literaturnyi protsess," *Voprosy literatury,* 1971, no. 9, pp. 4–16; A. Rashidov, "Nepokoi nastoiashchei zhizni (Lichnost' i tvorchestvo Chingiza Aitmatova)," *Zvezda vostoka,* 1973, no. 12, pp. 130–39; A. Gevorkian, "Tragicheskoe i ego khudozhestvennoe voploshchenie v povesti Ch. Aitmatova 'Belyi parokhod (Posle skazki)'," *Voprosy teorii i istorii literatury* (Samarkand University), vyp. 254 (1974), pp. 213–22. A few interesting books on Atimatov have come out, among them K. Asanaliev, *Otkrytie cheloveka sovremennosti. Za-*

metki o tvorchestve Chingiza Aitmatova (Frunze, 1968); M. Azizov, *Khudozhestvennye osobennosti iazyka povestei Ch. Aitmatova* (Makhachkala, 1971); a more Socialist Realist oriented book is Vl. Voronov, *Chingiz Aitmatov. Ocherk tvorchestva* (Moscow, 1976).

8. See *Verbliuzhii glaz,* pp. 106, 108, 112, 113–14, 118 for Il'ias' psychologically not very sound motivation in his betrayal of Asel for Kadicha.

9. Stanislavleva, "Dumy gor'kie i svetlye," (1966) *Chingiz Aitmatov (Stat'i i retsenzii o ego tvorchestve,* p. 239.

10. Ibid., pp. 239–40.

11. Chingiz Aitmatov, "Otvetstvennost' pered budushchim," *Voprosy literatury,* 1967, no. 9, p. 82.

12. L. Lebedeva, "Glavnoe v chelovecheskoi zhizni," *Druzhba narodov,* 1971, no. 1, p. 270.

13. See Taisa Napolova, "Natsional'naia samobytnost' pisatelia i dukhovnyi oblik geroia," *Volga,* 1972, no. 10, pp. 147–77, esp. pp. 165–66. See also Chingiz Aitmatov, *Posle skazki (Belyi parokhod)* (Frunze, 1971), esp. pp. 114–16 and compare it to the original version of "Belyi parokhod (Posle skazki)," Ibid., esp. pp. 99–100.

14. Abdyldabekov, ed., *Chingiz Aitmatov (Stat'i i retsenzii o ego tvorchestve).*

15. Chingiz Aitmatov, "Rannie zhuravli, Povest'," *Novyi mir,* 1975, no. 9, pp. 37–94.

16. See Ponomareff, *The Silenced Vision,* pp. 36–37. For a different viewpoint, see N. N. Shneidman, *Soviet Literature in the 1970's: Artistic Diversity and Ideological Conformity* (Toronto, Buffalo, London, 1979), pp. 39–41.

17. Chingiz Aitmatov, *Proshchai, Gul'sary! Povesti i rasskazy* (Frunze, 1967), pp. 557–68, esp. pp. 558–59, 562, 566, 568.

18. Ibid., pp. 547–56, esp. pp. 549, 552–53, 554, 556.

19. Ibid., pp. 526–46, here p. 526.

20. Ibid., p. 527.

21. Ibid., pp. 528, 529.

22. Ibid., p. 529.

23. Ibid., pp. 544–45.

24. Ibid., p. 546.

25. Ibid., pp. 499–525.

26. Ibid., pp. 510, 512, 516–17, 520–21.

27. Ibid., pp. 522–24.

28. Ibid., pp. 524–25.

29. See Chingiz Aitmatov, *Pegii pes, begushchii kraem moria. Rannie zhuravli. Povesti* (Moscow, 1977).

ANDREI BELYI'S THIRD SYMPHONY:
RETURN OR DEMENTED DEMISE?

RONALD E. PETERSON

Andrei Belyi's four "Symphonies," published from 1902 to 1908, have been the subject of scholarship and critical opinion; his Third Symphony, *The Return,* has been called the best of his four works in this "genre."[1] When Belyi wrote the Third Symphony in 1902, he drew heavily on his experiences as a student of the natural sciences at Moscow University. By the time *The Return* was published in November, 1904 (the title page has 1905), Belyi had begun to receive some attention and was on his way to a position as a leading Symbolist author and one of the major figures of early twentieth-century Russian literature.[2]

In 1922, when Belyi had assumed his influential position and had written much of his best work, he republished *The Return.* It was the only Symphony he reprinted after the revolution, and he valued it more highly than the other three as a work of literature.[3] Later, Belyi commented on the biographical context of the Third Symphony in his memoirs. He was nearing the end of his studies, simultaneously working "over a Bunsen burner and on *The Return,* begun in a histological teashop."[4] Describing the conditions under which he labored, he says: "I used to escape to a teashop and write *The Return* in a corner (on scraps of paper)."[5] In the work he satirizes the university and his professors, attacks the notion of positivism, and paints a gloomy, oppressive picture of his milieu at that time. He later summarized this aspect of the Third Symphony: "I fought with disheveled liberalism . . . with the dust of scientific cellars."[6]

There has been some disagreement about the work's story line, particularly in regard to what ultimately happens to the hero. Most readers would agree with the view advanced by Dmitrij

Tschižewskij that the first section of the book describes an idyll
on another planet, though some see the existence there as pre-
natal and genuine (Tschižewskij, R.V. Ivanov-Razumnik), and
others see it as a dream (G. Janecek).[7] No one would argue with
the notion that the middle section depicts the hero's daily life,
which is unpleasant in many ways. At the end, however, some
have written that the hero dies (Janecek), but others have claimed
that he returns to an original form of life (A. Kovač), that he
goes back to his "cosmic homeland" (K. Mochul'skii) or "native
cosmos," after experiencing his "earthly sufferings" (Z. Yurieff),
and that the Third Symphony is an example of rebirth through
death (S. Cioran).[8]

Because there are different interpretations of precisely what
goes on in the book's three parts, this question requires special
attention and a reasoned, reliable interpretation. One crucial
factor in arriving at this interpretation is the question of the protagonist's insanity. Khandrikov, the hero, feels threatened by
ominous, yet identifiable forces, which he seeks to evade. The
very real presence of these "malign spirits" could tend to make
the reader feel that perhaps Khandrikov's grasp on reality is not
so tenuous.[9] It is clear, however, from Belyi's autobiographical
letter to R.V. Ivanov-Razumnik in 1927, that the author's own
interpretation strongly favors the view that Khandrikov is insane.[10] As is always the case with Belyi's writings, one must be
cautious when using his statements. The view of the present author, nevertheless, is that Khandrikov's fears (though grounded
in reality) are exaggerated to the point of paranoia and a complete lack of common sense.

In addition, one very salient stylistic feature, its "symphonic"
structure, is a decisive factor in interpreting the work. From the
point of view of music, *The Return* can be said to have three
movements, recurring leitmotifs, and a final recapitulation of
the main theme. It is lyrical and has a good deal of repetition,
much like a musical composition, though Belyi changed the ge-
neric subtitle when he republished it in 1922, from *Symphony*
to *Novel (Povest')*.[11]

The Return has been called a Nietzschean tale; indeed, there
is a quite palpable influence of Nietzsche's *Also sprach Zara-*

thustra on Belyi's Symphony, not only in terms of theme (e.g., Eternal Recurrence), but also in the style. Belyi confessed his admiration for Nietzsche, "whose style resounded throughout my entire soul," in his memoirs: "From the autumn of 1899 I live Nietzsche — I give myself wholly to him — to his intimate glances, his phrases, his style, his syllables."[12] Belyi adapted Nietzsche's short paragraphs and brief chapters for *The Return,* and a good case has been made for his choosing the "symphonic" form because the German philosopher felt that his *Zarathustra* belonged under that rubric.[13]

The most important formal feature of the work, however, is the interplay of the two levels (*dva plana*) and the very obvious parallelisms. The transition from visions and dreams at a "higher" level of consciousness down to reality, sometimes in comic terms, as when, in Part II, Khandrikov, who has "evaporated" to another point in space is brought back when the flask he is heating breaks, is common for Belyi's works, even apart from *The Return.* A very good illustration of the two levels and of parallelism is central to an understanding of the work: at the beginning of Part II the hero wakes up from a dream about the sea; he hears the sound of the sea (he thinks), and then realizes that the sound is being made by the hiss of a samovar boiling water for his morning tea.

In the first part of the book Khandrikov dreams about a child who plays on the seashore of a different planet; he plays with his friend, a crab, and sometimes feels threatened by a sea serpent. He enjoys the tutelage and protection of a quite special old man, who gives him comfort but also warns him of the dangers to come. He hears a prophetic tale told by a man with green eyes, who wears a cap and brown rags, called the Tsar-Wind. The tale that the child hears is about someone named Khandrikov.

At the beginning of the second part, Belyi stresses again and again that his hero has awakened from a dream and strongly implies that the dream *is* Part I. He reinforces this notion later by depicting Khandrikov having a very similar dream about walking along a seashore with a protective, quite special old man (pp. 69–70). In Part II, Evgenii Khandrikov, a candidate for the Master's degree in chemistry at Moscow University, drinks

with a friend who resembles a crab, feels threatened by a train
that reminds him of a serpent, and is protected by a quite special
old man, the psychiatrist Dr. Orlov. Khandrikov also fears a
man wearing a cap and brown rags, with green eyes, a docent
in chemistry called Tsenkh. Khandrikov finally decides to retreat
to Dr. Orlov's sanatorium for the mentally ill, ostensibly to escape from Tsenkh.

Khandrikov's actions after the defense of his master's thesis,
when he attacks and ridicules not only positivism and science
but also Tsenkh personally, help to increase the feeling of enmity
between these two individuals. Previously Khandrikov had only
disliked Tsenkh, especially because of the latter's influential position at the University, but after "throwing the gauntlet at Tsenkh"
(p. 80) in a drunken frenzy he feels forced to flee quickly to Or-
lovka, the site of Dr. Orlov's sanatorium.

It is clear in Part III, however, that Khandrikov really belongs
in a mental institution. Here the action centers on his relationship with Dr. Orlov, who ultimately leaves him in much the same
way that the old man in Part I left the child. After this departure, Khandrikov develops the notion that he will be able to return to his imagined existence as a child by diving into a lake
and replacing his reflection, which seems like a child to him
(pp. 119–20). Khandrikov's insanity here is clearly a means of
escaping his everyday life, and this concept of escape can also
be applied to his dreams. During his waking hours Khandrikov
maintains "the hope that *everything around* him is a *dream*"
(p. 46).

At the end of Part III, Khandrikov plunges into the embrace
of his reflection (also a favorite image in Belyi's short prose).
Belyi describes Khandrikov choking and has a sea mew fly over-
head, "laughing at the impossible" (p. 123). There is, however,
what may appear to be a return to a "universal, ultimate truth."[14]
After Khandrikov's dive there is an additional chapter that tells
of a child being greeted by an old man, who proclaims this to
be the final return. This last little chapter has a certain amount
of ambiguity, but it seems clear that this scene is Khandrikov's
last insane vision as he is drowning. Once again Belyi is quite
unequivocal about this point in his letter to Ivanov-Razumnik

when he says that "Khandrikov drowns."[15]

One knowledgeable scholar, B.V. Mikhailovskii, has pointed to the parallelisms here: "*The Return* is distinctive because of its strong parallelism of images and situations on two contrasting levels." He has, uncharacteristically, concluded that Khandrikov's " 'holy madness' frees the hero from the power of time and space and opens the way to the return to the spirit, to the 'world of ideas'."[16] The parallelisms, in fact, point to the very opposite — that Khandrikov drowns and that there is no escape to an idealized life on another world.

In general, Belyi was very much drawn to repetition in his early prose and poetry, especially the exact repetition of epithets, sometimes even with italics, so that the reader could not miss the connection. In addition to the main parallels mentioned above, there are also examples of verbatim recurrences of perhaps less central, but nevertheless indicative, events and situations that reinforce the view that the parallels are indeed there for a purpose.

That purpose is to show that Part I is a dream of Khandrikov's which he apparently continues night after night: "The dream had ended . . . It left until the following night" (p. 45). This dream includes people and events from his life as a graduate student, some of his fears, and many of his wishes, especially for a protective figure. Part II shows Khandrikov dissatisfied and unhappy with his real life, and the root of his name, *khandra,* meaning "doldrums" or "melancholy," is significant. At the end of Part III, the now seriously ill Khandrikov commits suicide by leaping from a boat, obsessed by the constant vision of another life. Thus there will be no eternal repetitions, only the last return, the final conclusion of a life, Khandrikov's demented demise.

This reading of the Third Symphony is in fact quite consistent with views found in some of Belyi's early stories (e.g., "The Bush," "Adam") and poetry, and especially his first published work, the *Second Symphony, Dramatic* (Moscow, 1902). As T.Iu. Khmel'nitskaia has pointed out, it is characteristic for Belyi to combine inspired mysticism with merciless satire, and a good example of this characteristic is the Second Symphony, where Belyi makes fun of himself, of the people he associated with and revered, and of their mystical views, which he shared.[17] His Third Symphony is rather more somber than the Second, partly because of the death of Nikolai V. Bugaev, Belyi's father, in 1903; insanity and irony predominate instead. But because Belyi is able to use parody and satire on subjects dear to him, particularly in the early part of his career, this does not mean that he was dissatisfied with Symbolism as a literary movement or a world view. Belyi was a complex person, and some of his complexities are apparent in this clearly Symbolist book; a more thorough familiarity with this writer and his works cannot but help the reader to understand better the irony of *The Return,* both in the title and in the book itself.

Occidental College

NOTES

1. Valerii Briusov, "Andrei Belyi. Vozvrat. Tret'ia simfoniia," *Vesy,* 1, no. 12 (1904), p. 59; Anton Kovač, *Andrej Belyj: The "Symphonies" (1899-1908)* (Bern: Verlag Peter Lang, 1976), p. 210.

2. Andrei Belyi, *Vozvrat. III Simfoniia* (Moscow, 1905; the November, 1904, release date is from B.A. Bialik, ed., *Istoriia russkoi literatury kontsa XIX-nachala XX veka* (Moscow, 1971), vol. 2, p. 434.

3. Andrei Belyi, "Lettre autobiographique à Ivanov-Razumnik," published by Georges Nivat in *Cahiers du Monde Russe et Soviétique,* vol. 15, nos. 1-2 (1974), p. 55.

4. Andrei Belyi, *Na rubezhe dvukh stoletii* (Moscow and Leningrad, 1930), p. 403.

5. *Na rubezhe,* p. 444.

6. Andrei Belyi, *nachalo veka* (Moscow and Leningrad, 1933), p. 197.

7. Dmitrij Tschiževskij, "Andrej Belyjs Symphonien," in Andrej Belyj, *Četyre simfonii* (Munich: Wilhelm Fink Verlag, 1971), pp. xviii-xix; Razumnik V. Ivanov-Razumnik, *Vershiny* (Petrograd, 1923), p. 44; Gerald Janecek, Introduction to *Andrey Bely: A Critical Review,* ed., Gerald Janecek (Lexington, Ky: Univ. of Kentucky Press, 1978), p. 13.

8. Janecek, p. 13; Kovač, p. 176; Konstantin Mochul'skii, *Andrei Belyi* (Paris: YMCA-Press, 1955), p. 41; Zoya Yurieff, "Odezhda i materiia v tsikle simfonii Andreia Belogo," in *Andrey Bely Centenary Papers,* ed., Boris Christa (Amsterdam: Verlag Adolf M. Hakkert, 1980), p. 126; Samuel Cioran, *The Apocalyptic Symbolism of Andrej Belyj* (The Hague:

Mouton, 1973), p. 83.

9. Roger Keys, "Andrey Bely and the Development of Russian Fiction, 1900–1914" (unpublished essay).

10. Belyi, "Lettre autobiographique," p. 63.

11. Andrei Belyi, *Vozvrat. Povest'* (Berlin, 1922).

12. Belyi, *Na rubezhe,* pp. 468, 465.

13. Lena Szilard, "O vliianii ritmiki prozy F. Nietzsche na ritmiku prozy A. Belogo," *Studia Slavica Academiae Scientiarum Hungaricae,* vol. 19 (1973), p. 308.

14. Briusov, "Vozvrat," p. 60.

15. Belyi, "Lettre autobiographique," p. 56.

16. B.V. Mikhailovskii, "Symvolizm," in *Istoriia russkoi literatury kontsa XIX-nachala XX veka,* ed., B.A. Bialik (Moscow, 1971), vol. 2, pp. 257–58.

17. Tamara Iu. Khmel'nitskaia, "Poeziia Andreia Belogo," in Andrei Belyi, *Stikhotvoreniia i poemy* (Moscow and Leningrad, 1966), pp. 14–15. For more on irony and insanity in Belyi's stories, see Ronald E. Peterson, *Andrei Bely's Short Prose* (Birmingham: Birmingham Slavonic Monographs, 1980), p. 34, 39–40, 43, 51–52, and especially 54–59.

ANDREI BELYI'S THIRD SYMPHONY: MAJOR PARALLELISMS

Part I	Part II	Part III
Crab, fat comrade	Crab, fat physicist	
Old man, *quite special*, eyes like abysses, stooped shoulders	Old man, Dr. Orlov, *quite special*, eyes like abysses, stooped shoulders	Dr. Orlov and old man from Part I
Serpent, sea monster	Serpent, train resembles one	
Tsar-Wind, man wearing a cap and brown rags, with green eyes and a wolf's beard, insane	Tsenkh, man wearing a cap and brown rags, with green eyes and a wolf's beard, traces of former insanity	Tsenkh comes to visit Khandrikov
Child told about Khandrikov	Khandrikov is like a child with an overgrown beard	Khandrikov's reflection seems to be a child
Eagle, feathered man	Eagle, feathered man in modern clothes	
Sea, sound of sea and water	Sea, sound of sea is made by a samovar, water in the public baths	Lake by the sanatorium

ANDREI BELYI'S THIRD SYMPHONY: LESSER PARALLELISMS

Part I	Part II	Part III
Grotto of thoughts	Khandrikov's room and his laboratory resemble grottoes	
Hercules, constellation	Hercules, a picture on boxes	Hercules, constellation
Centaur in the sky	Professors resemble centaurs	Vision of professors as centaurs
Emblem of immutable Eternity on necklace	Emblem of immutable Eternity on a picture of Hercules attached to button of Orlov's coat	
Wreath of red roses		Wreath of white roses
White bird laughs at the impossible		Sea mew laughs at the impossible
Starfish on the seabed	Starfish on the floor is Khandrikov's son	
Citizen of the sea, bald, dives into water, creating a ruby whirlpool	An old man in the public baths dives into a pool, creating a ruby whirlpool	Bald attorney dives into the lake, creating a ruby whirlpool

OBERON'S MAGIC HORN:

THE LATER WORKS OF VALENTIN KATAEV

ROBERT RUSSELL

I

The transformation of Valentin Kataev from Soviet classic and author of such conventional Socialist Realist novels as *Vremia, vpered!* and *Za vlast' Sovetov* into the author of the modernistic *Sviatoi kolodets* (1966) and *Trava zabven'ia* (1967) and founder of a new literary school called "mauvisme" has been frequently discussed in critical literature.[1] While some critics of the "new" Kataev who emerged in the 1960s welcomed this change in manner of writing, others saw it as merely a nod in the direction of literary fashion.[2] By his work of the 1970s, however, Kataev has demonstrated that the change of direction which began in 1964 with the publication of *Malen'kaia zheleznaia dver' v stene* and first reached the consciousness of the wider reading public with the more ambitious *Sviatoi kolodets,* was not a superficial or temporary phase of his career but an important stage in his development. The works of the 1970s continue to reveal those features which surprised and disconcerted some critics of the works of the 1960s. Kataev has been a "mauviste" now for over fifteen years, and, however it is assessed, his later work can not simply be dismissed as a passing phase in the career of a man who has frequently changed his manner of writing to suit the prevailing literary fashion. His commitment to it is too prolonged and intense for that. The purpose of this paper is to examine the principal features of Kataev's prose of the 1970s and, where appropriate, to make comparisons with the works of the previous decade.

II

In the 1950s Kataev published a number of articles about the creative process which contain the theoretical seeds of the style of writing which he was later to practice and to name "mauvisme." These articles concentrate on four main points, all of which are prominent in the works of the 1960s and 1970s, namely: the importance of formal innovation; the role of detail; the musicality of prose; and the centrality to all literature of the author's personality. It is the last of these points, made in articles of 1953 and 1954, which proves to be the keystone of Kataev's later work. Creative individuality is described as "the fundamental basis determining the value of any type of conscious human activity, especially artistic."[3] More specific is the following paragraph, in which Kataev claims for the artist the right to interpret the world around him in the light of his own personality rather than in a general way that would be the same for everyone:

> But the artist's consciousness must not be like a mirror, reflecting in the same way once and for all. The artist's consciousness must not only reflect, but also creatively transform the world. A writer bereft of imagination and fantasy ceases to be a true artist.[4]

It is, of course, a truism that the personality of the author and his vision of the world determine the nature of a literary work, but it must be remembered that in the early 1950s, when Kataev wrote the articles containing these comments, Soviet literature was just beginning to emerge from a long period when an obvious display of a writer's subjectivity was not acceptable. So insistently does Kataev return to the theme of the centrality of the author's personality at this time that it clearly emerges as a plea for greater freedom of expression in literature.[5] By the time he put these ideas into practice, beginning with *Malen'kaia zheleznaia dver' v stene* and *Sviatoi kolodets,* the stultifying uniformity of Socialist Realism had crumbled considerably, and to some he appeared — in his insistence on his right to view the world in his own way and to place his own personality at the center of his creative work — to be pushing at an open door.[6]

The central theme of Kataev's work of the 1960s and 1970s is, then, the author himself, and in particular an exploration of the many thousands of factors, both personal and suprapersonal, which have gone into the making and development of Kataev as he is today. Taken as a cycle, his works since 1966 can be seen as a Proustian search for time past — the recreation in fragments, by means of memory and imagination, of the author's unique life.

Although Kataev's later works are frequently termed "memoirs," this is a description which he himself rejects, as in the following typical extract:

> In general I can not guarantee that the details in this work are correct. I beg the readers not to take my work as memoirs. I can not stand memoirs. I repeat: it is a free flight of my fantasy based on real events which may not have been entirely accurately preserved in my memory.[7]

In an interview given shortly after the publication of "Almaznyi moi venets" Kataev reaffirmed the point that factual accuracy was less important to him than the creative element deriving from his own personality:

> Working on "Almaznyi moi venets" I, as it were, refracted all the events and people through the crystal of my soul. I did not seek to achieve an accurate, photographic depiction. Some of it I made up.[8]

While recognizing that much of Kataev's later work can not be taken as purely factual, several critics have expressed or implied disappointment at his subjective approach.[9] It was never Kataev's intention, however, to limit himself to a factual account. In these intensely personal works, as one critic has put it: "the author is more interested in the psychological than the factographical aspect of existence."[10] His memory constantly interacts with his imagination to form that "magic crystal" which so fascinates him. (Pushkin, incidentally, is never far from Kataev's thoughts in his recent works. The reference to a magic crystal and the title of "Almaznyi moi venets" — *Evgenii Onegin* and *Boris Godunov* respectively — are merely two of the more obvious borrowings.) Using his memory of events and people as a starting point and allowing himself — as he puts it — "to be inspired by imagination and feeling,"[11] Kataev recreates rather than recalling, and always stresses the centrality of his own personality in his work. In *Malen'kaia zheleznaia dver' v stene,* his tale about Lenin, for example, he ascribes to his hero certain experiences and feelings which belong properly to himself, thereby retaining his central position in the tale, even in the presence of a fictionalized Lenin:

> How is it that I can so clearly imagine this typical Ile-de-France landscape in the summer of 1911; the hot breeze, the silky gleam of the clover field, the lilac-colored wrappers from Suchard Swiss chocolate lying discarded in the grass? . . . Probably because at that time almost everyone was fascinated by flying, and I myself, as a fourteen-year-old boy, would lie breathless with excitement among the wormwood trying to catch the magic moment when the miracle of flight would take place before my eyes.[12]

Here memory and imagination act together to form the image. It is a method that Kataev was to use more and more frequently in subsequent works. In *Razbitaia zhizn', ili Volshebnyi rog Oberona* (1972) he " 'creates' his childhood from the age of two,"[13] — embellishing and imagining rather than limiting himself to what he can recall; in *Kladbishche v Skulianakh* (1975) he "becomes" his own ancestors; in "Almaznyi moi venets" he emulates his own character — the mad Parisian sculptor Brunswick — and creates likenesses of his own great contemporaries, even giving them pseudonyms.[14] In all cases what is central is the creative power of the artist — Kataev himself.

III

We have seen, then, how Kataev's recent work has been self-orientated, its aim being to illustrate and explore the uniqueness of the author's existence. This principal theme of the formation of a unique individual gives rise to several ideas in the works of the 1960s and 1970s which, taken together, could be said to form the philosophical undercurrent of Kataev's work. With the exception of one or two short stories of the 1920s, Kataev's earlier work had not been noted for its treatment of philosophical questions, but in the last two decades metaphysical and biological considerations have come to play an important part. To a large extent Kataev's reflections on heredity, time, death, and the human soul are interrelated, and must of neccessity be treated together here.

Given his primary theme, it is scarcely surprising that Kataev should be keenly interested in genetics and heredity. Throughout his career he has frequently referred in his novels and short stories to inherited characteristics, particularly in the various fictional father/son relationships which are clearly based on his own life and that of his father. (One thinks here especially of the story *Otets*, published in 1928, and the tetralogy *Volny Chernogo moria*, 1936–61.) This subject is most extensively covered, however, in two works of the 1970s — *Razbitaia zhizn'* and *Kladbishche v Skulianakh*. In the latter work, on finding a journal kept by his grandfather, Kataev is struck by the similarity of the handwriting to his own:

> It is astonishing that at one time I too suddenly began to write this letter of the alphabet in the same way. Probably grandfather's genes were beginning to make themselves felt in me, just as surely as they had once been passed on in their turn to grandfather from great-grandfather.[15]

For the most part *Kladbishche v Skulianakh* deals with Kataev's maternal ancestors, the military family Bachei. But since their genes are responsible for only part of his character, he devotes some attention also to the other side of the family, the clerical Kataevs from Viatka:

> It ought not to be forgotten that I am a Bachei only on my mother's side. On my father's side I come from a Viatka clerical family. Thus, in me in a strange way north and south unite, as do Viatka and Skuliany, military and spiritual. . . . All of this . . . combines in me and has made an impression on my whole character.[16]

In leafing through his grandfather's and great-grandfather's papers Kataev is forced to consider the arbitrariness of his own existence at a given time and place. Had his grandfather been killed before his wedding (as was almost the case) "there would have been no grandfather, no grandmother, no mother, no me, no younger brother Zhenia in this wonderful, mysterious, unknowable world. I can not imagine this."[17]

The role of heredity and the chance combination of genes in producing the unique individual leads Kataev to a much closer identification than normal with his ancestors. Because of his view that time does not necessarily flow constantly in one direction from past to future, he feels strongly the link between generations, to the extent of "becoming" his grandfather and great-grandfather. The work opens with the surprising sentence: "I died of cholera on the banks of the River Prut in Skuliany, a historic place."[18] And it contains this clear statement on the transformation of one person into another, living at a completely different historical period: "Who is the grandson and who the grandfather? I turned into him and he into me and we both became some sort of single creature."[19]

If circumstances had so decreed, the unique individual who is the author might not have been born; similarly, at several points in his lifetime his existence might have been extinguished prematurely. In other words, the primary question of the existence of the unique individual is focused to a large extent on the nature of death, which is a prominent theme in all of Kataev's later works.[20] In *Trava zabven'ia* the young poet who is Kataev's autobiographical hero is nearly killed by bandits during the Civil War. Any one of the bullets which he can hear whistling past him could have "hit his head, shattering it completely and destroying irrevocably that divine world of love, beauty, and poetry which was what was known as the unique, priceless human life of Pchelkin."[21] Similarly, the young boy in *Razbitaia zhizn'* (another autobiographical hero) almost dies of scarlet fever, and later comes close to pulling a pan of boiling fat onto himself.

Like Iurii Olesha in *Ni dnia bez strochki* (whose influence on Kataev will be examined more extensively later in this paper), Kataev comes increasingly in old age to consider his own impending death and the possibilities of overcoming it. Faced with the almost weekly announcements of the deaths of his contemporaries Olesha nevertheless writes:

> Still I have an absolute conviction that I shall not die. Despite the fact that all around me people are dying—many, many people, young as well as my contemporaries—despite the fact that I am old, I do not for a moment admit the possibility that I will die.

> Perhaps I will not die? Perhaps all this—including life and death—
> exists in my imagination? Perhaps I am stretched out and infinite;
> perhaps I am the universe?[22]

The desperate search for an answer to the inevitability of death
strikes a pathetic note in this extract from Olesha. Kataev, too,
returns time and again to the theme of death, and, like Olesha,
he appears in places to deny its existence. Of course, he does
not doubt that he will die — the physical signs of aging (frequently
mentioned) are a constant reminder of his mortality. But that his
essence will irrevocably vanish at the point of death is unaccept-
able. So it is that Kataev has evolved a view of the human soul
which is certainly nonmaterialistic, and which resembles the age-
old tradition in Western philosophy and religion that "the 'true'
self, or soul, is a substance; that is, an entity separate and distinct from the changing body."[23] Kataev's conception of immortality appears now to be based less on the power of art to stop
time and allow the artist to live on after death through his work
(although his view can be seen in the works of the 1960s)[24] than
on a belief in the separateness and immortality of the human essence — the soul.

The young hero of *Razbitaia zhizn'* has a strange fainting fit
which the mature author now sees as an occasion on which his
soul left his body for a short while.[25] The soul of the narrator of
Sviatoi kolodets frequently leaves his body and becomes incar-
nated in other people and objects. While this particular example
(and others in "Kubik," the tale of 1969) may seem to be merely
a striking if rather pretentious way of conveying to the reader
the act of artistic depiction, the recurrence of the idea in *Kladbishche v Skulianakh* makes it clear that by the 1970s at any rate
the notion of an independent and immortal soul forms part of
Kataev's philosophy.

Indivisible from this concept of the soul is Kataev's view of
time as something which does not move inexorably onwards like
a river, but which can move backwards:

> Like any living or nonliving form of existence, I have neither a
> beginning nor an end. Like everything in nature I am eternal.[26]
>
> My human consciousness had long since been extinguished, but

it had been replaced by a new, eternal, inexplicable and inextinguishable consciousness which seemed immobile but at the same time capable of grasping the whole world of existence, the whole of its eternal movement. In it, in this strange nonhuman consciousness was contained the eternal past, the present, and the eternal future. In this world I continued my incomparable eternal existence.[27]

Sometimes I even think that the soul of my great-grandfather has settled in me and that all this happened to me.[28]

In the light of these reflections about the soul and reincarnation, Kataev's many comments on the nature of time, scattered throughout almost all of his recent works, must be seen as more than a device to justify the modernistic nature of his prose style. The concept of time held in these works is necessary to sustain Kataev's view of the soul. Time is not seen as an arrow pointing in the direction of death and ending when the target is reached. With a frequency which threatens to become tiresome the reader is reminded in work after work of Kataev's conviction that the "stream" and "arrow" metaphors normally used to conceive of time are incorrect, and that time does not flow constantly in one direction. In the modernist tradition of Proust, Joyce and Thomas Wolfe, and perhaps under the more direct influence of Olesha, Kataev emphasizes the dependence of time on memory. His "memoirs" of the 1960s and 1970s (I use the quotation marks because of Kataev's own rejection of the term) differ from those of, say, Ehrenburg and Pasternak in that historical time is almost entirely absent, and replaced by subjective time.[29] Kataev's concern is not so much to capture the feel of the age as to reconstruct, in a Proustian way, his self. In this task of reconstruction memory has a creative rather than a passive role to play. The one hundred and twenty or so episodes in *Razbitaia zhizn'* are not arranged chronologically. As Kataev said of this work while it was being written: "One story tells of a twelve-year-old boy, the next of a three-year-old child. And they are all me. I remember, and my memory structures the narrative."[30]

When the work referred to in this quotation was eventually published it bore the title *Razbitaia zhizn'*, literally *A Broken life*. In its English translation, though, the work bears the title *A Mo-*

saic of life, a change for which there is some justification, since
at one point Kataev does introduce the mosaic image:

> A sort of broken life, broken not morally, but "into pieces"
> physically, as a result of the eternal law of destruction and cre-
> ation. Perhaps it is more like the Byzantine mosaics which I saw
> many years later in Kiev and Constantinople. . . . Perhaps the
> heavy, multicolored board of my life, with all its picturesque de-
> tails, was laid out from something similar to the fragmented cubes
> of a sort of glittering smalt, turned first of all by someone into
> separate multicolored glass-like cubes, then collected into one
> picture, and finally scattered by time, losing form but not color,
> only to be turned again into one beautiful whole.[31]

The fragmentary nature of the work (and of other recent works
by Kataev) reflects a modern conception of time and simultaneously an attempt to reconstitute — as in a mosaic — the essential self from the fragments. In considering the conception of time
in modern literature Hans Meyerhoff has written:

> ["Stream of consciousness" or "free association"] is itself a strik-
> ing expression of the fragmentization of time in the consciousness
> of modern man; on the other hand, it is an attempt to overcome
> this fragmentization by showing that even this chaotic stream of
> time and experience contains certain qualities of duration, inter-
> penetration, continuity, and unity in terms of which some concept
> of the self may be saved.[32]

Significantly, the title of Kataev's work about his childhood has
two parts: the fragmentization is emphasized by the first part —
Razbitaia zhizn' — whereas the reconstitution into a work of art
("only to be turned again into one beautiful whole") is suggested
by the second part of the title: *Volshebnyi rog Oberona.*[33] At one
point Kataev explains that as a very young boy he was given a
book with the title *Oberon's Magic Horn* and that the particular
combination of words in this title struck a chord in him "thereby, perhaps, awakening the poet in me."[34] So, then, Oberon's
magic horn is a symbol for art. A few pages later Kataev explicitly links this term with the other part of the title — *Razbitaia
zhizn':*

> If these are all merely fragments from the picture of my life, dis-

rupted by time, then perhaps Oberon's horn possesses the magic power not only of summoning elves but also of uniting these fragments, separated and scattered without order, into one integrated beautiful whole, like a Byzantine mosaic?[35]

Kataev's work of the 1970s is, then, a highly personal quest for self, a Proustian search for lost time in which creative memory and imagination reconstitute the fragments of the past into a beautiful mosaic. In the absence of historical time and the prevalence of a nonmaterialist philosophy Kataev's later work is unusual in the corpus of modern Soviet literature.

IV

Several times in the course of this paper the name of Iurii Olesha has been mentioned in connection with Kataev's later work. Olesha was, of course, a close friend of Kataev's for many years, although they were estranged in the latter years of Olesha's life,[36] and Kataev has recently written of their friendship:

> Now one of us is eighty years old and the other is no longer in this world. He has been transformed into a legend. But a part of his soul is forever joined with mine. We were fated to become the closest of friends—closer than brothers. . . .[37]

The publication in 1965 of a posthumous collection of fragments by Olesha to which the compilers gave the title *Ni dnia bez strochki* was an event of considerable importance in Soviet literature. Its influence can still be felt very strongly in Kataev's work. It must be pointed out, however, that Kataev is not *imitating* Olesha; his articles of the 1950s and his tale of 1964 *Malen'kaia zheleznaia dver' v stene* show that he was working independently towards a similar manner. But the publication of *Ni dnia bez strochki* undoubtedly acted as a strong stimulus to the development of Kataev's later prose.

Olesha's work is fragmentary, yet, as critics have frequently pointed out, the fragments are, for the most part, rounded and polished, self-contained pieces of prose which fit together to form what Olesha himself describes as "a book with a subject, and a very interesting one at that."[38] There seems little doubt that, particularly in *Razbitaia zhizn'* and "Almaznyi moi venets," Kataev has learned from Olesha how to build a work up from rounded and polished fragments. (It is worth noting the author himself has referred to the episodes of *Razbitaia zhizn'* not as fragments, but as *rasskazy* and *novelly*.)[39]

Like Olesha, Kataev is concerned to recapture the physical experience of his childhood. Olesha's words "these notes are an attempt to restore my life . . . sensually" could equally apply to Kataev's vivid and sensual recollection of his early years.[40] Another feature of Kataev's later prose which may well have developed under the influence of *Ni dnia bez strochki* is the author's awareness of two distinct personas, his boyhood self and himself now, and his attempts to distinguish between the perceptions of these two figures. Throughout *Ni dnia bez strochki* Olesha takes care to separate his boyhood self (the protagonist of many of the episodes) from the mature adult who looks back and reflects after a lifetime of experience. The distinction is nowhere better illustrated than in the following extract, describing how the young Olesha's grandmother once took him to an examination hall where he was to sit a school entrance examination:

> It was not the writer [*literator*] whom grandmother took, but a little boy like all the others. He did not see all those things that the writer now remembers. Perhaps those things did not exist. And yet they *did* exist.[41]

Kataev similarly distinguishes carefully between the perception of his autobiographical hero (himself at an earlier stage) and the mature author, recalling and recreating. In *Trava zabven'ia* and "Kubik" he goes so far as to separate the autobiographical hero off from the mature author by giving the former a different name: Riurik Pchelkin. The interplay between the language and perception of the naïve young protagonist and those of the masterly old author form an important part of the texture of Kataev's recent prose.[42]

Finally, Olesha's last work undoubtedly influenced Kataev in its use of an open authorial position.[43] In his review of Olesha's work Kataev drew particular attention to this device, which he credited Olesha with inventing:

> Usually the process of the conception and construction of an artistic image takes place in secret, in the depths of consciousness. The reader only receives the results of this most complex and tortuous work of memory and imagination. Olesha has brought this process out of the secret depths of his consciousness and has made it — before the reader's very eyes — the subject of art, its very content. It would appear that before Olesha no one did this. It is his discovery. . . . The reader sees the miracle of the birth of a literary masterpiece.[44]

Examples of the open authorial position can be found in almost all of Kataev's recent works. The reader appears to be given access to the creative laboratory of the author's mind — to see for himself the raw material from which the finished work of art is made. In particular the reader is privy to the author's musings on the possible titles of the genre of the work he is writing: "Perhaps A Broken Life? Smalt? . . ."[45] *Trava zabven'ia,* "Kubik," and "Almaznyi moi venets" all begin with three dots, as if the work were merely a section of the author's thought stream caught on paper. Many of the paragraphs of these and other recent works begin and end in the same way, with three dots. The unfettered quality of Kataev's prose, to which the open authorial position contributes greatly, is to a large extent illusory, for the extracts are carefully crafted and the works develop in a way which is far from haphazard. Yet the open authorial position is more than a mere literary device; it is not just a means of endowing the works with that unfettered quality that distinguishes them. The open authorial position forms part of Kataev's principal theme: the very form of the works reveals their inward focus, their exploration of the unique individual who is the author.

This account of Valentin Kataev's later work would remain one-sided if it concentrated entirely on philosophical questions and on some of the technical aspects of "mauvisme." For Kataev epitomises a philosophical and ideological dualism which is typical of a number of nondissident Soviet intellectuals.[46] Despite all the similarities between his later prose and the work of Western writers and filmmakers, despite the quasi-religious nature of his philosophy, Kataev remains a committed Soviet artist who has written "I am a son of the Revolution. Perhaps a bad

son, but a son nevertheless."[47] To some extent each of his later
works contains an avowal of his loyalty not only to his native
land ("thrice-blessed land of my soul")[48] but also to its political
system. Kataev joined the Communist Party in 1958, and there
is little reason to doubt the sincerity of his ideological convictions. A recurrent theme in Kataev's work since 1966 has been
the relationship between the intelligentsia and the Revolution,[49]
and in particular the dilemma facing intellectuals at the time of
the Revolution: whether to support the Bolsheviks or emigrate.
In *Sviatoi kolodets* the narrator meets in America an elderly Russian widow whom he had loved before the Revolution, when they
were both very young. Following the death of her husband, this
émigré, who deliberately cut herself off from her native land, is
left entirely alone. Similarly, in *Trava zabven'ia* there is a strong
suggestion that Bunin's life in emigration was less happy and
successful than it would have been had he remained in the Soviet
Union at the end of the Civil War. (This suggestion is, at the
very least, naïve. Given Bunin's character and convictions, Kataev must be aware of what his fate would almost certainly have
been had he remained.) As a Soviet critic said in 1974: "In everything that Kataev has written in the last decade, up to and including the recent story 'Violet,' there is the theme of the inter-
dependence of the past and the present."[50] The decision taken
many years earlier to remain in Russia after the Revolution and
the later decision to became a *Soviet* writer are implicitly examined by Kataev in the contrast between his own fate and those
of the émigrés who figure in his works.

However, it is the contrast between Kataev's fate and that of
many of his contemporaries who remained in the Soviet Union,
such as Mandel'shtam and Babel', which has incensed several for-
iegn critics and has brought forth some very harsh words about
Kataev's morality. The author of a review of "Almaznyi moi
venets," for example, accuses him of writing the work with the
blood of his great contemporaries.[51] Ever since the appearance
of *Sviatoi kolodets* the controversy over Kataev's morality has
divided critics who are unanimous in their praise for his technical
mastery.[52]

Particularly important in this regard is the story *Fialka* (1973), which was turned into a play and produced on television.[53] Like the Klavdia Zaremba strand of *Trava zabven'is,* "Fialka" is a story of ideological commitment and treachery. The action of the story takes place in a retirement home for senior Party officials. The home's oldest and most respected inmate — Ekaterina Gerasimovna Novoselova, whose underground nickname was "Violet" — is visited by her former husband who wishes to see her again before his imminent death. Many years earlier she had helped him through college and nominated him for Party membership, and then, when he had begun to make a career as a Stalinist administrator, he became infatuated with a younger woman, denounced his wife to the secret police, and married the beautiful but heartless social climber. Now, mortally ill, he comes to ask his first wife's forgiveness. She meets him, but can not forgive him, and after his death she refuses to attend his funeral.

It is possible to read this story as an allegory of the path of the Revolution, with the idealistic side being represented by Ekaterina Gerasimovna and the slide into terrorism by Novoselov. In this reading virtue is eventually rewarded, and Ekaterina Gerasimovna's inability to forgive Novoselov expresses Kataev's own hatred of Stalinism. Perhaps the most striking feature of "Violet" is its tone of self-congratulatory rectitude. Despite the fact that Ekaterina Gerasimovna must bear much of the blame for what happened, since she helped her husband to his position of power, she emerges as blameless, and Kataev even endows her with his own sharp vision.[54] No clearer demonstration of the author's political orthodoxy could be provided.[55]

Kataev's later works appear to be a new departure for him. Yet to a large extent the conclusions to be drawn about them are those which can be drawn about his career in general. Kataev is basically an aesthete who is not content to remain a private writer, a lyricist pure and simple. It is interesting to speculate, as Nadezhda Mandel'shtam has done, on what might have become of this "very talented man, with a lively intelligence and a quick wit, who belongs to the most enlightened wing of the present-day best-selling Soviet writers"[56] if he had not felt obliged to conform to the demands of Socialist Realism. Yet to speculate in this way is ultimately fruitless, because Kataev is as temperamentally incapable of shaking off his "public" side as of discarding his "private" side. His inherent aestheticism has been held in check and modified by a need to publish and achieve public recognition and, in later years at any rate, by his commitment to his country and its political system.

University of Sheffield

NOTES

1. See, for example, B. Sarnov, "Ugl' pylaiushchii i kimval briatsaiushchii," *Voprosy literatury,* 1968, no. 1, pp. 21-49; R. Russell, "The Problem of Self Expression in the Later Works of Valentin Kataev," *Forum for Modern Language Studies,* 1975, no. 4, pp. 366-79.

2. Among the negative reviews is V. Smirnova, "No zachem?", *Literaturnaia Rossiia,* July 11, 1969.

3. V. Kataev, "Tvorcheskoe samochuvstvie," *Sobranie sochinenii* (Moscow, 1968-72), vol. 8 (1971), p. 368.

4. V. Kataev, "Novogodnii tost," *Sobranie sochinenii,* vol. 8, p. 346.

5. In addition to the articles mentioned see "Pero zhar-ptsitsy," *Literaturnaia gazeta,* 22 May 1959.

6. See, for example, Sarnov.

7. V. Kataev, "Almaznyi moi venets," *Novyi mir,* 1978, no. 6, p. 44.

8. V. Zhegis, "Goluboi fonar' vechnoi vesny," *Sovetskaia kul'tura,* 4 August 1978, p. 4.

9. See Deming Brown, *Soviet Russian Literature since Stalin* (Cambridge, 1978), p. 256; A. Subbotin, "Novaia zhizn' Maiakovskogo," *Ural,* 1968, no. 7, pp. 120-27.

10. Z. Vatnikova-Prizel, *O russkoi memuarnoi literature* (East Lansing, 1978), p. 151.

11. V. Kataev, "Razbitaia zhizn', ili Volshebnyi rog Oberona," *Novyi mir,* 1972, no. 7, p. 9. It is worth noting that Kataev is not alone among modern Russian writers in his "creative" approach to recalling the past. I. Shtok, for example, opens his work *Prem'era* with the words: "This is not a book of recollections. . . . It is a book of stories. Here are portraits of famous people, true facts, fantasy — things that did not happen to me but could easily have done. Some names have been changed because the actions of certain people have been ascribed to others. But in general this is the truth." Quoted by I. Shaitanov, " 'Neproiavlennyi zhanr', ili literaturnye zametki o memuarnoi forme," *Voprosy literatury,* 1979, no. 2, pp. 54-55.

12. V. Kataev, *Malen'kaia zheleznaia dver' v stene, Sobranie sochinenii,* vol. 9 (1972), p. 101.

13. Vatnikova-Prizel, p. 154.

14. Kataev explains his reluctance to use real names by pointing out that his work is not historically strictly accurate. It is not a history of literature or even a factually correct memoir. Rather it is a free creation in which fiction mingles with fact. At least one critic, however, has been incensed by this device, claiming that Kataev is afraid to name Mandel'-shtam, Olesha, Babel' and others. See M. Kaganskaia, "Vremia, nazad!" *Sintaksis* (Paris), no. 3, pp. 103–13.

15. V. Kataev, *Kladbishche v Skulianakh* (Moscow, 1976), p. 27.

16. Ibid., p. 225.

17. Ibid., p. 63.

18. Ibid., p. 3.

19. Ibid., p. 7.

20. On this theme see Phyllis M. Johnson, "Struggle with Death: The Theme of Death in the Major Prose Works of Iu. Olesha and V. Kataev," Ph.D. Dissertation, Cornell University, 1976.

21, V. Kataev, *Trava zabven'ia, Sobranie sochinenii,* vol. 9, p. 242.

22. Iu. Olesha, *Ni dnia bez strochki* (Moscow, 1965), p. 295.

23. H. Meyerhoff, *Time in Literature* (Berkeley and Los Angeles, 1968), p. 30.

24. On this see Russell, "The theme of Self Expression . . . ."

25. "Razbitaia zhizn'," *Novyi mir,* 1972, no. 8, p. 31.

26. *Kladbishche v Skulianakh,* p. 6.

27. Ibid., p. 176. See also p. 182.

28. Ibid., p. 206.

29. Vatnikova-Prizel, pp. 161–63. Vatnikova-Prizel also makes the interesting point that, taken as a cycle, Kataev's autobiographical works narrate his life in reverse order, beginning with old age in *Sviatoi kolodets* and working back to his ancestors in *Kladbishche v Skulianakh.*

30. V. Kataev, "Obnovlenie prozy," *Voprosy literatury,* 1971, no. 2, p. 131.

31. "Razbitaia zhizn'," *Novyi mir,* 1972, no. 8, p. 55.

32. Meyerhoff, p. 188.

33. For a more detailed discussion see Phyllis M. Johnson, pp. 288–98.

34. "Razbitaia zhizn'," *Novyi mir,* 1972, no. 8, p. 159.

35. Ibid., p. 171.

36. This is hinted at in A. Gladkov, "Slova, slova, slova . . .," *Rossiia, Studi e ricerche a cura di Vittorio Strada* (Turin), no. 1 (1974), pp. 185–240.

37. "Almaznyi moi venets," p. 6.

38. *Ni dnia bez strochki,* p. 171. On the self-contained quality of the fragments see E. Beaujour, *The Invisible Land: A Study of the Artistic Imagination of Iurii Olesha* (New York, 1970), pp. 176–77.

39. "Obnovlenie prozy," p. 131.

40. *Ni dnia bez strochki,* p. 40.

41. Ibid., p. 61.

42. For a detailed treatment of this point with regard to *Trava zabven'ia* see E.M. Ivanova, "Povestvovatel' i avtobiograficheskii geroi v *Trave zabven'ia* V. Kataeva," *Izvestiia voronezhskogo gos. ped. instituta,* 1972, vol. 125, pp. 142–59.

43. This useful term was suggested to me by E.M. Ivanova's article "Otkrytaia avtorskaia pozitsiia kak osobyi khudozhestvennyi priem v memuarno-avtobiograficheskikh proizvedeniiakh novogo tipa," *Uchenye zapiski Ivanovskogo ped. instituta,* 1972, vol. 105, pp. 163–77.

44. V. Kataev, "Proshchanie s mirom," *Sobranie sochinenii,* vol. 8, p. 437.

45. "Razbitaia zhizn'," *Novyi mir,* 1972, no. 8, p. 55.

46. Arkadii Belinkov makes a good case for considering Olesha in this way. See A. Belinkov, *Iurii Olesha: Sdacha i gibel' sovetskogo intelligenta* (Madrid, 1976).

47. *Trava zabven'ia, Sobranie sochinenii,* vol. 9, p. 331.

48. *Sviatoi kolodets, Sobranie sochinenii,* vol. 9, p. 235.

49. It is worth noting that when Kataev spoke to welcome the new Soviet constitution he did so on behalf of the intelligentsia. See *Literaturnaia gazeta,* 26 October 1977.

50. V. Kardin, "Siuzhet dlia nebol'shoi stat'i," *Voprosy literatury,* 1974, no. 5, p. 79.

51. Kaganskaia, p. 103.

52. See, for example, Sarnov, "Ugl' pylaiushchii . . ."; V. Dudintsev, "Dve magii iskusstva," *Literaturnaia gazeta,* 13 August 1966. For a positive view see V. Aksenov, "Puteshestvie k Kataevu," *Iunost',* 1967, no. 1, pp. 68–69.

53. V. Kataev, "Fialka," *Novyi mir,* 1973, no. 8, pp. 74–95; and "Fialka, P'esa v dvukh chastiakh," *Teatr,* 1974, no. 12, pp. 171–86.

54. On the identity of view between Kataev and his heroine see Kardin.

55. For a detailed discussion of "Fialka" see Kardin; and V. Iverni, "Sotsrealizm s chelovecheskim litsom," *Kontinent* (Paris), no. 7 (1976), pp. 393–417.

56. N. Mandelstam, *Hope against Hope* (London, 1971), p. 281.

SATIRICAL TRENDS IN RECENT
SOVIET SCIENCE FICTION

WALTER SMYRNIW

A salient feature of recent Soviet science fiction is the recurrence of various satirical tendencies in the novels and short stories of both major and minor writers. The phenomenon has certainly been noticed in the West, but in the main it has been interpreted quite unilaterally. In Western delineations of Soviet science fiction it is frequently asserted that Soviet authors utilize satire in order to ridicule the social, economic and the political system of the Soviet Union.[1] The promulgators of this view maintain that the writers of science fiction express this criticism primarily through allegorical satire. In fact some manage to discern anti-Soviet allegories even in those works which contain obvious satires of the capitalist system. Cyril Bryner, for example, states that "in reading these descriptions of the capitalist world one wonders whether they are not reverse images satirizing a communist world instead. . . ."[2]

Such political and ideological inferences are not limited to Western interpretations of allegorical satire in Soviet science fiction. Soviet literary scholars also assert that in the works written after the Second World War the Soviet authors frequently employ "allegorical imagery" in order to satirize the capitalist system and to show how "bourgeois democracy" fosters the rise of Fascism.[3] Regardless of whether the works are set in the West or on alien planets the Soviet critics invariably claim that by way of satire the science fiction authors ridicule solely the "negative social features which stem from the bourgeois way of life" and the "bourgeois ideology."[4]

In many instances both the Soviet and the Western allegorical inferences are not merely tenuous, but reflect an inadequate appreciation of the ambiguities which are inherent in science fiction allegories. Kingsley Amis was indeed most perceptive when he pointed out that "to read a science fiction utopia as one reads the traditional allegory, alert for one to one correspondence, is to misread it."[5] While many science fiction allegories lack the traditional "one to one correspondence" they contain open-ended allegorical formulas which are not subject to a single interpretation. In view of this A.F. Britkov could hardly avoid asserting the following about the Strugatskii brothers' *Khishch-nye veshchi veka* (Predatory Things of Our Age): "in the 'progress' of the Amazons it is possible to discern Fascism as well as the Maoist 'cultural revolution' and also the urban growth that is devouring the countryside, and whatever you like — and at the same time nothing at all."[6]

During the past two decades a number of Soviet science fiction writings have appeared which contain elements of allegorical satire. But inasmuch as these allegories are not based on a "one to one correspondence" their interpretations are as problematic and as controversial as those of abstract art. In many instances the elucidations of allegorical satire in Soviet science fiction reveal much more accurately the political and economic weltanschauung of the critics than the nature of the satire in the works.

Satire is, however, by no means always confined to allegorical techniques. There is an abundance of direct and explicit satire in Soviet science fiction of the 1960s and 70s. During these decades science fiction writers often employed forthright satire in the exposition of the negative features of science as well as of the views and life styles of scientists. Although not much attention was paid to it in literary criticism this tendency constitutes a substantial and a significant facet of the satirical trend in Soviet science fiction. Moreover, these science fiction works may be set in the Soviet Union, in the West or in extraterrestrial domains and the personages may be Russian, American or alien, and the actions may take place in the distant future or in our times, but the satirical depictions often have a direct bearing on Soviet as well as on international developments in the field of science.

In Soviet science fiction the authors scrutinize and often satirize the relationship between scientists and political authorities.

Hence it is not surprising that Aleksandr Admiral'skii queries whether from a government's point of view a scientist is regarded as a genius or a criminal; and in his story "Genii" (The Genius) Admiral'skii replies in the affirmative to both possibilities. For his discovery of an efficient and an economical mode of transportation for people and cargo a scientist named Urg was hailed as a genius by the head of state and consequently acclaimed as such by fellow scientists. But the author goes on to point out that the scientists, and even the whole academy of science, did not understand the operative principles of Urg's discovery, and nevertheless did not bother to question their colleague or his invention as long as the state endorsed the device. However, as soon as the horrible side effects of this invention became apparent the state authorities immediately denounced Urg as a criminal and incarcerated him for life. And once again the other scientists merely concurred with the political decision. During the secret trial Urg himself admitted that he knew about harmful side effects of his invention and that by concealing them he was transgressing the social and moral norms. But Urg declared that he felt that it was his right and privilege to disregard all laws inasmuch as he was a scientist and a genius. By means of this episode the author conveys how the other scientists as well as the government itself manifested a relativistic attitude towards ethical norms and how all their actions were based on a morality of expedience.

Sever Gansovskii's story "Den' gneva" (The Day of Wrath) also entails a poignant satire on the state's support of scientific undertakings which lead to disasterous consequences and loss of life. The featured scientist, named Fidler, conducted genetic experiments in order to breed a creature with a supermind. He succeeded in breeding apes which were much more intelligent than Homo sapiens, but a large number of them escaped from the laboratory and, roaming through the countryside, they devoured not merely all the animals but many humans as well. In spite of this the government made no attempt to prosecute Fidler. On the contrary, it even provided personal guards who protected him as though he were a most precious commodity and fully supported his further research. The author cites an obvious reason for this. The creatures which were produced by Fidler's genetic engineering, the so-called *otarki,* were used by the Ministry of War, for they were most capable in solving abstract problems and functioned as biological computers.[7] Gansovskii's satire is directed against both the state support of military research and the attitude of the scientists who are so obsessed with research that they value it more than human life. A victim of Fidler's experiments emphasizes this moral flaw by stating: "First of all one should be a human being and only after that a scientist."[8]

In Soviet science fiction Gansovskii is not alone in pointing out the inhumanity and at times the sheer savagery of the scientists serving the interests of the state. A vivid example of this tendency is a story about a prison escape on an alien planet. The escape was but a hypnotic illusion produced by scientists in order to motivate the prisoner to work harder for the state even during the last few days of his terminal illness. At the conclusion of the story, elated by the success of the experiment and smiling with pleasure, the scientist reveals the "sharp teeth of a vampire."[9] In complete contrast to the light-hearted and paradoxical humor in his other writings, Il'ia Varshavskii utilized sarcasm and sardonicism for the conclusion of his "Pobeg" (The Escape) in order to deride the scientists' contribution towards the ultimate form of exploitation through mind control.

The theme of psychological control and exploitation recurs frequently in Soviet science fiction. Some authors have used it in a satirical vein. In "Akvariumy" (The Aquariums) Boris Zubkov and Evgenii Muslin ridicule with great effect the use of subliminal suggestion techniques to compel an entire population to purchase large quantities of completely useless articles. And in a more recent work, "Fabryka heniiv" (A Factory of Geniuses), Volodymyr Hrybenko derides the utilization of advanced psychology and computer technology for the decoding and transcription of the brainwaves of brilliant individuals in order to establish a factory that would specialize in the mass production of geniuses.[10]

In dealing with the notion of mind control the majority of authors emphasize through the setting, the names of the personages, and explicit comments that theirs is a satire of the inevitable results of the so-called bourgeois democracy and of capitalists who work on various developments in war technology. When lampooning the role of scientists in this area Soviet writers suggest that only Western scientists are unscrupulous and irresponsible men of knowledge. Such assertions as the following are not uncommon in Soviet science fiction: "In the world where everything is bought and sold the relationship between science and authority is based entirely on a commercial premise. Science offers an increase in income, the greater productivity of labor, political and military influence, and personal power. . . . Corrupted through money and bourgeois ideals the scientists offer their services without worrying as to how and to what purpose the results of their work will be utilized."[11] Conversely, Soviet scientists are not censured for contributing to the invention and production of weapons. But in the same context they are often praised for their contributions to peaceful applications of scientific discoveries. This satirical formula was utilized by Anatolii Dneprov in his story "Kraby idut po ostrovu" (The Island of the Crabs), and in his novel *Goluboe zarevo* (Pale Blue Glow), as well as by Iurii Harasymenko in his story "El'fy doktora Shtillera " (The Elves of Dr. Shtiller), and by Anatolii Stas' in his "Vulytsia chervonykh troiand" (The Street of Red Roses).

There are, however, some deviations from this satirical pattern. Some authors present a general and a much more impartial assessment of the scientists' contribution to war technology and of their involvement in political affairs. At times these writers do not single out the work of a particular scientist, but direct their satire against the general involvement of scientists in the field of warfare. The negative results of scientific pursuits are sometimes pointed out obliquely through depictions of the devastations which result from various superweapons. This device is quite apparent in the novel *Obitaemyi ostrov* (An Inhabited Island)[12] by Boris and Arkadii Strugatskii. By means of vivid descriptions of the effects of nuclear warfare which has completely devastated the countryside, of horrible mutations among the survivors, and of automatic weapons which function with extraordinary efficiency even twenty years after the end of the war, the Strugatskii brothers mock and scorn implicitly all scientists who contribute to the production of destructive devices. A similar denunciation is conveyed through Vasyl' Berezhenyi's tale

"Arkheoskrypt" (Archeoscript) which contains an account of
how the scientists produced a bomb powerful enough to destroy
an entire continent and reduce a large part of another to an utter
wasteland.[13]

When lampooning the involvement of scientists in aggressive
and pernicious activities Oles' Berdnyk consistently localized his
plots on alien planets. But he always singled out those characters
who were responsible for the malicious deeds. In his novel *Slia-
khy Tytaniv* (The Ways of the Titans) Berdnyk describes how
"with the help of machines a group of scientists became the rulers of the whole world."[14] This coup d'état was initiated by a
scientist named Ro who ultimately became the absolute dictator
of the whole galaxy and strove to eliminate all biological life
forms and replace them with machines which carried out his every command unquestioningly. A similar exposé occurs in Berdnyk's *Strila chasu* (The Arrow of Time). There the author out-
lines how an alien physicist named Sei Nur started a series of
nuclear reactions in volcanos by means of which he could control the rotation of their planet. Sei Nur intended to use this vast
power to enslave the entire planet and to establish "a caste of
thinkers, scientists and creators" who would "dictate their will —
the will of the gods — to all people."[15] When this physicist realized that he would not succeed in usurping political authority he
set off explosions which led to the disintegration of the whole
planet. The satirical intent of this episode is obvious from the
comments of the alien narrator who emphasizes the absurdity
of action and the lust for power which is manifested by some
scientists.

Berdnyk also employed satire in his portrayals of tyranny and
aggressiveness in the realm of science itself. A vivid example occurs in his *Zorianyi korsar* (The Star Corsair). There he describes
how at a "Congress of Thinkers" the chief co-ordinator of the
council of scientists, Ariman, exceeded his rights and privileges
by incarcerating all scientists who opposed his project, one that
entailed among other things a psychological exploitation of beings at a lower cultural level. Ariman's personal tactics and his
tyrannical undertakings are rendered with obvious ridicule, especially in view of the author's repeated references to the so-

called "Cosmic Charter" which guarantees personal freedom for all intelligent creatures of the universe.[16]

Although Soviet writers refrain from ridiculing directly any lust for power among scientists of the USSR or their involvement in military technology and the means of mind control, they nevertheless manage to satirize these activities in general through the use of foreign or alien settings. An opposite tendency prevails, however, in satires on scientists engaged in peace-oriented activities. Science fiction writers employ predominantly Soviet settings and character types when ridiculing the life styles and professional aspirations of scientists. Writers like Gennadii Gor endeavor to lampoon the highly idealized image of the scientist. As Gor puts it, "many conceive of scientists as romantics and eccentrics, as they are frequently depicted by writers in accordance with an established tradition, and inasmuch as they are not very well acquainted with this milieu. But in actual fact scientists are just as fond of ordinary things as the representatives of the most humdrum professions."[17] Thoroughly familiar with the milieu of scientists the Strugatskii brothers ridicule the various benefits in the field of science. They cite two undesirable tendencies. Some professionals pursue a career in science because "the institute is warm and cozy; the work is clean and well respected; the salary is good, and the people are splendid; and besides, nobody has ever died from shame. . . . One could still have some pity for these. . . . But there are others, with hollow eyes. They know quite well which side of the bread has been buttered. In their own way they are real experts on human nature. Calculating and unscrupulous, aware of the immense range of human weaknesses, they know quite well how to turn all misfortunes into personal advantages and indeed, they are quite tireless in this endeavor. . . . And quite frequently they attain substantial success and significant eminence in their principal goal — the building of a future in one separately leased apartment and on one personal plot on a collective farm fenced off from the rest of humanity with barbed wire."[18]

A career in science offers many rewards, but it requires an adherence to well-established routines. Consequently, scientists are not adequately prepared to cope with unknown and unexpected phenomena. Ridiculing this inadequacy, Gennadii Gor asserts that the scientists "are least of all prepared to perceive something completely unexpected, something extremely paradoxical, which is almost impossible and borders on a miracle. They detest all hoopla and sensations — some do it because they are fond of absolute truth, and others (the majority) owing to an attachment to the habitual, to the accessible and to that which is in concordance with ordinary logic."[19] In his story "Minotavr" (Minotaur) Gor goes on to demonstrate how a specialist in logic and symbolism rejected the logical premises of a visitor from outer space because they were incongruous with the logical patterns known on earth. In their depiction of responses among scientists to contacts from an extraterrestrial entity the Strugatskii brothers point out that if the contact threatens the lives of the scientists, the majority of them are not only prepared to abandon their careers, but also to "throw it [their work] all into the incinerator."[20] The Strugatskiis describe how in a group of scientists threatened by a mysterious force only one individual is dedicated and courageous enough to face the unknown entity and to live at a remote metereological outpost in order to study the phenomenon from outer space though its enigma may not be unravelled for a billion years.

Not only the various activities of scientists, but the general aims of science are at times scrutinized and satirized in Soviet science fiction. Dmitrii Belinkin, for example, ridicules the lack of teleological orientation in science and points out that "knowledge is power, a weapon, and if the scientist does not care where it's aimed, what makes him different from a mercenary soldier?"[21] Belinkin satirizes the myopic, theoretical orientation of science which requires continuous research, but ignores such basic issues as the ultimate purpose and the final consequences of scientific pursuits. In the same vein, by utilizing satire in his "Podorozh v antysvit" (The Journey into the Antiworld) Oles' Berdnyk ridicules attempts to experiment with antimatter in order to build more powerful bombs or to be able to travel to a parallel universe in order to use this space for undetected spying on the enemy.[22] In his tales and novels Berdnyk frequently resorted to a teleological criterion in examining the ultimate results of the peaceful applications of scientific knowledge. In *The Star Corsair*, for example, he satirizes the belief that the ultimate objective of science should entail a complete satisfaction of material needs. He lampoons this notion by describing how a "Central Synthesizer" that was developed on the planet Aoda brought about a social, psychological and a physical degeneration of all the inhabitants by providing the population of the planet with free food and other material goods. The inventors of the synthesizer believed that the machine would free the people from menial work and enable them to devote themselves fully to creative tasks. But the invention gave rise to quite contrary results. By eliminating the need to struggle the machine also deprived the people of a stimulus which was essential to their development. Consequently, "the majority of the people have lost the ability to speak. They have but one desire: enjoyment, lighthearted contemplation, spontaneous reproduction and vegetative existence."[23] By means of this ludicrous depiction of the ultimate results of a well-intended undertaking Berdnyk accentuates the teleological impotence of both natural and social sciences.

The Strugatskii brothers devoted an entire novel to the discussion of teleological inadequacies in science. Set in the twenty-second century *Dalekaia raduga* (Far Rainbow) contains many statements about future scientific problems which have a direct bearing on the present lack of foresight in science. The Strugatskiis shock the contemporary advocates of unlimited possibilities in science through such statements as "science is a labyrinth as far as you're concerned. Dead ends, dark alleys, sudden turns. You don't see anything but walls. And you don't know anything about the final goal. . . . The measure of your success is not the path to the finish line, but the path from the start."[24] The authors illustrate this deficiency by showing how the scientists of the future can neither foretell nor control the immense forces of energy generated by advanced physics. On a planet called Rainbow, "a planet colonized by science and set up for physics experiments,"[25] the scientists had spent ten years exploring the so-called "zero-physics" which involved the instant transmission of matter over interstellar distances of space. Although they did

manage to transmit small amounts of matter to Earth they also
generated thereby a very destructive moving wall of energy called
the "Wave." The scientists spent ten years surveying this phenomenon, took six thousand photographs of its manifestations
and yet, as one narrator of the novel puts it, "the Wave is mortally dangerous. . . . The trouble is that the physicists never know
how it will behave ahead of time. For example, it can dissipate
at any moment . . . or not dissipate."[26] In the *Far Rainbow* it
is apparent that even their advanced mode of scientific enquiry
will not enable the scientists to foresee the emergence of new
phenomena, such as the new and enormous Waves of energy
which ultimately not only destroyed all experiments, but also
annihilated all life forms on the planet. In this work the authors
seek to demonstrate that the global catastrophe resulted partly
from the complacency of the best physicists on Earth, but also
to a large measure from the impossibility of predicting ultimate
results through scientific experimentations.

Although Aleksandr Solzhenitsyn is not a regular contributor
to science fiction his play *Svecha na vetru* (Candle in the Wind)
warrants inclusion in this genre. Like many science fiction works
this play is set in an unspecified time and place, and it entails
various scientific notions which are relevant to the present and
the future existence of man. In the vein of other science fiction
writers Solzhenitsyn dwells in *Candle in the Wind* on such problems as the moral premises of scientific pursuits and the govern-
mental support of scientific research. But on raising repeatedly
such questions as "What is science for?"[27] Solzhenitsyn inevitably touches on teleological issues in the field of science. Hence
Candle in the Wind contains not merely such poignant questions
as "why are we doing all this? . . Why do we need science at
all?"[28] but also outright ridicule of the scientists who are not in
the least concerned about the final results of their work. Furthermore Solzhenitsyn illustrates how even in well-intended, thera-
peutic applications, as for example Alda's "neurostabilization,"
the ultimate results cannot be predicted through previous scientific experiments. There was a temporary remission of Alda's
neurosis, but as a result of the treatment her soul, "a marvel of
nature . . . turned into a stone."[29] In this play the full force of

Solzhenitsyn's satire is directed against such scientists as Philip Radagise who, albeit aware of the possible consequences of his research, i.e. the destruction of the very nature of the human soul and potential political tyranny through the mind control of all people, nevertheless "continue their experiments on human beings. . . ."[30]

In both Soviet and Western media it has been pointed out that mankind has reached a stage of development in which ninety percent of all scientists are alive at present and that the majority of scientific discoveries have been made during the last fifty years. Although it is usually not mentioned it obviously follows from these data that at least ninety percent of all errors and the greatest blunders were made by men of science during this period. On examining Soviet science fiction satire it becomes clear that authors are very much aware of some of the errors and problems in science and that they do make an effort to illustrate them in their works. Moreover, from the satirical exposés of both major and minor Russian and Ukrainian science fiction writers during the past two decades it is quite plain that the satirical trend in this genre is not confined to allegorical criticism of the Soviet regime. These satirical tendencies further confirm that Soviet science fiction authors are by no means mere heralds of the various achievements and dazzling promises of science and technology. On the contrary, in the realm of satire the Soviet writers have proven themselves discerning and serious critics of various shortcomings in science. A comprehensive examination of their satire confirms that regardless of whether they ridicule the relationship between the scientists and political rulers, scorn the contributions of the scientists to the means of mind control and to war technology, sneer at the personal and professional aspirations of the careerists in science, or deride the ultimate results of scientific pursuits, Soviet science fiction writers tend to dwell on the inadequacy, or even on the utter lack of generally accepted ethical norms in the field of science.

In keeping with a long-established tradition in satirical writings science fiction authors do not merely point out various shortcomings, but they also endeavor to indicate the need to introduce reforms. Hence a number of writers stress that it would be indeed desirable to formulate an ethical code similar to the Hippocratic oath which would guide and censure the behavior of all professional scientists. They point out that even in the distant future when science will enable men to make gold from other substances and to control psychologically the population of an entire planet by an "exposure to hypnotic radiation from three equatorial satellites,"[31] it will still be very difficult to devise a code of ethics even for a relatively primitive society. Such a code should ensure personal liberties and at the same time subdue within each man the enemy which is the source of egoistic and destructive impulses. The authors suggest that for man it is indeed "hard to be a god"[32] in the realm of ethics.

Writers like Gennadii Gor, Il'ia Varshavskii, Arkadii and Boris Strugatskii make extensive use of humor in their satirical expositions, and this of course augments substantially the effects of their ridicule. But by and large the satire of Soviet science fiction entails somber attacks against the incongruities, absurdities, and inherent dangers in the field of science. Yet in spite of the serious tone a number of authors either imply or state explicitly that "there is still a billion years to the end of the world . . . there's a lot, an awful lot that can be done in a billion years if we don't give up and we understand and don't give up."[33] Satire enables Soviet science fiction writers to behold critically and skeptically the various developments in science and technology without resorting to morbid pessimism or prophesies of an ultimate doom from science.

McMaster University

NOTES

1. Brian Ash, *Who's Who in Science Fiction* (London, 1976), p. 187; see also Baird Searles, et al., *A Reader's Guide to Science Fiction* (New York, 1979), p. 171; Hedrick Smith, *The Russians* (New York, 1976), pp. 386–87; Cyril Bryner, "The Future of Soviet Science Fiction," *Survey,* 18, no. 1, pp. 172–82; D. Rudnev, " 'Zamknutyi mir' sovremennoi russkoi fantastiki," *Grani,* 25 (1970), no. 78, pp. 175–76.
2. Cyril Bryner, "The Future of Soviet Science Fiction," p. 175.

3. A.F. Britikov, *Russkii sovetskii nauchno-fantasticheskii roman* (Leningrad, 1970), pp. 204–07, 210, 212.

4. Liudmyla Polushkina, "Prvadyvist' neimovirnoho: notatky pro suchasnu ukrains'ku fantastyku," *Dnipro,* 45 (1971), p. 138.

5. Kingsley Amis, *New Maps of Hell* (New York, 1960), p. 104.

6. A.F. Britikov, *Russkii sovetskii nauchno-fantasticheskii roman,* p. 280.

7. S. Gansovskii, "Den' gneva," *NF: Al'manakh nauchnoi fantastiki* (Moscow, 1964), no. 3, p. 174.

8. Ibid., p. 183.

9. Il'ia Varshavskii, "Pobeg," *Fantastika 1968* (Moscow, 1969), p. 91.

10. Boris Zubkov and Evgenii Muslin, "Akvariumy," *Fantastika 1968,* pp. 126–35; see also Volodymyr Hrybenko, *Fabryka heniiv* (Kiev, 1976), pp. 83–89.

11. Anatolii Dneprov, "Goluboe zarevo," *NF: Al'manakh nauchnoi fantastiki* (Moscow, 1965), p. 30.

12. This work was translated into English under the title *Prisoners of Power.*

13. Vasyl' Berezhnyi, "Arkheoskrypt" in his *U promini dvokh sonts'* (Kiev, 1970), p. 58.

14. Oles' Berdnyk, *Shliakhy Tytaniv* (Kiev, 1959), p. 172.

15. Oles' Berdnyk, *Strila chasu* (Kiev, 1960), p. 148.

16. Oles' Berdnyk, *Zorianyi korsar* (Kiev, 1971), pp. 167–74.

17. Gennadii Gor, "Minotavr," *NF: Al'manakh nauchnoi fantastiki,* 1967, no. 6, p. 68.

18. Arkadii Strugatskii and Boris Strugatskii, *Ponedel'nik nachinaetsia v subbotu* (Moscow, 1979), p. 115.

19. Gennadii Gor, "Minotavr," pp. 68–69.

20. Arkadii Strugatskii and Boris Strugatskii, *Za milliard let do kontsa sveta.* Translated into English by Antonina W. Bouis under the title *Definitely Maybe: A Manuscript Discovered under Unusual Circumstances* (New York, 1978), p. 139.

21. Dmitrii Belinkin, "The Ban," in his *The Uncertainty Principle* (New York, 1978), p. 52.

22. Oles' Berdnyk, "Podorozh v antysvit," in *Z dalekykh planet* (Kiev, 1963), pp. 53–55.

23. Oles' Berdnyk, *Zorianyi korsar,* p. 99.

24. Arkadii Strugatskii and Boris Strugatskii, *Far Rainbow* (New York, 1979), p. 18.

25. Ibid., p. 105.

26. Ibid., p. 68.

27. Aleksandr Solzhenitsyn, *Candle in the Wind* (New York, 1974), pp. 52, 111, 146.

28. Ibid., p. 111.

29. Ibid., p. 130.

30. Ibid., p. 141.

31. Arkadii Strugatskii and Boris Strugatskii, *Hard to Be a God* (New York, 1973), pp. 198, 203.

32. Ibid., p. 205.

33. Arkadii Strugatskii and Boris Strugatskii, *Definitely Maybe,* p. 142.

PART II

CRITICISM

INTRODUCTORY: RUSSIAN LITERARY CRITICISM IN THE TWENTIETH CENTURY

SIDNEY MONAS

As Alexander Piatigorsky points out in his brilliant if somewhat gnomic paper, Russian literary criticism in the *nineteenth* century tended to usurp the place of philosophy and to deal with literature as if it were life itself and with life as if it were literature. This confusion may have been due, as Piatigorsky suggests, to the relatively anemic quality of the Russian Enlightment, whose aim was the socialization and objectification of knowledge, to the absorption of the ideas of German Hegelianism minus, as Piatigorsky states, the actual texts, or generally to the "latecomer" quality of Russian culture, or to the constraining nature of the censorship and the relatively unconstrained position of literature and discourse about literature that tended to lay upon it a certain burden of *literature oblige*. In any case, the phenomenon itself is unmistakable. Just as Russian literature in the nineteenth century was marked by a psychological and philosophical depth, a certain quality of transparency and holism, that distinguished it from the rest of the European nineteenth century, Russian literary criticism spoke with an authority not simply about literature but about life itself, about society, man, and nature, took upon itself the tasks of philosophy, social criticism, and even in part theology (Piatigorsky's remarks about Slavophile "historiosophy" are very much to the point here) in a manner that no European critic, not even St. Beuve or Mathew Arnold, would have dared. The educated, or "cultured" Russian, whatever his profession, tended to look at life through the glass of literature. References to life were extraordinarily mediated by *literary* reference, and the distinction between literature and life, for the cultivated, tended to disappear.

Piatigorsky's concept of "culture" is somewhat odd. He calls it, simply, "A body of texts," but surely rather more is meant. His is not the strictly anthropological usage of the word — though, as I am aware, even here there is more than one usage — and he distinguishes culture rather severely from *byt,* the habitual pattern of daily life. His concept is perhaps closer to Mathew Arnold's, which might be expressed as "The best that has been created, written, and preserved by mankind," or a continuously developing, communal sense of that. Culture thus would imply the ongoing moral aspirations of a society as embodied in texts. It may include clashing or contradictory aspirations, yet given sufficient perspective, they may be seen to form something of a pattern or a coherent whole.

He also uses the term "civilization" which, in somewhat the German tradition, he distinguishes from "culture" as a different realm. The distinction is, I would take it, not altogether Spenglerian. Civilization is not, as in Spengler, the late, ossified form of culture, creativity petrified into method. It is rather the realm of *manners,* perhaps also of method and methodology, as distinct from the realm of *morals* and moral aspiration. It is not a late form of culture, but exists side by side with it.

Given the position of literary criticism in Russian culture and given the holistic nature of Russian literature, it was inevitable that the relationship between culture and Christianity be raised with a special poignancy. Nowhere is this more apparent than in the dramatic contrast between the sweeping "historiosophy" of the still very literary Russian philosophers — Berdiaev, S. Bulgakov, and P. Florensky are striking examples — and the careful, diffident, precise tone that T.S. Eliot took such pains to establish in those philosophical attempts of a major poet, *Notes towards the Definition of Culture* and *The Idea of a Christian Society,* works which in the late 1940s and early 1950s shocked and repelled many of his "modernist" or "esthetic" admirers. (R.P. Blackmur, for instance, far more judicious than most, entitled a review of the latter *"Non possumus,"* thereby alluding humorously to Eliot's pseudonym, "Old Possum," used in some of his light verse, which Blackmur also considered somewhat clumsy and outside Eliot's real talent.)

While Piatigorsky is not without admiration for the breadth and profundity of cultural self-awareness that he sees as, in part at least, a product of this process of the "literarization" of Russian culture and especially of Russian philosophy, he emphasizes the handicap it has posed for the development of professional philosophy and for any perspective that requires an extracultural stance.

It is in these terms that he sees the justification for Russian structuralism and the so-called Tartu school of semiotics, of which he has been and in a sense still is a member. It is the science of the sign, Piatigorsky might say, that enables a Russian, if he have the wit and the strength of character to use it properly, to stand outside the boundaries of cultural self-awareness, not by casting off his culture, but by employing a methodology appropriate to the concept of culture as a body of texts.

In the context of a cultural scene that has been forcibly and repressively dominated by Socialist Realism — very much, in its roots, a product of the nineteenth-century phenomena that Piatigorsky treats, though its nineteenth-century founders were innocent of the administrative-police methods by which it has been imposed — the Russian structuralists seem to offer the only methodological alternative. One cannot help thinking in this connection of their long and fruitful controversy with the formalists, a debate which in a way nobody could win, since it was simply repressed by external authority rather than resolved. It is the structuralists who have emerged, however, and who now are once again creative and inventive, having absorbed and transmuted what was most valuable in the formalists, their concern for the specifically literary in literature, with what made literature the thing it was rather than something else, and with what therefore made literary criticism something different from philosophy or social thought. Of course, there are gaps in the story. We have not mentioned the roles of Roman Jakobson and Yury Tynianov, nor that of the Prague Linguistic Circle and Jan Mukarovsky. One cannot in any case omit that of the presiding spirit of Russian semiotics, Mikhail Bakhtin, who appears increasingly as a numinous figure, not "merely" a great Dostoevsky scholar, or a literary historian who knocked almost all of the French, German, and English scholarship on Rabelais into a cocked hat, but a philosopher of language of the first magnitude.

The figure that J. Michael Holquist so brilliantly presents strikes me — especially when read beside Piatigorsky's paper — as Janus-faced, an image he himself, with his powerful emphasis on double-voicedness and his insistence on the necessity of the presence of "the other" before a "self" can be constituted, would probably like. There is the Bakhtin, who, as "Medvedev" and "Voloshinov," debated the formalists, criticized Freud, and wrote *Marxism and the Philosophy of Language*. This is the Bakhtin of "official" and "unofficial" consciousness, of the ineluctably socio-ideological nature of the word and the inevitably social nature of language and of art. It is also the Bakhtin who, as opposed to the followers of Saussure, emphasizes the diachronic as opposed to the synchronic, and *parole* as opposed to *langue,* the individual speech-act or utterance as opposed to the abstraction of an overall linguistic system. It is the Bakhtin whom Holquist has elsewhere called "the poet of openness," the Bakhtin of "the dialogic imagination." But Holquist indicates here also another Bakhtin, even less familiar and more intriguing, the Bakhtin who inspired Fedotov and Father Florensky and the "god-builders," the religious thinker and great anti-authoritarian cultural guru who founded a subculture that had intimate links with that period of cultural self-awareness Piatigorsky writes about and who, at the same time, invented a series of intimately linked concepts for transcending it. One is immediately struck by the appositeness of "the holiness of matter" — quoted by Holquist from the Russian religio-literary tradition — to the Bakhtinian idea of "carnival" as elaborated in his book on Rabelais, the immortal ongoing body of the people and its impulse at once to "degrade" by immersion in the lower bodily stratum and to resurrect, to endow with its own vitality a continuing life.

Clearly, not only the Tartu school is immensely indebted to Bakhtin, but the scholarship and approach of D.S. Likhachev as well — himself the founder of the most notable contemporary school of Russian medievalist literary scholars. Ewa Thompson's paper is sharply critical of Likhachev, largely on grounds of what I presume she interprets as nationalist presumption.

Likhachev applies, in one of his best-known works, the Bakhtinian concept of "carnival" to Russian humor of the seventeenth century, where Thompson feels it is inapplicable. As she points out, the basic notion behind the West European "carnival" (Bakhtinian or not!) is that *temporarily,* the world is turned upside down; strongly patterned hierarchies are reversed, the norms are suspended. The European "carnival" humor is thus based on the notion of reversal and temporary suspension. She sees here a relationship between "laughter" and "authority" that allows for a temporary reversal without any profound innate hostility; that is, authority does not consider laughter in itself unholy, and laughter while it reverses the rules keeps them arranged in a tightly formal pattern. The instances she cites do, certainly, seem to indicate differences that Likhachev ignores or smooths over.

Still, one may doubt that Western authority, in spite of what seems a relative tolerance, was as comfortable with the laughter of "carnival" as Thompson assumes. The devil was always there, and played a role. The "diableries" of the Mystery Plays were an intimate part of carnival, and the devil was always threatening to get out of hand. As Bakhtin has pointed out, the seventeenth century (about which Likhachev writes) was *not,* in the West, a good time for carnival, but rather the time of its repression, withdrawal, conversion into minor, less threatening forms ("masquerade," for instance) and while Bakhtin gives no elaborated reason for why this happened, surely disapproval of church and state had much to do with it. According to Bakhtin, the period of the Renaissance was the high point of the carnival spirit in Western Europe. Before that, it had its ups and downs. And its historical roots precede Christianity, so that the tolerance or disapproval of the Church, while certainly an important influence, cannot be held as the decisive factor in its existence or nonexistence.

The very sharp and specific focus of Thompson's paper, however, and the aptness of her examples, provides a salutary critique of the too hasty, too wishful, nationally aspiring projections into literary texts that even a great concept like Bakhtin's may inspire in a great scholar like Likhachev.

"BAD FAITH" SQUARED:

THE CASE OF M.M. BAKHTIN

MICHAEL HOLQUIST

In the year 1929 three important events occurred in the life of the Russian thinker M.M. Bakhtin. The first was the publication of his book *Marxism and the Philosophy of Language*; the second was his arrest and subsequent exile to Kazakhstan; the third was the publication of another of his books, *Problems of Dostoevskii's Poetics*. Each of these events had its curious twist. The arrest and exile were never made official: there were never any formal charges brought and no trial. The only procedures were a lengthy interrogation (which Bakhtin found quite interesting), and a certain amount of uniquely Soviet plea-bargaining, i.e. should he be sent to certain death in the forced labor camps of the Solovki islands, or merely exiled to a remote area for a fixed period. In the end he got off with six years exile, but because the whole thing was officially a nonevent, Bakhtin could never be — officially — rehabilitated. The Dostoevskii book, which appeared while Bakhtin was already in jail undergoing questioning, was highly praised by, among others, Anatolii Lunacharskii, who made strong claims for the work in a long review article. Thus you have a book written by a man imprisoned for being politically suspect advanced as a model by the Soviet Minister of Education.

Strangest of all, however, are the facts surrounding the other book Bakhtin published that year (a second edition came out in 1930), *Marxism and the Philosophy of Language*. Before dwelling on some of these facts, I will briefly outline the main thesis of the book. The reason is that I hope to apply some of its own dicta about the nature of language in general to the specific language of the text of *Marxism and the Philosophy of Language* itself. By examining closely the interplay between the book's loudly proclaimed ideology and the silent conditions of the cultural context it enacts, I shall hope along the way to suggest some of the complexities in these key terms.

Marxism and the Philosophy of Language has had a resonance among professional linguists — and among those who have attempted to reconceptualize other disciplines on a linguistic basis — because it is the first systematic attack on the Saussurian vision of language to offer a counter model as powerful as the structuralism it so energetically opposes. Simply stated, what Bakhtin does is to turn Saussure on his head: the primacy that attaches to the two enabling conditions of structuralist linguistics, the privileging of synchrony and the conception of language as an abstract system Saussure termed *langue,* is taken away and bestowed on their previously scorned opposites, diachrony and the level of actual utterance Saussure called *parole.* Instead of a Leibnitzian timelessness and a Cartesian logic, Bakhtin insists that the royal road to understanding language must pass through the messiness of history and the vagaries of individual performance. Those who would study language must rethink the nature of their subject: not only *what* it is, but *where* it is. Language is not to be found laid up in a Platonic dream of order, but in the hurly-burly, the give and take of speech in everyday life. "The actual reality of language — speech — is not the abstract system of linguistic norms, . . . and not the psychophysiological act of its implementation, but the social event of verbal interaction implemented in an utterance. . . ."[1]

Bakhtin locates the roots of Geneva school linguistics in the old European philological tradition. Philology had always been, of course, the study of *dead* languages, such as ancient Greek, or *phantom* languages such as proto-Indo-European. Linguistics is the child of philology, and as such "it has always taken as its point of departure an utterance that was finished, monologic — the ancient written monument [which it considered] the ultimate realism" (72). Bakhtin goes on to say, "Despite the vast differences in cultural and historical [characteristics], from the ancient Hindu priests to the modern European scholar of language, the philologist has always and everywhere been a decipherer of alien, 'secret' scripts and words. . . . The first philologists and the first linguists were always and everywhere *priests*. History knows no nation whose sacred writings or oral tradition were not to some degree in a language foreign and incomprehensible to the profane. To decipher the mystery of sacred words was the task meant to be carried out by the priest-philologists'' (74).

Because it is so deeply embedded in the historical role of the alien word, philology has been blind to its own complicity in that role. Philology has thus been unable to break out of its obsession with esoteric languages and turn attention to familiar speech, the living native language.

It is no wonder then that Saussure "privileges" the abstract, extrahistorical *langue* over the vivid specificity of speech: of all conceptions, *langue* is the one that most radically distances the word from the mouths of actual men. Not only does "linguistics [study] a living language as if it were a dead language [but it treats the] native language as if it were an alien tongue'' (77).

The place where language resides is not where linguistics seeks it: it is not *elsewhere,* other in space or past in time. Language, the word alive with human meaning, is *here and now,* it lives in concrete utterance. But to admit as much is to court another danger: if Saussure erred by defining the word too mechanically, others in the history of linguistics have gone to the opposite extreme and located language in the individual psyche of speakers. Romantic linguistics, represented in the twentieth century by such figures as Wundt and Vossler in Germany, Croce in Italy, and in Russia by the followers of Potebnia, "considers the basis of language . . . to be the individual creative act of speech. . . . The laws of language creativity . . . are the laws of individual psychology'' (48).

The great weakness of this school is its inability to assimilate the undeniable fact that language does have its systematic aspects. Phonetics, grammar, and syntax are not merely phantoms in a Genevan obsessional fantasy, they constitute the normative, given side of language, even where it is defined as utterance. Language, among other things, *is* systematic, standing before the individual user as a set of inviolable norms. The individual acquires the system of language from his speech community completely ready-made. Any change within that system is beyond the range of his individual consciousness.

Bakhtin does not question this systematicness as such. But the peculiar status the systematic aspect of language has in *reality* must be reconceived. It does not exist as a set of rules chiselled into tablets by an academy, of course, nor as a preinscription into some mysterious collective mind (pace Chomsky). The normativeness of language rules is similar rather to any other system of *social* norms, which is precisely why linguistics can serve as a kind of *ars generalis* capable of restructuring the social sciences, as it has in France since the 1950s. The systematic nature of language is analogous to a system of moral norms, of judicial norms, of norms for aesthetic taste . . . and so on. What this means is that, "it exists only with respect to the subjective consciousness of individuals belonging to some particular community governed by such norms. Of course these norms vary. . . . But the nature of their existence as norms remains the same — they exist [it bears repeating] only with respect to the subjective consciousness of members of some particular community" (66).

Thus the Saussurians err by hypostasizing into neo-Platonic forms rules that are, after all, merely human; the Vosslerians err by assuming that every individual is capable of somehow generating these rules out of the pure *energia* of his own subjectivity. Language is not, then, a set of laws that is completely objective in the sense, say, that the laws of thermodynamics are objective. Nor, on the other hand, is language completely a *subjective* phenomenon, distinctive to individual persons, in the way, say, my fingerprints are uniquely my own.

Where, then, shall we seek terms that are capable of subsuming in one global system the two seemingly contradictory faces of language that the Saussurians and Vosslerians have treated independently: the undeniable normativeness of the extra-individual system on the one hand and on the other the undeniable conviction each individual speaker has that his words are in some sense *his own*. Bakhtin's answer is to follow out the systematic implications of his dictum that language is housed in the *social:* it is born, lives, and dies in actually spoken dialogs between real people who exist in historically realized institutions.

The study of language should properly seek its subject in the subjective consciousness of real speakers of living languages. When it does it will immediately discover that "the speaker's focus of attention is [oriented by] the particular, concrete utterance he is making" (67). In other words, "What is important for the speaker about a linguistic form is not that it is a stable and always self-equivalent *signal,* but that it is an always changeable and adaptable *sign.* . . . But doesn't the speaker also have to take into account the point of view of the listener and understander? Isn't it possible that here, exactly, is where the normative identity of a linguistic form comes into force?" (68).

This is, of course, the crux of any linguistic system. Bakhtin's answer is both simple and very complicated. It avoids the complete solipsism of Lewis Carroll's Humpty Dumpty, while at the same time resisting the temptation of a premature hypostasis à la Saussure: "The center of gravity lies not in the identity of the form but in that new and concrete meaning it acquires in the particular context. . . . The task of understanding does not basically amount to recognizing the form used, but rather to understanding it in a particular, concrete context, to understanding its meaning in a particular utterance, i.e. it amounts to *understanding* its novelty and not to *recognizing* its identity . . ." (67–68).

Anticipating George Herbert Mead's and C. Wright Mills's concept of the "generalized other," Bakhtin points out that "The word is [always] oriented toward an addressee, toward who that addressee might be. . . . Each person's inner world and thought has its stabilized *social audience* that comprises the environment in which reasons, motives, values and so on are fashioned. . . . The word is a two-sided act. It is determined equally by whose word it is and for whom it is meant. The word is precisely the product of the reciprocal relationship between speaker and listener, addresser and addressee. Each and every word expresses the one relationship to the other. I give myself verbal shape from another's point of view, ultimately from the point of view of the community to which I belong. A word is a bridge thrown between myself and another. If one end of the bridge depends on me, then the other depends on my addressee. A word is territorially *shared*

by both addresser and addressee, by the speaker and his inter-
locutor'' (85–86).

This dialogic aspect of the word is fundamental to Bakhtin's
whole system. It implies much more about my need always to
account for the presence of the other to whom I speak than formal grammars reveal in such crude registers as pronouns. This
is true even when the pronomial system is as sensitive to such
differences as it is in Palaung, a language spoken by a small
tribe in the northern Shan States of Burma, which has eleven
pronouns (whereas in English we have three plural pronouns,
Palaung has eight).[2] In such languages you cannot avoid indicating very precisely the borders between those included or *excluded* from being implicated in the meaning of any statement.
The very complex rules governing the use of even such minimal
pairs as you/thou have been shown by Paul Friedrich to be absolutely ubiquitous and of enormous complexity.[3] And Erwin-
Tripp has expanded the analysis to show that even in a language
such as American English, where there is no second person sin-
gular, the kinds of distinctions such a pronominal option makes
available in say French or German are nevertheless present in
the way Americans address each other in names (Bill vs. William)
and titles (Brown vs. Mr. Brown).[4] Anthropologists often note
that in distant places such as Java "it is nearly impossible to say
anything without indicating the social relationship between the
speaker and the listener in terms of status and familiarity."[5] But
the same is increasingly recognized to be the case closer to home.
English lacks fully worked out vocabularies of hierarchy, but
we are no more able to avoid recognizing rank in our speech than
the Javanese. As an example of this, let me cite an item from a
recent *San Francisco Examiner,* in which an invitation to an army
social is quoted as addressed to "Officers with their ladies and
enlisted men with their wives."[6]

Recent work in such areas as sociolinguistics (especially by Dell
Hymes and William Labov) and ethnolinguistics (especially the
work of C.O. Frake and the group around the journal *Alcheringa*)
have done much to further elucidate Bakhtin's emphasis on the
dialogic aspect of the word. But they, as well as philosophers
who have devoted their attention to speech act theory (Austin,

Searle, Grice) and even innovative sociologists (such as C. Wright Mills and Erving Goffman) have all tended to reduce the variegated complexities of a *parole*-based concept of language to a homogenizing set of rules of one sort or another. The rules may be deduced from observation of actual *performance* and their terms may be *social* rather than logical, but the "scenarios," "frames," and "tree diagrams" which result tend to obscure the wider implications of recognizing that "the immediate social situation and the broader social milieu wholly determine — and determine from within, so to speak — the structure of an utterance" (*Marxism and the Philosophy of language*, p. 86).

To put it another way: in the years since 1929 there has been no shortage of studies which demonstrate the dependence of language as a system on the other (but internecine) system of its social context, and that "the structure of the utterance and of the very experience being expressed is a social structure" (*Marxism and the Philosophy of Language*, p. 93). Labov has shown that lower class black children in New York are perfectly capable of interpreting sentences spoken in standard English, but use only substandard English when speaking among themselves.[7] And even more dramatically E.M. Albert has shown that among the Burundi of East Africa, "a peasant may command the verbal abilities stressed and valued in the culture but [he] cannot display such [abilities] in the presence of a herder or other superior. In such cases appropriate behavior is that in which their words are haltingly delivered or run on uncontrolled, their voices are loud, their gestures wild, their figures of speech ungainly, their emotions freely displayed, [and] their words and sentences clumsy."[8] It would seem, then, that the new sciences of socio- and ethnolinguistics — having recognized the home of their subject in social organization — would finally have developed a set of procedures adequate to Bakhtin's insistence on the dialogic nature of the word.

But such is not the case, since most sociolinguists separate the practices they initially recognize as dependent *on* specific cultural contexts *from* those contexts: the distinctive speech of young blacks in Bedford-Stuyvesant or Burundi peasants in East Africa is studied as a contribution to our understanding of language with a capital L, rather than for what they might reveal about these societies as such. Language in current linguistics is not treated, in other words, as part of a living social totality even when it is derived from societal practice in given cultures. The professional caution of sociolinguists has created a conceptual gap that their less timorous colleagues in other departments have been more than eager to fill: some of the most ambitious attempts to create cultural models based on the social essence of language have been made not by linguists or social scientists, but by literary critics anxious to place those texts which occupy their professional interest in a more comprehensive world of discourse, a universe that increasingly seems to be constituted entirely of texts of one sort or another.

Such critics concur with many assumptions which are obvious on the conceptual surface of *Marxism and the Philosophy of Language*. But none of them, it seems to me, is capable of accounting for the peculiarities which marked the production of *Marxism and the Philosophy of Language* as a specific text in a given place at a given time. They all will agree on the need to refer to a social genesis, to an ideological context for understanding the meaning of any specific text. But none of them will be able to account for the particular kind of double-voiced configuration that *Marxism and the Philosophy of Language* enacts in its relationship to time, place, and particular mix of ideologies in which it was written.

Before going on, then, to indicate what seem to me to be gaps in some current models of culture, let me briefly sketch certain peculiarities attendant on the appearance of *Marxism and the Philosophy of Language* in 1929 and which I believe call into question the comprehensiveness assumed in such models.

A first peculiarity is the fact that the book, while written by Bakhtin, was published under the name of his friend, Valentin Nikolaevich Voloshinov. This is not the only case of plagiarism in reverse to be laid at Bakhtin's door during the 1920s. He published another book (*Freudianism: A Critical Sketch,* 1927) and an article ("Discourse in Life and Discourse in Art," *Zvezda,* 1926, no. 6, pp. 244–67) under Voloshinov's name; a book attacking the Formalists under the name of his friend P.N. Medvedev

(*The Formal Method in Literature Study,* 1928); plus an article on Vitalism in a science journal under the name of another friend, the eminent biologist I.I. Kanaev (also in 1926).

This is not the place to rehearse the long and complex proofs of Bakhtin's authorship of these books and articles. Suffice it to say that there is no doubt that he is their begetter (I do not say "onlie," because in Bakhtin's theory there *are* no "onlie" begetters). But it is germane to our argument to dwell for a moment on his reasons for entering into what might be called, in his own terminology, such a *polyphonic* arrangement with his friends. These reasons are complex, and different in the case of each book or article, but essentially they all boil down to expediency: Bakhtin was notorious in Leningrad intellectual circles as a *tserkovnik,* a man vitally interested in religious matters; he was close to such figures as A.A. Meyer, K.A. Polovtseva and G.P. Fedotov of the *Voskresenie* group, which gathered weekly for prayer and discussion. Since early in his career, while still living in retreat from the capital in Byelorussia (1918–1924), Bakhtin had been working on a *magnum opus* that he hoped would succeed in doing for the Russian religious tradition what Hermann Cohen had failed to do in his last book (*Religion der Vernunft,* 1918) for *Judaism:* that is, to recast all of West European metaphysics in the light of religious thought; to show, as it were, that philosophy had in a sense always been anticipated by religion. The problems metaphysics had not solved within its own categories could be shown to be resolvable within theology. This intention resulted in an enormous book Bakhtin wrote during the early 1920s about moral philosophy.

Only portions of this manuscript have survived, written in pencil on crumbling student note pads.[9] It bears no title, but internal evidence suggests it might be called *The Architectonics of Responsibility,* since it is devoted to the problem of how I give shape to the world through the values I articulate in my deeds. The work contains a full-blown axiological theory having clear ties both with Neo-Kantianism and with Husserlian phenomenology. The theory is couched in its own highly idiosyncratic language that exploits Russian for its unique coining capacities, much as Heidegger plays with German and Greek.

We shall not have time to dwell on this work, but in order to proceed it must be kept in mind that *it contains in embryo every major idea Bakhtin was to have for the rest of his long life.* The whole *conception* of the work, a kind of phenomenological meditation on Christ's injunction to treat others as you would yourself be treated, was wildly at odds with the time and place in which Bakhtin lived. He attempted to publish a watered-down version of one section in 1924, but the journal that had been foolhardy enough to accept it (*Russkii sovremennik*) was closed down before the fragment could be published. Bakhtin's problem, then, was to find ways he could translate his idiosyncratic religious ideas into a language and a genre that would be publicly acceptable in the Soviet Union at a time when that country had already begun its march into the dark night of the 1930s.

The problem became even more urgent in the latter half of the 1920s, since Bakhtin could find no work. He and his wife lived the most ascetic of lives, existing for long periods on little more than strong tea and smoking endless even stronger cigarettes in an effort to keep warm. At this point the theoretical epicenter of his work — how to reconcile modern linguistics with the Biblical assurance that the Word became flesh — overlapped with his own most pressing practical needs: how was he to find an appropriate ideological flesh for the spirit of his own words so that he could sell his work before wasting completely away.

His solution was the conception of a number of books, each of which would convey only one aspect of the general theory of his *Architectonics,* but all of which could be presented in the Marxist idiom of the day. Thus a major thesis of his axiology had been that human existence is the interaction between a given world that is always already there (*uzhe stavshee bytie*) and a mind that is conjoined (*priobshchen*) to this world through the activity (*postupok*) of enacting values. It would be possible, for instance, to define the given aspect of the world as the "socio-economic base." A central obsession in the axiology is the relationship between the "I" and "the other." In the *Architectonics* this irreducible duality is seen as a consequence of the need to *share* being (his term for human existence is *sobytie bytiia,* the "coexistence [but a word that also means *event*] of being"). But the necessity of always accounting for others can also be treated as the primacy of the *social.* In the Freud book Bakhtin says "dialectical materialism [demands that] . . . human psychology be socialized."[10] We might add this is not only the demand of "dialectical materialism," but of Bakhtin's own system of ethics as well, in which there is no "I" without "the other."

Marx sometimes appears in the works published in the late twenties as an honored philosopher who very early saw the systematic implications of man's social being. Thus his *Sixth Thesis on Feuerbach* is quoted with approval: "The essence of man is not an abstraction inherent in each separate individual. In its reality it is the aggregate of social relationships [*Freudianism,* p. 5]." But this emphasis on the collective and social dimension in human beings is not, of course, an exclusively Marxist attitude. Another area where such a position is an enabling a priori is, obviously, the study of language: Zellig Harris relates that after Leonard Bloomfield read *Capital* in the 1930s he "was impressed above all with the similarity between Marx's statement of social behavior and that of linguistics."

But Marxist terms are most often present in Bakhtin's books from this period as a kind of *convenient,* not necessarily *inimical* — and above all, *necessary* — flag under which to advance his own views: if the Christian word were to take on Soviet flesh it had to clothe itself in ideological disguise. But there is nothing in his argument that depends exclusively on a set of assumptions that are specifically Marxist.

But of course it would have been impossible for Bakhtin himself, in the right circle of the Leningrad intelligentsia, to publish self-dramatizingly Marxist works, even had he wished to: everyone knew of his religious beliefs. But two of his *friends* could publish such works without straining credulity: Voloshinov because he was a relative unknown, a minor poet, amateur musicologist and student of linguistics about whose personal convictions very little was generally known; and Medvedev, because he was not only a Marxist, but a well-known and energetic member of the Party, former chairman of the Central Committee in Vitebsk province, and in Leningrad a frequent go-between in the Party's dealings with people in the theater and other intellectuals. Each of these men had his own reasons for entering the deception: Voloshinov because he wanted to help his beloved friend and mentor; Medvedev because he felt such a book might raise his stock both in the Party and among the ranks of the intelligentsia. So it was that the three books were published as if they were contributions *to* Marxist theory put forward *by* committed Soviet Marxists. The parts Voloshinov and Medvedev were assigned required both actors to have well established *emplois.*

Did Bakhtin — as so many others — have completely to *misrepresent* his beliefs in order to publish in the conditions obtaining in the Soviet Union? The answer, while it must, of course, be highly qualified, is that he did *not.* The Voloshinov and Medvedev books are, among other things, investigations into the mystery of the voice; they probe the surprising complexities that lie hidden in the apparently elementary question, "*Who* is talking?" When discussing the phenomenon of "reported" or "indirect speech" (*chuzhaia rech'*, literally in the "speech of another"), there is a point in each of the books where Bakhtin leaves an opening in the surface rhetoric he has woven around his argument. He creates a kind of authorial loophole (*lazeika*), in which he describes exactly what he is doing.

In *Marxism and the Philosophy of Language* one such loophole is constituted by his discussion of the situation that occurs in fiction when the character and author speak with a *single* voice: "The absolute of acting out we understand to be not only a change of expressive intonation — a change logically possible within the confines of a single voice, a single consciousness — but also a change in voice in terms of the whole set of features individualizing that voice, a change of persona ('mask') in terms of a whole set of individualizing traits of facial expression and gesticulation, and, finally, the complete self-consistency of this voice and persona throughout the entire acting out of the role . . ." (156–57).

In other words, the text of the book *Marxism and the Philosophy of Language* itself constitutes the kind of dialogic space Bakhtin is talking about within the book *Marxism and the Philosophy of Language*: Bakhtin, as *author,* manipulates the *persona* of Voloshinov, using his Marxist voice to ventriloquize a meaning not specific to Marxism, even when conceived as only a discourse.

The recurring motifs of *Marxism and the Philosophy of Language* — "the concrete utterance," "the living word," and "the word in the word" — bespeak in their Marxist context an emphasis on the here and now, on the intensely immediate exchange between living people in actual historical and social encounters. Does not this emphasis on the material world of the present preclude any religious interpretation?

Some background is necessary here: such motifs are present in the Russian *religious* tradition as well, even the insistence on materialism. Nicolas Zernov has recently pointed out, "the fundamental conviction of the Russian religious mind is the potential holiness of matter. . . ."[11] This concern for the materiality of things is nowhere more insistently present in Orthodoxy than in its ancient obsession with the corporeality of Christ, the emptying out of spirit, *kenosis,* when the Word took on flesh during the life of Jesus. From the time of their conversion as a nation the Russians have venerated Christ not as the Byzantine Pantocrator, but as a humble man, a tradition exemplified by "God-Manhood," not only for such would-be mystics as Merezhkovskii, but even for political radicals such as Gor'kii, who preached God-building (*bogostroitel'stvo*) from the rostrum of the Writers' Union Congresses as late as the 1930s.

There is no time to trace this "kenotic" tradition in any detail, but we should keep in mind that the first Russian saints, Boris and Gleb, were canonized not because they were martyrs for the faith. The motivation for their deaths was cold-bloodedly political: they were assassinated by their brother Sviatopolk to insure his inheritance of their father's throne. But they submitted humbly and meekly to the knives of their attackers, and it is this humility, this following of Christ's example (Russians shy away from the idea of "imitatio") for which they were made saints. G.P. Fedotov, a member of the Voskresenie group which Bakhtin frequented, in his history of the Russian religious mind (written after Fedotov's emigration) points out that St. Theodosius, founder of the greatest of the old monasteries, was opposed to any mysticism. In this, he "is the spokesman of ancient Russia. . . . The terms in which he speaks of his love for Christ are quite remarkable: the Eucharistic bread speaks to him not only of Christ, but especially of Christ's flesh."[12]

This tradition was kept alive in Russian religious experience throughout the centuries: at times the obsession with Christ's corporeality was manifest in extreme forms, such as the sect of the *Khlysty,* an Orthodox version of Tantrism, whose sexual orgies were an inveterate feature (and whose importance in the twentieth century was highlighted by the central role of Rasputin at the Court of the last Romanov czar).

Bakhtin's work in axiology was a philosophical contribution to this tradition: its thesis is that men define their unique place in existence through the responsibility they enact for their own Being, the care (in the Heideggerian sense of *Sorge*) they exhibit for others and the world in their deeds. Deed is understood as meaning *word* as well as physical act: the deed is how meaning comes into the world, how brute factuality is given significance and form, how the Word continues to become flesh. This context helps to explain the somewhat puzzling conclusion to *Marxism and the Philosophy of Language,* whose final words concern "the present alarming instability and uncertainty of the ideological word. . . . This stage in the vicissitudes of the word . . . can be characterized as the stage of *transformation of the word into a thing. . . .* The ideologues of this process, both here [!] and in Western Europe, are the formalistic movements in poetics, linguistics, and the philosophy of language. One hardly need mention here what the underlying social factors explaining this process are [or] . . . the only ways . . . a revival of the ideological word can come about — the word with its theme intact, the word permeated with confident and categorical social value judgment, the word that really means and takes *responsibility* for what it says" (159).

Marxism and the Philosophy of Language, if treated as an utterance, that is a statement whose meaning depends on the unrepeatable historical and social context in which it was pronounced as well as on the repeatable words of the text, is, then, a very complex example of the transcoding possibilities of in-

direct speech, *chuzhaia rech'*, the speech of the other: Bakhtin
has appropriated the code of one ideology to make public the
message of quite another ideology.

Bakhtin's ventriloquism raises several thorny questions, but
the one I'd like to concentrate on is the issue of linguistic deter-
minism. How can we systematically account for his ability to
use terms from one ideology to body forth a message born in a
different ideology? Most models for conceiving the relationship
between an individual consciousness and the expressive means
society makes available to such consciousness will not help us
here. This is so, it seems to me, because even the most powerful and sophisticated of these presume the *necessity of false consciousness*. Pierre Macherey,[13] using Althusser, has concluded
that authors can never express the truth of their placement vis à
vis the reigning myths of their own time and place: their texts
will always be incomplete in the sense that they will leave out
the author's complicity in his own web of — unavoidable — mis-
recognitions. Thus Jules Verne might "figure" [consciously pro-
mote] the ideology of the colonializing French bourgeoisie of
the Third Republic, but a discerning critic will be able to perceive a gap in his texts where, unknown to the historical subject
Jules Verne, he is "representing" a powerful critique of that
ideology. There are, as it were, two voices, two ideologies to be
found in a single text, but only as it is constituted by the astute
reader who can overcome its own delusion, the delusion of the
author, that it (he) is monologic.

Clearly, such a theory cannot account for Bakhtin's very consciously wrought creolization of different ideologies in the texts
he published as Voloshinov. In his case we get the very opposite
of what Macherey proposes: it is the *author* who knew more
about the ideologies concealed in the gaps of his text than the
"discerning readers" in the Soviet censorship. The science of
ideologies most capable of accounting for Bakhtin's dialogic
practice is, not surprisingly, his own.

In his book on Freud, Bakhtin redefines the distinction between
the conscious and the unconscious. This part of the argument
is initiated by a bold act of substitution. The distinction between
unconscious and conscious is seen as a difference not between

two different kinds of reality, but as variants of the same phenomenon: *both* are aspects of consciousness. So, instead of going further in the mistaken assumption that there is an ontological difference between the two, we should rather perceive the distinction as *ideological:* the unconscious is a suppressed, relatively idiosyncratic ideological realm (insofar as ideology can ever *not* be shared), whereas the conscious is a public world whose ideologies may be shared openly with others. "Freud's unconscious can be called the 'unofficial conscious' as distinct from the ordinary 'official conscious'."

"The language of the unofficial conscious is inner speech, while the language of the official conscious is outward speech, but they both operate according to the general rules of all human verbal behavior. And *the verbal component of behavior is determined in all fundamentals and essentials of its content by objective social factors. . . .* Therefore nothing verbal in human behavior (inner and outward speech equally) can under any circumstances be reckoned to the account of the individual subject in isolation; the verbal is not his property but the property of his *social group* (his social milieu) . . ." (83).

There is, of course, a *hierarchy* of causes and effects that stretches from the content of the individual psyche (*individual,* but never isolated) to the content of a large system of culture. But the route between the two extremes is a highway governed by the same rules of the road: "At all stages of this route human consciousness operates through *words* . . ." (87). It follows that "Any human verbal utterance is an ideological construct in the small. The *motivation* of one's behavior is juridical and moral behavior on a small scale; an exclamation of joy or grief is a primitive lyric composition; pragmatic considerations of the causes and consequences of happenings are germinal forms of scientific and philosophical cognition; and so on and so forth. The stable, formulated ideological systems of the sciences, the arts, jurisprudence and the like, have sprung and crystallized from that seething ideological element where broad waves of inner and outward speech engulf our every act and our very perception" (88).

But if there are important similarities between the modus operandi of individual psyches and whole culture systems, there are also important differences. In outlining these we become aware of the reasons for Bakhtin's substituting unofficial/official consciousness for Freud's unconscious/conscious distinction.

While the systems of the individual psyche and of whole societies are both ideological through and through, ideology has a different status in each. The primary difference consists in the achieved, stable quality of official ideologies that are shared by the group as a whole. They are, in Bakhtin's own terminology, "finished off" (*zavershen*), the source of what he will call in his 1930s version of the same distinction the discourse of authority ("*avtoritetnoe slovo*").[14] Because of its rigidity, it is ever present, it is "prelocated discourse" (*prenakhodimoe slovo*), the language, then, of the fathers, a past that is still very present.

Over against this fixed system of values Bakhtin poses another system, which he calls behavioral ideology: "that inner and outward speech that permeates our [individual, 'personal'] behavior in all its aspects" (88). As opposed to broadly based social values, behavioral ideology is "more sensitive, more responsive, more excitable and livelier" than is an ideology that has undergone formulation and become 'official'." It is *not* finished off, and corresponds to what in the 1930s Bakhtin will call innerly-persuasive discourse (*vnutrenno-ubeditel'noe slovo, Voprosy*, 157 ff.). It is unfinished, not completely formulated, because it is the world made ideological from the point of view of a developing individual consciousness which lives in "the absolute future" of possibility. Behavioral ideology is shaped by the laws of what Bakhtin has called horizon (*krugozor*), societal ideology by the laws of surroundings (*okruzhenie*).

The opposition Bakhtin sets up here, although carefully camouflaged in Marxist terminology and neutral adjectives (i.e., "social," "behavioral") is still the master opposition at the heart of his *Architectonics:* the conflict between a set of values grounded in the self and a set of values grounded in the other. What Bakhtin is saying with his distinction between behavioral ideology (which is, of course, a euphemism for the operations of the *ja dlia sebia,* the "I for myself") and social ideology (a euphemism for the operations of alterity, *drugost'*) is that there is a gap between the two. Individual consciousness never — even among the most wholly committed ideologues — fully replicates the structure of the society's public values. This was the great mistake of the "vulgar Marxists" such as Pereverzev, who believed that everything about even such idiosyncratic figures as Gogol and Dostoevskii could be explained by their social origin, that there is no gap between individual and class consciousness. In his *Architectonics* Bakhtin explains the gap in ontological terms: the self and the other are seen to constitute two different realities that can never fuse on a single plane. In the Freud book the explanation for the gap is developmental, i.e., the more primitive behavioral ideology is still inchoate: when it finds its highest expression it will be fixed in the *shared* values of an official ideology, a perhaps necessary dissembling if so radical a distinction is to be maintained at all. But, even so, the clear implication is that the traffic between the social and the individual is not all one way: an ideology, once formulated, has an enormous impact on the individuals comprising the society whose values it defines. But the *opposite* is also the case, for "in the depths of behavioral ideology accumulate those contradictions which, once having reached a certain threshold, ultimately burst asunder the system of the official ideology" (88).

Bakhtin quickly backs away from the larger implications of the gap between self and other to return to his criticism of Freud. What Freud calls consciousness Bakhtin has renamed official consciousness because its content is in relatively close accord with the socially approved values of the culture as a whole: "On these levels of behavioral ideology, inner speech comes easily to order and freely turns into outward speech or, in any case, has no fear of becoming outward speech" (89).

But, "other levels corresponding to Freud's unconscious lie at a great distance from the stable system of the ruling ideology. They bespeak the disintegration of the unity and integrity of the system, the vulnerability of the usual ideological motivations" (89).

What Bakhtin has done is to realize in a recognizably Russian scenario Freud's metaphor of censorship: the unconscious, as unofficial conscious, operates like a minority political party opposed to certain aspects of the reigning politics of a culture.

The more of these it opposes, the more "censored" it is, because the difference between its values and those of the majority will be expressed as a difference of languages; the less the unofficial party has in common with the official ideology, the more restricted will be its expressive means. Insofar as the minority cannot *share* its values, it is condemned to a relative silence. It is as if an Eskimo revolutionary group, seeking independence from the United States, were to flood New York City with manifestoes written in Athabaskan — even though *willing* a conflict with the majority culture, they are condemned to inaction by the structure of communication, the architectonics of value. In a very real sense, what Bakhtin is doing may be likened to the efforts of early Christians to spread their message by parable. The clandestine church in Leningrad during these years was called "the catacomb church" because its members felt they lived in times very similar to those first-century sectarians who met by night in cellars below the imperial marble of a hostile Rome. It is here we should seek the reasons Bakhtin feels compelled to revise Freud's scenario of conflict between the official and unofficial conscious. When he writes "the wider and deeper the breach between the official and unofficial conscious, the more difficult it becomes for motives of inner speech to turn into outward speech . . . wherein they might acquire formulation, clarity and vigor" (89), he is describing his own dilemma, the increasing gap between his own religious and metaphysical ideas and the Soviet government's ever more militant insistence on adherence to Russian Communism. Bakhtin says, "Motives under these conditions begin to . . . lose their verbal countenance, and little by little really do turn into a 'foreign body' in the psyche," but it is clear he means as well that they become foreign bodies in the state as well.

His daring insistence on the uniplanar coexistence of the rules of governance in the psyche with the rules for governance in the state is not only a new way to conceive Freudian theory. It explains as well Bakhtin's practice of sending out transcoded messages from the catacombs. He has just said that the gap between official and unofficial conscious can become so great that finally the content of the unofficial conscious is snuffed out.

But if we remember that the traffic between the terminus of an individual psyche and that of a whole culture moves in *both* directions, a more optimistic scenario can be conceived for unofficial forces: it is not true "that every motive in contradiction to the official ideology must degenerate into indistinct inner speech and then die out — it might well engage in a struggle with that official ideology [and] . . . if it is not merely the motive of a déclassé loner, then it has a chance for a future and perhaps even a *victorious future*. . . . At first a motive of this sort will develop within a small social milieu and will depart into the underground — not the psychological underground, but the salutary political underground." And as if to underscore the applicability of such a scenario to his own case, he goes so far as to emphasize that this is *"exactly how a revolutionary ideology in all spheres comes about"* (90).

We live in an age of wildly proliferating theories. Attempts to frame a science of ideologies are especially numerous. Bakhtin's is assured of a central and honored place among these for two reasons. The first and obvious one is the comprehensiveness and intrinsic power of his dialogic model. The second is the close fit between the theory and the praxis that was Bakhtin's life: Who should know more about base and superstructure than a man from the underground?

Indiana University

NOTES

1. V.N.Voloshinov, *Marxism and the Philosophy of Language,* tr. Ladislav Matejka and I.R.Titunik (New York: Seminar Press, 1973), p. 94.
2. R.Burling, *Man's Many Voices* (New York: Holt, Rinehart, Winston, 1970).
3. P.Friedrich, "Structural Implications of Russian Pronomial Usage," *Sociolinguistics,* ed. W.Bright (The Hague: Mouton, 1966), pp. 214–33.
4. S.M.Erwin-Tripp, "Sociolinguistics," *Advances in Experimental Social Psychology,* ed. T.Berkowitz (New York: Norton, 1969), vol. 4, pp. 93–107.
5. C.Geertz, "Linguistic Etiquette," *Sociolinguistics,* ed. J.B.Pride

and Janet Holmes (Harmondsworth: Penguin Books, 1972), p. 167.

6. Cited by J.J.Gumperz, "Sociolinguistics and Communication in Small Groups," *Working Paper* no. 33, Language Behavior Research Laboratory, 1970, University of California, Berkeley.

7. W.Labov, *The Social Stratification of English in New York City* (New York: Center for Applied Linguistics, 1966).

8. Hymes, in Pride and Holmes, p. 276.

9. A portion of the existing MS. (one out of five sections) has been published under the self-consciously neutral title "Author and Hero" in the latest collection of Bakhtin's writings to appear in the Soviet Union. See "Avtor i geroi," *Estetika slovesnogo tvorchestva,* ed. S.G.Bocharov, S.S.Averintsev (Moscow: Iskusstvo, 1979), pp. 7–180.

10. V.N.Voloshinov, *Freudianism: A Marxist Critique,* tr. I.R.Titunik (New York: Academic Press, 1976), p. 22.

11. *Russian Religious Renaissance of 20th Century* (London, 1963), p. 285.

12. *The Russian Religious Mind* (Cambridge, Mass.: Harvard University Press, 1946), vol. 1, p. 129.

13. *A Theory of Literary Production,* tr. Geoffrey Wall (London: Routledge, Kegan Paul, 1978).

14. *Voprosy literatury i estetiki* (Moscow: Khudozhestvennaia literatura, 1975), p. 155. The University of Texas Press has now published four of the major essays in this volume under the title of *The Dialogic Imagination,* ed. M.Holquist, tr. Caryl Emerson and M.Holquist (Austin, 1981).

PHILOSOPHY OR LITERARY CRITICISM

ALEXANDER PIATIGORSKY

> Can we entrust such an important
> matter as culture to our reason?
>
> Are we not fearful to death of words
> like "decadence" or "regression,"
> which we tend to shun and for which
> we substitute words like "unhappiness"
> or "misfortune," but never "defeat"?[1]

It might seem almost needless to say that from the point of view of philosophy, "literature" appears as a far more concrete object than either "life" or "culture," if only for the simple reason that literature consists of concrete and discrete texts.

As far as Russia is concerned, the initial stage of Russian literary criticism not only happened to coincide with the spread of German speculative philosophy, but, more importantly, having assimilated German philosophical *ideas* — and it was ideas far more than *texts* that the then still very young literary criticism took to itself — it could not but turn them into a kind of culture, thereby separating them from their own speculative context and methodology. The function of philosophy was to provide "cognition of reality," and yet the reality of life was present in the form of a literary text only, and philosophy itself had therefore to wait until the early 1870s for the appearance of Vladimir Soloviev, the first "professional" in Russian philosophy.

One might even go further and say that literature itself came to be regarded as the reality of life. This in turn could be interpreted as one of the indirect consequences of the absence in Russia of that complex European phenomenon, the Enlightenment, a process of intense and sustained efforts to socialize knowledge and objectify the world. Gogol criticism is perhaps a case in point, and Rozanov's commentary on this critical tradition, while itself partaking somewhat of the malaise it analyzes, is apt. None of Vissarion Belinsky's contemporaries was surprised that he treated those notorious letters of Gogol as reality, and not as literature. Rozanov writes more than a half a century later: "From Gogol, there commenced in our society that *loss of a feeling for reality.*"[2] And this was not meant as a metaphor. Rozanov postulated a philosophical principle separating *literature as life* [i.e. "reality"] from the *ethical* criteria of literature as *related* to life. A little further, he wrote:"His [Gogol's] imagination — not properly related to reality, and not properly related to any ideal [Belinsky would surely have written *idea*] — *corrupted* our society and our souls, filling them with deepest suffering. What prevents us from becoming aware of it? Or are we already so completely corrupted that we cannot help but love real life less than . . . the play of shadows in the mirror?"

So literature is not a "reflection" of life — we might recall Lenin's *Lev Tolstoy as a Mirror of the Russian Revolution!*[3] — for it *forms* life, shapes it, makes life real or unreal, natural or artificial, correct or incorrect, or even, moral or immoral. Literature molds our society as though, without it, society would have become "empty" and devoid of meaning.

It was eleven years after those words had been written that Rozanov, in a total reappraisal of the role and function of literature, announced that literature must be literature and nothing more.[4] This implied in turn that philosophy must be philosophy. Yet in the early years of the present century, Rozanov still treated literature as reality or at least as a form of self-awareness without which reality itself could not be reflectively grasped by an external observer.

Neither Belinsky nor Rozanov was an external observer of literature, of course. Nor was Rozanov's mightiest adept, Andrei Siniavsky, when he wrote in 1974 that the subjects under discussion were on his original theme, a belief in the power of words,"[5] however ironic this might have sounded. Neither Belinsky nor Rozanov nor Siniavsky could be considered philosophers. But it was under the impact of Belinsky's pronouncement that Gogol's destiny unfolded outside of literature itself, and Siniavsky's scrutinizing symbolico-mythological analysis in *V teni Gogolia (In the Shadow of Gogol)* stands not far from Rozanov's initial statement. And it was not Chernyshevsky whom Rozanov opposed to Dostoevsky in *Koroby (Baskets)!*

This quasi-Hegelian approach — I say "quasi" because the very notion of a *phenomenology* of the idea was missed — has marked the whole history of Russian literary criticism (the few brilliant exceptions were mercilessly brushed aside) making it serve as a substitute for philosophy and, therewith, not permitting the latter to develop into an independent aspect of Russian culture. One might say, having taken concrete literary texts as its own objects, Russian philosophy did not become concretized with respect to its method and object, and remained embedded, imprisoned in culture, without the capacity of standing outside its own culture while taking it as an object. This is to say that it had to be confined to the realm of cultural self-awareness (*samoosoznanie*) and self-cognition (*samopoznanie*) which in some other cultures (in German, and partly in French) had been mastered during their respective periods of Enlightenment.

Self-awareness as formulated by N.A. Berdiaev with regard to Russian philosophy might be represented there in two quite distinct, though often overlapping, variants.

First, self-awareness could be based on the idea of historic tradition (cultural above all) reduced in its turn to the idea of a *Volksgeist,* more Schellingian than Hegelian. Culture would in this case remain, as it were, "undecoded" and remain apprehended thereby as an instance (or stage) of *historic consciousness.* This was especially typical of Khomiakov and the early Slavophiles.

Second, self awareness could be based on the idea of *reality* (the reality of the idea, of reason, or of life) taken in all of its idealistic as well as materialistic implications, and applied first of all to literature, by both philosophers and literary critics. And indeed, in Russian philosophizing, a literary text was (unconsciously sometimes) conceived of as a *natural object* of philosophy, while in Russian literary criticism, philosophy (now explicitly, now implicitly) was regarded as the *natural method* by means of which a literary text was to be analyzed, ratiocinated, and "returned to culture." This attitude has not by any means been outmoded; even today, it is adopted by many.

Literary criticism functioned as philosophy, and philosophy served as the "inner focus" of literary criticism. They were so utterly intermingled in Russian culture as to be indistinguishable, and this is particularly true if they are observed in historical retrospect.

In the late 1940s, all the major universities in the USSR were ordered to establish departments, sections, and chairs of Russian philosophy. During the following decade, dozens of books were published and hundreds of dissertations were defended on the "philosophies" of Herzen, Belinsky, Dobroliubov, Chernyshevsky, Pisarev, etc. (while religious Russian philosophy was "strictly forgotten" or "abolished"). It is a bitter irony that the cynical and ignorant ideologue-leaders of that period simply could not have known that all the "progressive and democratic" literary critics had indeed been, at least in their main intention and attitude towards literary texts, "philosophers" of a peculiarly home-baked variety.

Even when the separating out of professional philosophy began, even after a philosophy developed that had its own objects and methods, it could not immediately dispose of literature as its primary point of departure; or, at least its pretext. In such an emphatically eschatological context as that of Soloviev's *Three Conversations,* Lev Tolstoy figures not only as the object of a metaphysical critique, but also as the embodiment and personal manifestation of a certain objectively fixed esthetical and literary pattern. Furthermore, Berdiaev in *Ghosts of the Russian Revolution* (*Dukhi russkoi revoliutsii,* Berlin, 1922) construes his ontological scheme of Russian history on the basis of "antinomian" dialogues from *The Brothers Karamazov.* Even Lev Shestov in the essays of *In Job's Balances* demonstrates his concept of "Revelation through Death" by using the plots and situations of Dostoevsky's fiction and especially of Tolstoy's "Master and Man."

Observing the beginning of the nineteenth century from the perspective of the end of the twentieth, it is amusing to note that P.Ia. Chaadaev, the main precursor of Russian "Westernism" seems to have been, at least in his "philosophy of culture," very close to Slavophilism. For both Chaadaev and Khomiakov, "Russian reality" seemed to lack something essential — a unifying factor that could unite culture on the one hand and the "real life" of people on the other. Chaadaev saw this unifying factor in "Christian civilization," while Khomiakov saw it in the *sobornost'* of Christian-Orthodox Church Unity. (According to Berdiaev, neither concept really belonged in the realm of philosophy, properly speaking, but rather to that of cultural self-awareness.) The "culture" problem thus is not merely a constant of Russian philosophy, but seems at times almost its obsession.[6]

The recent discussion of "Christian culture" in Moscow and in emigrant circles abroad merely returns us to the problem which began to take shape with Chaadaev and continued through Leontiev to Berdiaev and S. Bulgakov: Is there such a thing as a *Christian* culture? If so, what does it mean? Can *any* culture be, or become, Christian?[7] Here, too, the *criteria* of what constitutes a culture, and partly even what constitutes Christianity, have remained mostly literary.

A moment of the utmost importance in the development of this culture theme is that of *cultural relativism*. It has been, indeed, a touchstone for Russian philosophers, almost all of them tending to converge on the notion, at least in their private view. They might say, "We've had enough for the time being," or, to paraphrase Nekrasov slightly, "We've had enough poets; — let's have a few citizens now!" It should be clear that what we mean here by "cultural relativism" is *not* that values are relative to the cultural system in which they are embedded, but that *culture itself* is a relative value, and that by culture what is still largely meant is *literature*.

It was perhaps Rozanov who treated culture most relativistically, insisting that it was "as bad as Gogol," for culture (i.e. literature) "binds us in a knot and returns us to . . . what is not Christ, but what is rather . . . life." At the end of his life, Rozanov made a sharp distinction between "Great Literature," with a capital L, understood as culture, and "simple literature" which assumed some of the features of what we might call *civilization* as opposed to culture. Thus, in relation to Christ, literature was seen as nothing; while, in relation to life, literature was considered more than a little something.

To the early Sergei Bulgakov, culture was a reflection of men's faith or faithlessness in God, and it was focused through literature. That is, according to the early Bulgakov, apart ftom the question of faith in God, there is no culture at all. In other words, culture is not faith itself, but it is *a way* in which men either have or do not have faith.[8]

To Berdiaev, it seemed a far more complex problem. Rozanov's position seemed to him "cultural nihilism," and sheer neglect of tradition. Yet Berdiaev himself regarded culture as the *static* aspect of creativity; as a creative impulse already frozen and thus belonging to the past. His metaphysical evaluation of culture, however, finds itself repeatedly in blatant contradiction with his factual, empirical attitude, in the context of which culture always plays the role of the highest among relative values. This often led him astray from philosophy and made him a rather mediocre historian or publicist.

In the context of the sophiological, eschatological approach (from which Berdiaev deviated) the value of culture (qua literature) was seen in the fact that it must carry within itself the *noumenal meanings* to be revealed to this (or to some other) stage of history, apart from which it had no use at all. I would assert that the position of V. Ivanov and Gershenzon to the effect that "culture is above the level and beyond the realm of reason," could be regarded as a kind of delayed reflex to this approach.

One cannot in any case, metaphysically speaking, call Russian culture as a whole "Christian," for that would inevitably force one to see so many exceptions that one could not apply the rubric even as conditionally true. And the main point would be that the very *idea* of the Christian character of Russian culture became possible only after it had been worked out and intensely reflected upon in Russian literature — at least twenty years before it emerged in Russian philosophy and Free Theology. From a formidable presence in literature, it passed into philosophical speculation while carrying with it all the traces of its literary origin. Those thinkers who branched off from Dostoevsky — above all, Leontiev and Rozanov — would certainly have rejected any notion that Russian culture as a whole is Christian (each for his own reason, of course), and rejected it "from the threshold." And this idea would not even have existed in philosophy had it not been presented in literary formation.

And was Berdiaev not right when he wrote of Rozanov: "He was a brilliant thinker, he was a genius, but he never was a Christian"? And was Rozanov not right when he wrote of Leontiev: "He was a great thinker, but he never was a man of the Church (*tserkovnyi chelovek*); he did not love the Church"? And these days when V. Borisov so bitterly reproaches G. Pomerants and B. Shragin for their "rationalistic" neglect of certain aspects of Russian history and historicity, he is also right. But they are all wrong in that none of them is yet able to detach himself from his own culture, from considering it as the only and unique one, nor has any of them reflected on his cultural position as "a certain position." Examined from that perspective, each of the persons mentioned above would have to be seen as a *writer,* doing one and the same thing as the others — *literature.*

This "literariness" of Russian philosophy has contributed a good deal to another quite typically Russian tendency, an overwhelming subjectivism. In philosophical polemics one finds it commonplace to treat a thinker as if he were a personage from a novel or a story, while in literary polemics it is equally common to treat a fictive personage as if he or she were necessarily the bearer of an abstract idea. This has often resulted in a methodological confusion, an erratic mixture of ethical, esthetic, and metaphysical criteria. Moreover, no philosophical concept, no matter how abstract or speculative, can be dealt with otherwise than as embodied in a person, whether living or dead, real or imaginary. For such is the traditional method, often unconsciously applied, of "fixing" objects in Russian philosophy. It is a method whose very character has been predetermined by the "personalism" of Russian culture as reflected and transformed through literature.

Further, this philosophical literariness has always led to the attempt to discover in the discrete literary texts an *objective historical content;* and Russian history itself has been transformed into an object of religious philosophy, that is, into an *historiosophy.* From the angle of the historiosophical approach, Russian literature appears as a series of historical prophecies or predictions, from Lermontov's *"Predskazanie"* through Dostoevsky to Blok and Bely.[9] Russian philosophy was discovering Russian history in the *literary* texts, appropriating and "fixing" it then as its own object.[10] One should not therefore be surprised that to V. Soloviev it was Lev Tolstoy, and not Pobedonostsev or John of Kronstadt who served as a landmark for this particular period of history.

Unlike Hegel and Marx who believed they themselves were engaged in creating the essence of history, Russian religious philosophers have cultivated the intuition that it was Russian literature that had a direct access to history; and that the philosopher's task was to decipher the anagrams of poetic images into a meaningful metaphysics of events. Even S. Bulgakov and P. Florensky could not resist the temptation of doing this.[11] It was as if history, formless and unreflected in itself, could reveal itself only through the medium of literary texts, though the texts of a "real" or "true" literature, without the prior existence of which no philosophical reflection was possible. And this tendency has not yet become obsolete.[12]

This eternal return of Russian philosophy of history to Tolstoy, and even more so, to Dostoevsky, provided this philosophy on the one hand with a strong cultural foothold, yet on the other kept it confined with regard to its objects within the limits of cultural self-awareness. There remains, however, an enormous methodological obstacle: from a complex of literary texts, one can conceive a particular type of culture; but no possible succession or sequence of these same texts enables one to conceive *a particular type of history*. Perhaps another way of saying this is that there is no possible historiosophical illusion that could prey on Russian literature all the way. Even given the great tension that surely exists in the relationships between modern Russian religious philosophy and modern Russian structuralism — varying from open hostility to secret admiration — one may well wonder how many steps there really are between "type of culture" and "type of history."[13]

University of London

NOTES

1. This paper was read at Garmisch by Sidney Monas and has been edited and slightly abridged by him with the author's express consent; indeed, at his urging. The first quotation in the epigraph is from M.O. Gershenzon to V. Ivanov, *Perepiska iz dvukh uglov* (Moscow, 1921), p. 15. The second is from a letter by N. Ardatovskii to A. Dmitriev, ca. 1959 (unpublished). For the author's basic approach to the problems of "culture" and "text" and the idea of culture as a collection of texts, see Ju.M. Lotman, A. Piatigorsky, "Le texte et la fonction," *Semiotics,* 1969, no. 1, pp. 205–17.

2. V.V. Rozanov, *O Gogole* (Moscow, 1906 [repr. by Prideaux Press, Letchworth, England, 1970]), pp. 15–16.

3. N.A. Berdiaev wrote: "The art of Tolstoy was not prophetic, but *he was himself revolution."* See *Istoki i smysl russkogo kommunizma* (Paris, 1955), p. 71. (The Russian text dates of course from the 1930s.) Is this not a step forward from Lenin?

4. In the supplement to *Koroby,* written ca. 1918.

5. A. Siniavskii, "Literaturnyi protsess v Rossii," *Kontinent,* no. 1, 1974.

6. The culture problem seems to have been indispensable to Berdiaev, whether with regard to social history or with regard to personal characteristics. For example, he wrote that Socialism does not bear within itself any new type of culture; see *Filosofiia neravenstva,* 2nd ed. (Paris, 1971). "But the level of culture of the 'thinking realists' was low, much lower than that of the idealists of the forties." (*Istoki i smysl,* p. 45). "During the years spent in the West, Plekhanov became a sufficiently cultured person, yet his *type* of culture was not very high. . . ." (p. 78). "Lenin's culture was not of a very high type . . . lower than that of Plekhanov's. . . ." (p. 97).

7. For an approach to the same problem and even the same set of problematics, but within the context of a rather different cultural tradition, from which "literature" is fastidiously excluded, even though the author is one of the two or three great poets of the English speaking world in the twentieth century, see T.S. Eliot, *Notes towards the Definition of Culture,* New York, 1949; see also, by the same author, *The Idea of a Christian Society.*

8. S. Bulgakov, *Tikhie dumy* (Moscow, 1918), especially the chapter *"Trup krasoty"* ("The Corpse of Beauty").

9. This comes across clearly in the fourth chapter of Berdiaev's *Istoki i smysl,* though without a pause for reflection on how this manifests

itself in his own attitude. I think the most brilliantly stupid example of a "prophetic literary text" can be seen in A. Belyi's *Revoliutsiia i kul'-tura* (Moscow, 1917), particularly pp. 6, 7, 24.

10. See P. Florenskii's article on Blok in *Vestnik russkogo khristian-skogo studencheskogo dvizheniia: Le Messager* no. 114 (1974).

11. Ibid.

12. A contemporary Moscow philosopher, V. Trostnikov, called Sol-zhenitsyn "prophet," genuinely believing that a prophecy has some equivalence with "the national" or "the collective," "the extra-personal." See *Vestnik russkogo khristianskogo studencheskogo dvizheniia: Le Messager,* no. 128 (1979), p. 361. More surprising is that even such a brilliant modern Russian theologian as the Rev. A. Shmeman expresses this same idea, *Le Messager,* no. 130. It is as if all of them had forgotten that such a "literary" application of a strictly theological term seems to stand much closer to a typically German and Romantic notion of *Volksgeist* than to any private theological opinion, permissible or possible within the framework of Russian theology.

13. V. Borisov, a contemporary Moscow historian and philosopher, while criticising severely the idea of a logically compulsory principle of historic process, admits nonetheless a kind of "diachronic typology." See "In Search of a Lost History," *Vestnik russkogo studencheskogo dvizheniia: Le Messager,* no. 125 (1978), p. 132.

D. S. LIKHACHEV AND THE STUDY OF
OLD RUSSIAN LITERATURE

EWA M. THOMPSON

In *"Smekhovoi mir" drevnei Rusi,* D.S. Likhachev interprets the humorous literature of Old Russia and applies to it the concepts and ideas associated with the European Middle Ages, in particular, with the carnival festivities in medieval Europe. He asserts that the two kinds of humor are in many ways synonymous:

> Древнерусский смех относится по своему типу к смеху средневековому. . . . Авторы средневековых и в частности, древнерусских произведений чаще всего смешат читателей непосредственно собой. . . . Снижение всего образа, саморазоблачение типичны для средневекового и в частности, древнерусского смеха.[1]

Similar views have been voiced in the programmatic book *Poetika drevnerusskoi literatury:*

> Если характеризовать древнерусскую литературу, пользуясь методом «больших скобок», то следует признать, что она принадлежала по своей структуре к типу литератур средневековых (свойственных ранее и литературам Запада).[2]

While the comments in *"Smekhovoi mir".* . . may be in a certain sense true of European medieval culture, they are misleading at best, and false at worst, when applied to seventeenth-century Muscovite humor (all but one of Likhachev's examples come from that century. Likhachev is profoundly mistaken in his mechanistic application of the concepts of one culture to another, and he leaves us with a distorted picture of the way in which humor functioned in Muscovite society. I propose to substantiate these statements by comparing typical examples of medieval and Muscovite humor.

One of the characteristic manifestations of medieval humor was the carnival and the celebrations and customs it had generated. The French *Mardi Gras,* the Bavarian *Fasching* and their equivalents in other European countries, are the contemporary remnants of this period of festivities preceding Lent during which the customary social, political, and religious hierarchies were temporarily suspended and their opposites were temporarily introduced. The historian of carnival festivities Enid Welsford observes that during that period, "mighty persons were humbled, sacred things profaned, laws relaxed and ethical ideals reversed, under the leadership of a Patriarch, Pope, or Bishop of Fools."[3] In twelfth-century France, the Feast of Fools was celebrated during which a complete reversal of ordinary custom occurred. The lowest deacon of the cathedral was declared bishop or pope or king — depending on the locality — and led his fellow deacons into the stalls of the higher clergy. Then a burlesque mass was performed: censing was done with pudding and sausages, and brays and howls replaced the usual responses of the faithful during mass. On occasion, mock consecrations of bishops were performed. In 1498, the citizens of Tournai captured some clerics of Nôtre-Dame and "consecrated" them as bishops. In other localities, the "abbatial cross" was handed to the citizen who had done the most foolish deed of the year. Similar make-believe ceremonies took place regarding the political order, to mention only the tradition of the carnival kings and queens. In apparent irreverence toward the actual monarch, a commoner was "elected" king by a crowd of people celebrating the carnival.

Civil and religious authorities showed great indulgence toward these antics. Suffice it to say that at medieval universities, which were the barometers of medieval attitudes, students got more days off for the carnival than for Christmas or Easter.[4] Given the authoritarian nature of medieval society, such tolerance seems highly unusual. How can it be explained? To answer this question, let us consider some aspects of the relationship between humor and law in medieval Europe.

The carnival pranks and mock celebrations seemed funny to the citizens of medieval Europe who saw in them a temporary relaxation of norms, a world upside down, a make-believe reversal of what they knew was the actual order of things. As Ernst Curtius points out in his *Europäische Literatur und lateinisches Mittelalter,* there existed in medieval Europe the topos of "the world upside down,"[5] which was one of the principal devices of medieval humor. This topos generated laughter for the reasons later defined by Kant in his reflections on humor as the sudden transformation of a strained expectation into nothing.[6]

Out of such traditions François Rabelais' *Gargantua* and *Pantagruel* were born. These books are loaded with examples of the medieval humorous topos of "the world upside down." Among the examples are the circumstances of, and occurrences during, Gargantua's and Pantagruel's birth and education, Pantagruel's visit to the land of Satin and his founding of the Abbey of Thélème. Let us have a look at this last example.

The Abbey of Thélème represents a total reversal of the medieval idea of the monastery. It admits both sexes, everyone is free to come and go as he pleases, only good looking and young men and women are admitted, and everybody is governed by what occasions and opportunities might arise. The motto of the monastery is "Do as thou wilt."

Such stories seemed funny to the readers of Rabelais because they described a world upside down, one which the laughing person did not take seriously because it was governed by the rules which ran counter to those generally believed to be true. If we accept Kant's definition of humor, it also follows that the concept of law must have been firmly imbedded in, and accepted by, the minds of medieval Europeans, and departures from it seemed unreal and therefore funny.

Let us now look at the works of the seventeenth-century Russian humor and try to determine whether the topos of "the world upside down" which was so central to medieval humor generated laughter in Moscow. According to Likhachev, the narrative "Kaliazinskaia chelobitnaia" is a typical example of Muscovite humor. It tells the story of the archimandrite Gavriil who introduced in his monastery "unusual" customs and rules: he ordered his monks to get up early, go to church and pray; he made them fast and wear shabby clothes; and he spent money on incense and candles instead of food and drink. The monks complained about these innovations to the bishop and demanded reinstitution of the old ways.

Like the description of the Abbey of Thélème, "Kaliazinskaia chelobitnaia" is meant to be funny. But let us not miss the fact that while in the first case, we were asked to laugh at a departure from the rules, in the second we are requested to laugh, as it were, at the rules. The narrative tone of "Kaliazinskaia chelobitnaia" does not convey hostility toward, or condemnation of, the roguish monks. No moral can be drawn from the story unless it be a conclusion that one should sidestep the rules if one has an opportunity to do so. If we were to judge the seventeenth-century Russian humor on the basis of "Kaliazinskaia chelobitnaia," we would have to say that in Old Russia, humor was associated with disregard for the rule of law. By laughing at someone who according to the rules was a perfectly good and reasonable abbot, the readers of "Kaliazinskaia chelobitnaia" partook of the attitude which belittled the rules and "the world as it is supposed to be" and accepted as normal "the world upside down." In "Kaliazinskaia chelobitnaia," the object of ridicule is the world according to the rules, the ideal world. Let us see whether this kind of humorous topos was in any way recurrent in Old Russian literature.

The seventeenth-century narrative "Skazanie o roskoshnom zhitii i veselii" is a description of an ideal world where everything is plentiful and where rivers flow with milk and honey. It is, in short, the Russian version of Ovid's *Aurea prima sata est aetas, que vindice nullo, / Sponte sua, sine lege fidem rectumque colebat.* But unlike Ovid's description of the Golden Age, "Skazanie" is meant to be funny. This is indicated by the roguish "road directions" provided at the end:

> А прямая дорога до того веселья от Кракова до Аршавы и на Мозовшу, а оттуда на Ригу и Ливлянд, оттуда на Киев и на Подолеск, оттуда на Стекольню и на Корелу, оттуда на Юрьев и ко Брести, оттуда к Быхову и в Чернигов, в Переяславль и в Черкасской, в Чигирин и Кафимской. А кого перевезут Дунай, тот домой не думай.[7]

Here we have another indication that in Old Russian literature, the ideal world rather than the imperfect and deformed world fulfilled the role of a humorous topos.

Another example is "Povest' o Shemiakinom sude," a story which enjoyed wide popularity in numerous editions of *luboch-nye kartiny* in the seventeenth, eighteenth, and nineteenth centuries.[8] Once there were two brothers, one rich and one poor. The poor one has been sponging on the rich one for years: *"Bo-gatyi zhe ssuzhaia mnogo let ubogova . . ."* until the rich one lost his patience and sued his brother for negligent treatment of a borrowed horse. On his way to the courthouse, the poor brother's continuing negligence caused the death of two people. He now faced three suits instead of one. When he arrived at the courthouse, he showed the judge a stone wrapped up in a piece of cloth. The judge thought that it was a bribe and ruled in the poor brother's favor in all three cases. When the time came to offer the bribe, the poor brother told the judge that he meant to kill him if he had ruled against him. The judge was so pleased to have avoided such a fate that he let the poor brother go undisturbed. Having extorted some money from his former victims (in addition to the favorable ruling from the judge), the poor brother left for home: *"Ubogii otyde v dom svoi, raduiasia i khvalia Boga."*

What are we laughing at here? The poor brother is cruel, selfish, and dishonest. Yet he is the winner, whereas those in the right: his brother, the priest, the bather whose father was killed, and the law itself, have been ridiculed. Again, laughter is linked to a defiance of rules and norms.

Another example: in the narrative "Skazanie o krest'ianskom syne," a thief robs a peasant's house. While doing so, he mutters pious words which later turn out to be blasphemies, and the peasant (thinking that an angel from heaven came to visit him) allows him to go away with his bounty. One is left with the "moral" that the clever use of blasphemy is the surest road to fortune. Again, this tale suggests that in Old Russia, denigration of norms and rules and ideals was a common component of humorous works.

The same can be said about the best known work of seventeenth-century Russian humor: "Povest' o Frole Skobeeve." In fact, it has been said already, by the English scholar Anthony Stokes:

"The tale has not even the excuse of describing scandalous behavior as a dire warning to sinners. The rogue and thief, as Frol
is called throughout, prospers, leaving as the only possible moral
that seduction is the surest road to fortune."[9]

Stokes could have said it, *mutatis mutandis,* of the majority
of works of seventeenth-century Muscovite humor. They all suggest that "the world according to norms" is to be ridiculed or
disbelieved, and that "the world upside down" is to be accepted
as normal.

Whence comes this repetitious defiance of the rules and why
did the topos of "the world according to the rules" acquire humorous overtones in Muscovite literature? And why did a reverse
ordering take place in Western and Central Europe? The reasons
for this are complex, and many of them have been discussed by
such diverse scholars as Richard Pipes and Iurii Lotman in their
respective works.[10] For our purposes, the most relevant reason
is the Muscovite interpretation of the Byzantine religious tradition. Briefly, in Old Russia there developed an association between humor and sinfulness, humor and defiance of the law. In
this context, humorous works tended to ridicule the law rather
than uphold it. The opposite was true in the rest of Europe.

The roots of this contempt toward laughter go back to Byzantine Christianity which frowned upon merrymaking and humor
to a much greater extent than did the Western Church. Two favorite saints of Russian Orthodoxy: John Chrysostom and Ephraim of Syria, wrote exhortations against laughter and merriment.
While it is true that Ephraim's teachings were directed at monks
rather than lay people, it is also true that in Russia, such teachings were understood as referring to the laity as well as to monks.[11]
Thus Ephraim was probably an indirect source for the joyless life-
style recommended by the sixteenth-century book of household
rules *Domostroi.* In contrast, the saints who were popular in the
West tended to tolerate, and even approve, of gaiety: Benedict tac-
itly permitted moderate laughter, Anthony's discourse was spiced
with godly wit, and Martin used to tell "devout jests." Similarly,
the scholastics generally argued in favor of laughter and jest.[12]

Byzantine austerity contributed to the emergence of a hostility
toward laughter in the social conventions of Muscovy. Silvester's

Domostroi tells us that playing the *bandura,* laughing and dancing are the surest roads to hell. *Domostroi* recommends austerity and joylessness in private households in general, and in the parent-child relationships in particular. It advises fathers not to smile at their sons but instead, to show them a severe and gloomy countenance.[13] *Domostroi* indicates that spontaneous joy and laughter were considered indecent in Muscovite society. It is therefore no accident that the sixteenth-century travellers to Muscovy were struck by the absence of merrymaking in the everyday life of that country.[14]

Eventually, these customs were codified into law. In 1648, the teen-age tsar Aleksei Mikhailovich issued several edicts in which corporal punishment (*knut*) was promised to those who laughed, joked, sang songs in public or in private, to those who played cards, chess, and other social games; and even to those who swung on the swing.[15] These edicts were directed not only against the minstrel-entertainers (*skomorokhi*) but also against private households. In 1672, in violation of his own edicts, Aleksei asked the Moscow clergyman Gottfried Gregorii to assemble a theatrical troupe for court entertainment. Gregorii fulfilled the request and organized the first Russian court theater, which performed some highly stylized Biblical and historical plays at the Moscow court. Aleksei was so worried about his own trespass that he sought the advice of his confessor who promptly released him from the orders imposed on himself by himself. The Moscow theater lasted for four years only. After Aleksei's death, the new tsar Fedor closed it down. The court theater reopened only during the reign of Peter the Great. This reopening was one of the many indications that the links between old and new Russia, specifically, between laughter and defiance of the law, were weakened during the reign of this monarch.

The persecution in Muscovite Russia of the *skomorokhi* provides further support for my thesis about Muscovite humor. As Russell Zguta pointed out in his study of the subject, throughout the Muscovite period the *skomorokhi* were treated with more or less effective hostility by both the church and state authorities.[16] This hostility was rooted in the belief that the *skomorokhi* were carriers of pagan traditions. It seems entirely probable, however,

that the attitude toward the *skomorokhi* was reinforced by the
universal hostility toward merrymaking in Muscovite Russia.

In the 1551 collection of church regulations *Stoglav,* a special
chapter was devoted to the condemnation of the entertainment
inspired by the *Skomorokhi.* The *Stoglav* states the following:

> В мирских свадьбах играют глумотворцы и арганники, и гу-
> сельники, и смехотворцы и бесовские песни поют, и как к
> церкве венчаться поедут, священник со крестом будет, а пред
> ним со всеми теми играми бесовскими рищут, а священницы
> им о том не возбраняют и не запрещают.
>
> *Ответ.* К венчанию бы ко святым Божиим церквам скомра-
> хом и глумцом пред свадьбою не ходити, а священником бы
> о том запрещати с веиким запрещением, чтобы такое без-
> чиние никогда же неименовалося.[17]

Enforcement of this rule had lagged until the mid-seventeenth
century when the *skomorokhi* were practically eliminated from
Muscovite life. In his edicts of 1648, Tsar Aleksei banned them,
and the Church excommunicated them in 1657. Nor did the Old
Believers lag behind in condemning mirth and entertainment: in
his autobiography, the leader of the Old Believers Avvakum says
that he once encountered a troupe of itinerant *skomorokhi* and
proceded to break up their instruments and set their bears free.
This was certainly an act of charity toward the bears, but hardly
toward the *skomorokhi.*

It is significant that in Ivan IV's later years, which were marked
by violence and despotism, the tsar spent much time in the company of the *skomorokhi.*[18] He once forced Archbishop Pimen to
parade about the city in the company of *veselye liudi* (which was
another name for the minstrels). The association of tyranny and
merriment must have further strengthened the social convention
of Muscovite Russia according to which sin and mirth were somehow related.

The assumption that humor and the denigration of "the world
as it is supposed to be" are two sides of the same coin exerted a
profound influence on the humorous literature of Old Russia,
and it made this literature different from its counterpart in Western Europe. In contrast, the idea of culpability of laughter qua
laughter has never taken root in Western societies with their yearly

carnivals and long tradition of spontaneous merrymaking to which neither the church nor the state objected in a strenuous manner.

One result of this situation was the development in Russia of humorous literature which ridiculed the law and "the world according to the rules." In Muscovite Russia, humor acquired the taste of the forbidden fruit and it *became associated with breaking the law.* This is why derision at "the world as it is supposed to be" and denigration of "the world according to the rules" or "the ideal world," became a recurring topos in Old Russian humorous literature. This topos was the humorous writer's revenge on rules and customs that denied him the right openly to practise his craft. He lashed out against all laws, throwing the hammer after the hatchet as it were, and he ridiculed all those who did not seek to circumvent the rules.

The fact that the humorous topos of "the world as it is supposed to be" developed in Muscovite literature indicates that in a very fundamental way, this literature differed from the literature of medieval Europe. Medieval literature affirmed the rules in the very act of laughing at them, whereas Old Russian literature denigrated the rules and held them up to ridicule. Old Russian literature and Western medieval literature thus represent two different categories in the humorous literature of the world. Likhachev's attempt to present them as stemming from the same social customs obscures rather than clarifies this important literary issue.

Rice University

NOTES

1. D.S. Likhachev, A.M. Panchenko, *"Smekhovoi mir" drevnei Rusi* (Leningrad: Nauka, 1976), p. 9.

2. D.S. Likhachev, *Poetika drevnerusskoi literatury* (Leningrad: Nauka, 1967), p. 16.

3. Enid Welsford, *The Fool: His Social and Literary History* (London: Faber and Faber, 1935), p. 199.

4. Will Durant, *The Age of Faith* (New York: Simon and Schuster, 1950), p. 929.

5. Ernst R. Curtius, *Europäische Literatur und lateinisches Mittelalter*

(Bern: Francke Verlag, 1948), p. 106.

6. Immanuel Kant, *Werke* (6 vols.; Wiesbaden: Im Insel Verlag, 1957), vol. 5, pp. 437–38.

7. *Russkaia demokraticheskaia satira XVII veka,* ed. V.P. Adrianova-Peretts (Moscow: Nauka, 1977), p. 33.

8. Wiktor Jakubowski, "Piśmiennictwo zjednoczonnego państwa moskiewskiego," *Literatura rosyjska,* ed. M. Jakóbiec (Warsaw: PWN, 1970), vol. 1, p. 140.

9. Anthony Stokes, "Literature of the Seventeenth Century," John Fennell and Anthony Stokes, *Early Russian Literature* (London: Faber and Faber, 1974), p. 258.

10. Richard Pipes, *Russia under the Old Regime* (New York: Scribner's, 1974); Iurii Lotman, "O dvukh tipakh orientirovannosti kul'tury," *Stat'i po tipologii kul'tury* (Tartu, 1970), pp. 86–98.

11. The fact that the Byzantine exhortations against laughter among monks were interpreted in Russia as pertaining to the laity as well was pointed out to me by Professor F.J. Thomson of the University of Antwerp.

12. Curtius, *Europäische Literatur . . . ,* pp. 421–23.

13. *Domostroi* (Moscow: Universitetskaia Tip., 1882; reprinted by Bradda Books, 1971), pp. 57–62, 68.

14. "The Account of George Turberville," eds. L.E. Berry and R.O. Crummey, *Rude and Barbarous Kingdom* (Madison: University of Wisconsin Press, 1968), p. 76.

15. A.M. Skabichevskii, "Asketicheskie nedugi v nashei sovremennoi peredovoi intelligentsii," *Russkaia mysl',* vol. 21 (October 1900), p. 24.

16. Russell Zguta, *Russian Minstrels: A History of the "Skomorokhi"* (Philadelphia: University of Pennsylvania Press, 1978), pp. 45–80.

17. *Stoglav,* ed. D.E. Kozhanchikov (St. Petersburg: Akademiia Nauk, 1863), pp. 135–36.

18. N.M. Karamzin, *Istoriia gosudarstva rossiiskogo* (St. Petersburg: Evdokimov, 1892; reprinted by Mouton, 1969), vol. 9, p. 105.

SCHEDULED PUBLICATIONS FROM THE
SECOND WORLD CONGRESS FOR
SOVIET AND EAST EUROPEAN STUDIES
GARMISCH - PARTENKIRCHEN, 1980

ENGLISH-LANGUAGE PUBLICATIONS: Published for the International Committee for Soviet and East European Studies by a number of different publishers; General Editor, Roger E. Kanet, University of Illinois at Urbana-Champaign.

I. Humanities and History: Berkeley Slavic Specialties, P.O. Box 4605, Berkeley, California 94704 U.S.A.

1. East European Literature: Selected Papers from the Second World Congress for Soviet and East European Studies, edited by Evelyn Bristol, University of Illinois at Urbana-Champaign. ISBN 0-933884-26-5 (paper)

2. Russian and Eastern European History: Selected Papers from the Second World Congress for Soviet and East European Studies, edited by R.C. Elwood, Carleton University. ISBN 0-933884-28-1 (paper)

3. Religion and Communist Society: Selected Papers from the Second World Congress for Soviet and East European Studies, edited by Dennis J. Dunn, Southwest Texas State University. ISBN 0-933884-29-X (paper)

4. Russian Literature and Criticism: Selected Papers from the Second World Congress for Soviet and East European Studies, edited by Evelyn Bristol, University of Illinois at Urbana-Champaign. ISBN 0-933884-27-3 (paper)

5. Soviet Investment for Planned Industrialization, 1929–1937: Policy and Practice. Selected Papers from the Second World Congress for Soviet and East European Studies, edited by R.W. Davies, The University of Birmingham. ISBN 0-933884-32-X (paper)

II. International Relations: Pergamon Press, Inc., Maxwell House, Fairview Park, Elmsford, N.Y. 10523 U.S.A.

6. Soviet Foreign Policy and East-West Relations, edited by Roger E. Kanet, University of Illinois at Urbana-Champaign (summer, 1982, ca. 200 pp.).

III. Politics: Praeger Publishers, 521 Fifth Avenue, New York, N.Y. 10175 U.S.A.

7. Politics and Participation under Communist Rule, edited by Peter J. Potichnyj, McMaster University, and Jane Shapiro Zacek, New York State Governor's Office of Employee Relations (1982).

IV. Politics: George Allen & Unwin, P.O. Box 18, Park Lane, Hemel Hempstead, Herts HP2 4TE England.

8. Leadership Selection and Patron-Client Relations in the USSR and Yugoslavia, edited by T.H. Rigby, Australian National University, and Bohdan Harasymiw, The University of Calgary (1982).

V. Information Science: Published by Russica Publishers, Inc., 799 Broadway, New York, N.Y. 10003 U.S.A.

9. Access to Resources in the '80s: Proceedings of the First International Conference of Slavic Librarians and Information Specialists, edited by Marianna Tax Choldin, University of Illinois at Urbana-Champaign (1982, 110 pp., $7.50) ISBN 0-89830-049-5.

VI. Economics:

10. Planning, Efficiency and Development in the Soviet-Type Economies: Selected Topics, edited by Zbigniew M. Fallenbuchl, University of Windsor, and Gertrude Schroeder Greenslade, University of Virginia.

VII. Law: Martinus Nijhoff Publishers, P.O. Box 566, 2501 CN The Hague, The Netherlands.

11. Perspectives on Soviet Law for the 1980s, no. 24 in the series *Law in Eastern Europe,* edited by F.J.M. Feldbrugge and William B. Simons, Rijksuniversiteit te Leiden (1982).

VIII. Education: Published as a special issue of *Slavic and European Education Review International,* c/o Editor, Office of East/West Education, Bowling Green State University, Bowling Green, Ohio 43403 U.S.A.

12. Soviet Education Policy: Perspectives and Problems, edited by Patrick L. Alston, Bowling Green State University.

IX. Philosophy: D. Reidel Publishing Co., P.O. Box 17, Dordrecht, The Netherlands.

13. East European and Western Developments in the Philosophies of Science, Technology, Society and Human Values: Selected Papers from the Second World Congress for Soviet and East European Studies, edited by Peter P. Kirschenmann, Vrije Universiteit Amsterdam, and Andreis Sarlemijn, Technische Hogeschool Eindhoven.

GERMAN-LANGUAGE PUBLICATIONS: Published for the Deutsche Gesellschaft für Osteuropakunde in the series *Osteuropaforschung;* General Editor, Wolfgang Kasack, Universität zu Köln. All volumes published by Berlin Verlag, Pacelliallee 5, 1000 Berlin 33, Germany.

1. Politische Kultur, Nationalitäten und Dissidenten in der Sowjetunion, edited by Georg Brunner and Horst Herlemann, Universität Würzburg (summer 1982, 164 pp., DM 20,-) ISBN 3-87061-248-7.

2. Sicherheitspolitik und Internationale Beziehungen der Sowjetunion, edited by Georg Brunner and Horst Herlemann, Universität Würzburg (summer 1982, 88 pp., DM 15,-) ISBN 3-87061-249-5.

3. Modernisierungsprobleme in der Sowjetunion, edited by Georg Brunner, Universität Würzburg (1982, ca. 100 pp., DM 15,-) ISBN 3-87061-250-9.

4. Literatur und Sprachentwicklung in Osteuropa im 20. Jahrhundert, edited by Eberhard Reissner, Universität Mainz (summer 1982, 216 pp., DM 28,-) ISBN 3-87061-245-2.

5. Bildung und Erziehung in Osteuropa im 20. Jahrhundert, edited by Oskar Anweiler, Ruhr-Universität Bochum (summer 1982, 215 pp., DM 28,-) ISBN 3-87061-251-7.

6. Grundrechte und Rechtssicherheit im sowjetischen Machtbereich, edited by Georg Brunner, Universität Würzburg (summer 1982, 137 pp., DM 18,80) ISBN 3-87061-252-5.

7. Wirtschaftsrecht, Internationaler Handel und Friedliche Koexistenz aus osteuropäischer Sicht, edited by Georg Brunner, Universität Würzburg (summer 1982, 128 pp., DM 18,80) ISBN 3-87061-243-6.

8. Wirtschaftsprobleme Osteuropas in der Analyse, edited by Heinrich Vogel, Bundesinstitut für ostwissenschaftliche und internationale Studien (1982, ca. 280 pp., DM 38,-) ISBN 3-87061-254-1.

9. Internationale Osteuropa-Forschung, edited by Arnold Buchholz, Ständiges Sekretariat für Koordinierung der Bundesgeförderten Osteuropaforschung (summer 1982, 104 pp., DM 18,80) ISBN 3-87061-229-0. (This volume will also be published in English.)

10. Kunst, Architektur und Musik in Osteuropa im 20. Jahrhundert, edited by Hans-Jürgen Drengenberg, Freie Universität Berlin, with the cooperation of Milka Bliznakov, Virginia Polytechnic Institute and State University, John E. Bowlt, University of Texas at Austin, Joachim Braun, Bar-Ilan University, and Peter Spielmann, Museum der Stadt Bochum (1983).

FRENCH-LANGUAGE PUBLICATION: Special issue of the journal *Revue d'Études comparatives Est-Ouest: Économie, Planification, Organisation;* 27, rue Paul-Bert, 94204 Ivry/s/Seine, France.

"Europe de l'Est: Économie officielle et économies parallèles," *Revue d'Études comparatives Est-Ouest,* XII, no. 2 (June 1981).

COPYRIGHT NOTICES

BERKELEY SLAVIC SPECIALTIES

P.O. Box 4605

Berkeley, California 94704 U.S.A.